Where shall we go for dinner? A food romance

Where shall we go for dinner?

A food romance · Tamasin Day-Lewis

WEIDENFELD & NICOLSON

First published in Great Britain in 2007
by Weidenfeld & Nicolson
10 9 8 7 6 5 4 3 2 1

Text copyright © Tamasin Day-Lewis 2007
Design and layout © Weidenfeld & Nicolson 2007

Illustrations by Marion Deuchars

A CIP catalogue record for this book is available from the British Library.

ISBN-13: 978 0 297 84429 7
ISBN-10: 0 297 84429 6

The Orion Publishing Group's policy is to use papers that are natural,
renewable and recyclable products and made from wood grown in
sustainable forests. The logging and manufacturing processes are expected
to conform to the environmental regulations of the country of origin.

Design director David Rowley
Editorial director Susan Haynes
Edited by Corinne Roberts
Designed by Ken Wilson | point918
Index by Elizabeth Wiggans
Printed by Butler and Tanner, Frome

Weidenfeld & Nicolson
The Orion Publishing Group Ltd
Orion House
5 Upper St Martin's Lane
London WC2H 9EA
www.orionbooks.co.uk

An Hachette Livre UK Company

For Julia, fellow romantic adventuress

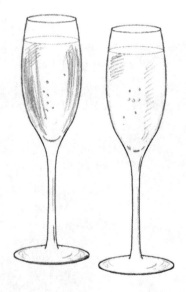

When I first set out on this great adventure with Rob I had no idea where it would take us, who we would meet along the way or what we would eat. There was no plan, no road map for the forthcoming year, but we knew that each dinner, each sortie, each trip, could become a landmark, might make a chapter, and that even the places we knew and loved we would be revisiting with a keener eye, a fresh palate and a sense of expectation.

Sharing a good dinner is one of the chief pleasures of life, particularly when you're sharing that dinner with the special person you share your life with, but this book had to be rather more ambitious. It also had to tell a story. It was conceived as a year of travels and discovery which could also encompass the great delight of simple suppers and bread broken with friends and family at home. It is part memoir, part love story, but the glue that holds it together is food, a shared passion and some-thing that binds our life together in the obvious but all the unobvious ways too.

But how could my story begin and end with this year's adventure? The truth is, it couldn't. A deep archive of food memories began to surge up, past into present. I remembered how Rob and I first met and how our food romance began. Further back in time were the memories of my childhood; the cooks and food that influenced me most. I began thinking about the part food had always played in shaping the big events of my life. In fact, it is most often remembering or recreating a particular dish that leads me back to a time, a place, an occasion, and defines that occasion, that memory, for me.

Since I first learned to cook, the expectation of each and every dinner has remained a source of pure pleasure. It doesn't matter whether I am roasting road-kill badger in Somerset to Rob's disgust and dismay, or we are walking down Sullivan Street in New York to dine on fried chicken at the Blue Ribbon, we always set out in hope of the perfect dinner.

We may find it at a small café serving cinghiale in the hills of Santo Stefano Belbo in Piemonte, or snacking on falafel in a warm wad of pitta bread at Mamoun's, a hole in the wall in Greenwich Village. It may be a brunch of black Russian rye bread and wild smoked salmon while climbing in the Pyrénées, or an unexpected breakfast with a fresh burrata maker in a cheese shop in Puglia.

Sometimes we try too hard and don't find it at all, but even the disappointment is food for thought, and often a better story to dine out on afterwards. And there is always tomorrow.

Where *shall* we go for dinner?

§1   *Supper at Harvest Time*

The first of the white truffles are,
like a crime passionelle, probably
the most emotive of foods in the
culinary lexicon. Like a high-class
whore, they are at once secret,
clandestine and stratospherically
expensive. Battles are fought, won
and lost over them, but their beauty
is never disputed. You pay richly for
your slice of heaven …

Looking through my notebook, I find the words 'Supper at Harvest Time' and am reminded of the mid-September sun over the hills last autumn, high above Santo Stefano Belbo in the Langhe, and of how Rob and I came to be sitting at the tiny café table at La Cristina in Valdivilla, the village at the top of the hill.

We have come for the cinghiale, the wild boar, for it is that time of year, and Mario has promised he will cook it for us tonight, but he has implored us to try some of his fresh porcini first, crisped in egg and breadcrumbs. We'll start with a glass of Moscato d'Asti to get the gustatory juices flowing and, if we can get that far, we'll finish with a late-ripening peach from a bough a few paces away from where we are sitting on the tiny Strada del Moscato d'Asti that runs through the Asti vineyards. They'll serve it the local way, in slices in a wine glass with a libation of beaded Asti bubbles winking at the brim.

We have already spent three days in the little town of Bra, celebrating the goat at the biennial Slow Food Cheese Festival and scouting out new cheeses for Rob's New York cheese shop, Murray's, on Bleecker Street. We have eaten only at simple, small restaurants, delighting in menus that barely vary from place to place, but follow the rhythms of the seasons, each individual stamping his imprimatur on a dish to make it his own. Nothing has felt repetitive though everything has been more or less the same.

It is the most enviable and envied part of our jobs, our lives, this licence to take off somewhere, often with only the name of a tiny dairy, a small producer, a restaurant, an ingredient, and trespass on the food and cooking of a region until it's time to leave, replete with new ingredients and recipes.

I am happy to travel for hours – though the threat of the carbon footprint is increasingly turning my job into a war crime

— or head miles off course, incurring the wrath and scepticism of a whole carload of hot, quarrelsome passengers, for a holy grail that may, or may not live up to its culinary reputation, when they'd rather pull up at a gas station and scarf a greasy crocque-monsieur.

When I met Rob, five years ago, I realised I had finally met my match: someone as greedy as I am (the word greedy is unacceptably pejorative to him, whilst it is a badge of honour to me), yet with a palate as pleasingly fine-tuned and refined as a Formula One car. He is highly critical, knowledgeable and every bit as obsessively prepared to travel a distant dirt track in hope, if just to be proved wrong. After all, they don't all end in the perfect lunch.

Our trip last year in the early autumn convinced us that every season in the Langhe is about a handful of dishes: a breath-takingly simple carpaccio of veal; homemade tagliatelle with fresh porcini from the surrounding woods; the first white truffles, their raw scent seeping from thick cream, butter, eggs or rice; cinghiale, rich, dark and braised to tenderness with a square of soft, sloppy, golden polenta to soak its juices into beneath; the last of the local white peaches or hazelnuts pounded to a paste and baked into an intensely flavoured torta di nocciola from the nuts in the hazel groves where dogs and their owners dig secretly for hidden troves of the mighty white truffle.

We had driven half way up the twisted road that climbs high above Santo Stefano Belbo, a hill, if viewed from below, that resembles the local bonet, a tantalisingly wobbly chocolate concoction shaped like a 1930s cloche, to a swish, Michelin-starred spa hotel, the Relais San Maurizio, to spend a final few nights of luxury, but this particular night we left the comfort and sanctuary of what was probably the summer palazzo of a debauched Italian count for La Cristina, the trat at the top of the hill. For a menu offering the same six dishes that have been intrinsic to the region at least since the first flood. The great food historian Anna Del Conte believes that a lifetime spent perfecting half a dozen traditional Italian dishes is a lifetime well spent and who am I to disagree? It is probably the secret to life.

As with all the best discoveries, La Cristina happened quite by chance. When we arrived at the Relais San Maurizio, I had left the hotel and run the three kilometres to the top of the hill through the gathering heat. The nebbiolo, the famous local mist, had not yet burned off and all the surrounding hills seemed to hang suspended, inanimate. Tomatoes had begun to droop on the branch by the side of the road, so exhausted by their growth and the heat that their swollen crimson orbs were beginning to crack and split open. Pear trees, apple trees, figs and quinces were spilling ripe fruit onto the wayside ensuring that no poor traveller should pass by hungry. In a show of almost obscene fecundity and excess the pomegranate and squat peach trees seemed to stagger under their burden of fruit. The narrow verge was littered with produce, courgettes in flower, rainbow chard and earthed-up banks of fat leeks. The rest was vines, as far as the eye could see, stepped terraces of old, gnarled roots from which shot hieroglyphics of leaves. The first tractors were beginning to head off into the vineyards to pick, returning at full tilt, their trailers crammed with dusty clusters of dark grapes.

Facing me at the junction at the top of the hill was an unambitious looking small sign, 'La Cristina, Trattoria Pizzeria'. It was closed, but I went and scanned the menu anyway and thought it looked quite promising. Running back past it 30 minutes later, the first scent of cooking was casting its own nebbiolo onto the street, so I went inside to investigate. I let the girl at the desk know I wanted to go into la cucina and she brought me through to where her father Mario was removing a huge metal dish of darkly braised meat from the oven. He told me it was cinghiale to be served with polenta in the evening, the sight and scent of it enough for me to tell them that there would be two of us for lunch.

We struggled up the hill in the midday sun on the hotel's bikes and decided to sit in the small garden to eat where 'la Cristina', Mario's daughter, told us what papa was cooking for lunch.

The dish of vitello tonnato was a classic rendition: thinly sliced pink veal with a sticky emulsion of tunny mayonnaise spiked with capers, and we dug into it feverishly after our climb. Next, two bowls of taglierini with porcini; perfect, slippery egg-yellow noodles and a creamy ragu sauce into which the fungi had released a stream of black, bosky juice. A sliced white pesche in Moscato had a clear, sweet, slightly acidic fragrance and ended this cheap, simple lunch – 25 euros for the two of us – faultlessly.

It may have been downhill all the way home, but the sun and the lunch and the lazy bubbled Moscato sent us shooting down a muddied sidetrack through a burst of golden quince trees to recover in a field of tall grass surrounding a derelict stone house.

Intimations of Marvell's magical and sensual poem *The Garden* sprang to mind, it could have been written for the place, the hour, the season:

> *What wondrous life is this I lead!*
> *Ripe apples drop about my head;*
> *The luscious clusters of the vine*
> *Upon my mouth do crush their wine;*
> *The nectarine and curious peach*

Into my hands themselves do reach;
Stumbling on melons as I pass
Ensnared with flowers, I fall on grass.

The following night we returned for the cinghiale. Mario and Cristina welcomed us like old friends, clearly delighted that we'd found their food delicious enough to return for. Large parties of local farmers began to arrive in a state of visible, sons-of-the-soil exhaustion straight from the vineyards as we ate our velvety-dark wild boar with its pale slop of polenta, its fagiolini and its patati. We had started with the fried porcini, such spankingly fresh porcini that the ill- and oft-used 'morning gathered' sobriquet could have been invented especially for them. As is the way in these tightly knit places, the foreigners were acknowledged, and later, when glances met, nodded to with a glimmer of approval and shared enthusiasm once we had been observed to be greedily appreciative of the food, the drink, the chef, his daughter. 'Supper at harvest time' had been defined by this evening's experience, its warmth, its abundance, its generosity of spirit, its inclusion of us, the outsiders.

On the night we arrived at the Relais San Maurizio, we'd headed downstairs to the dining room to a very different experience. The restaurant was in the hotel's cellars and featured a typically sophisticated Michelin-star menu. We asked what we should order and were told the agnolotti which, as is common to the region, were stuffed with veal, pork and rabbit. Here the pasta is known as 'plin' which means pinch, as that is exactly what you do with the crocus-coloured sheets when you've filled them, to seal in the stuffing.

We sprinkled Parmigiano over the silky-wet pillows; we speared them, we tasted them, we looked at each other in amazement. The Parmigiano was better than anything either of us had ever tasted, full, rich, grainy without being over-salt; buttery, intense. It turned out to be a two year old Bonati, made by Giorgio Bonati at Basilicanova in Parma. Rob has imported it ever since. Now when he comes to Somerset, he brings a great, crumbly hunk of it wrapped in layers of waxed paper, concealed in the foot of his bag, releasing its deep salt scent, I imagine, the length of the aircraft.

The agnolotti were no less remarkable, in fact they were the best we ate over the whole 10 days, and naturally we asked what the secret was.

'Lidia is 75,' our waiter began. 'She has been making agnolotti the same way for 48 years. If you would like to watch her, come to the kitchen tomorrow evening at around 6pm.'

The restaurant kitchen is, to me, the most exciting place on earth. It is a place of glamour, of mystery, of heat, of pain, of theatre and the kitchens of the best chefs offer the chance to learn someone else's secrets, to find out how to do something differently that you could never have thought out for yourself.

The following evening we presented ourselves to the kitchen. The chefs were standing at their stations in a whirl of preparation for the evening performance. One short, stocky figure was sitting calmly on a bench somewhat removed from, but clearly a part of, the bustle, bent over a work table, moving slowly, precisely, rhythmically. It was quite obvious that she was treated with awe, with respect, as senior even to the head chef by the deference accorded her and the hush that stilled the more usual din and thrum of the huge restaurant kitchen. We were introduced. I watched as the little gobbets of meat were pushed in precise amounts with an old spoon onto the pasta before Lidia pinched them and ran her little wheel over them to separate each full bundle.

'How do you manage such a precise quantity in each?' I marvelled.

'After 48 years I should have got the hang of it by now,' Lidia said, her brown, robin's eyes twinkling with humour, as she showed me the old, bent spoon which had clearly been her only tool, bar her fingers, for the last four dozen years.

There were more secrets. The meats had to be cooked separately so that they retained their identity. They were roasted first before being added to a soffrito of vegetables. The little pillows of agnolotti had to be transferred not fully drained, and served in the damp napkin they were removed to. The snippets of a lifetime's wisdom were, as I had hoped, generously and freely given with the pride of one who would rather the student went home and made the dish the proper way than went home, failed, blamed themselves and never attempted the dish again. In my somewhat shorter lifetime of cooking experience I have found that it is always the best cooks who are the most generous and specific with their knowledge; they take pride in sharing their secrets, their recipes, their skills, whereas the second-raters are intent on guarding their precious dishes like state secrets and intimidating the rest of us into believing we couldn't cook them anyway.

This wasn't the only recipe I asked about. Accompanying a gluey-sweet tender cheek of veal, ganascino arrosto di vitello, was a brace of figs wrapped with a scarf of thinly sliced lardo. Roasted in a hot oven, the fat had begun to weep and crisp into the hot, yielding flesh of the figs. Three minutes in a red hot oven is all it took I was told, and when I returned home I made the dish with the wide ribbons of pata negra fat from the great acorn-fed Spanish pigs, and christened it 'piggy figgy'. Like the smell of bacon frying in a pan, there is really nothing to beat the scent of hot, sweet pork fat spitting into a plump, ripe fig and disgorging its porcine fattiness and flavour into the seeded flesh. A twist of chopped thyme, the leaves bruised to release their oils, is the only addition I make, and a scrunch of black pepper.

We set out on our bikes again the following morning, switch-backing up and down the narrow funnels of lanes that ran like thread through the vineyards and gradually beginning to get some sense of the lie of the land and the contours of the hills. Low down in a sunken pudding basin of a valley we found a tiny village with a disproportionately enormous church at its centre. The village was marked 'Madonna'. There was no obvious sign of life until we got to what looked like a rather basic village shop that was evidently closed. Closed and firmly shuttered. Attached to the shop was a restaurant, the Campagna Verde, again, firmly closed, and the old man who came out to sweep from its shuttered interior spoke no English and seemed none too keen to find anyone inside who could. Rob went up to the door of the shop and spotted the cardboard sign which spelled out the word 'salume' in faint, sun-blonded letters.

It is one of the things he bemoans most, the fact that he isn't allowed to import the traditionally cured meats that the Italians are famed for to sell at Murray's. Rob gets so excited when he finds the real thing that there's absolutely no holding him. It looked like the chef whose restaurant and shop we had stumbled upon also made his own salume. We'd be camping out in the heat for the matinée or even the evening performance if no one appeared in the meantime.

We hammered on the shop door and waited. The girl who finally opened the door seeming none too pleased at the disturb-ance looked distressingly like a 1950s Italian film star and was clearly not new to the word temperament. She was arrestingly beautiful and as sexy as a cat. Rob would have to be the one to win her over. Once he had ascertained through her broken English and his Italian which is entirely confined, as is mine, to ingredients and Italian menu-speak, that her husband made the salume in his kitchen and it was the best in the area, he started with the killer flattery. It worked.

'You should be in the movies. What are you doing here in this shop, in this village, you look like Sophia Loren, like Monica Vitti, like a film star? We are going to discover you, my girlfriend here is a food writer and she writes cook books, could we come into the shop and see your husband make the salume? What is your name?'

'Mirella,' the girl replied, rolling her r's deliciously and preening. 'My husband is not making his salume today, he has to cook a big dinner for the harvest tomorrow, he is in the kitchen stirring the mostarda Piemonte, it has been on for two days, he can't leave it.'

'My girlfriend always loves to go into the kitchen to see what's going on and we'd like to book a table for dinner tomorrow,' Rob continued.

'I'm not sure if I'll have room,' Mirella said, bridling. 'The whole village is coming, I'll have to look and see, come with me.'

We were led through the restaurant to the kitchen where great vats of sticky purple sludge were bubbling precariously near to the tops of the gigantic pans and the chef, Mirella's husband Massimo, was moving from one to the other with an oar-length paddle, stirring and watching, stirring and watching. He looked as quiet and gentle as she was excitable and mercurial, and seemed perfectly happy to have an Inglese and an Americano poking their noses into his pots and pans and asking questions.

After inspecting the contents of the great vats – I knew about mostarda di Cremona and mostarda di Venezia, but I had never heard of this jammy grape-harvest gloop – we were invited to sit at a little table in the corner of the kitchen where Massimo brought us a scoop of the boiling brew that he'd ladled onto a plate to cool down and set a huge wheel of Castelmagno, a local raw cow's milk cheese, down next to it, inviting us to taste the two together.

The fact is some things always taste better where they come from. Get them home and their exotic foreignness seems to lose its appeal, seems out of place and they just don't taste the same. This was the best breakfast you could ever wish to eat after a cycle ride in the Langhe hills in the autumn. As Massimo sliced wafers of the pale, crumbly, pasty cheese with its mildly mush-roomy, lactic undertones from the wheel for us to spread the warm, fruity mostarda onto and we got talking about his cooking, the dinner he was making for the grape pickers the following night and his favourite local dishes, our passion and curiosity finally won through and he invited us to dine in the restaurant the following night, saying there were some special things he wanted to cook for us.

I couldn't help but wonder how many chefs in England would have given two complete, albeit curious and clearly pretty well informed strangers the same welcome and sat them down in their kitchens to let them try their latest dish just because they happened to have knocked on their door at harvest time in time for elevenses.

We finished eating, talked shop and salume, toured the kitchen, shook hands until the morrow and remounted our bikes sustained by Massimo's mostarda and Castelmagno, and looking forward to what we knew would be a memorable dinner.

The following night Mirella had transformed herself from

shop girl to patronne. She was made up for the movies and
dressed for the part and she had adopted a sort of haughtiness
that she clearly felt befitted the role of wife of the village chef
and restaurant owner. The Campagna Verde may have been
a small village restaurant attached to a shop in the middle of
nowhere, but Mirella was like the female equivalent of a bull-
fighter, out in the arena, world-class, ready to run with the
crowd, gather the plaudits, please her public.

We weren't allowed to order, we were captive while Mirella
brought one dish after another out from the kitchen, arriving
first with a basket crammed full of outsize fresh porcini, their
stalks still earthy where they had been wheedled out of their lair,
their scent penetrating our nostrils, just to show us what we were
in for, in case we had had any doubt about the standard of the
ingredients or what miracles Massimo was about to perform
behind the swing door.

We ordered a bottle of the local Barbera Asti Montivenere '99,
Castiglione Tinella, and awaited our food.

There were deep-fried puffs of potato beignets, so light they
could have been blown like dandelion clocks across the plate;
Massimo's home made salami served hot and steaming and garlicky from the pan in which he had fried fat chunks of it, which
sent Rob into ecstatic eulogy; tiny puff pastry tarts filled with
fontina; fagottino gorgonzola which turned out to be fat little
parcels running with a fonduta of cheese, spinach and mushroom
when you cut into them; there were agnolotti, the emphasis of
flavour being the veal rather than the pork or rabbit; a plate of
porcini fritti, the mushroom sealed by a light crumb, as sensual
and simple as a dish could be, crisp fried river fish with pignoli –
pine nuts, tomato, dill and chervil; there was a plate of rare duck
breast served with slices of roast vegetable, and finally a poached

pear drowned in Barolo and a hazelnut torta whose pralinéed centre was as intense as dark chocolate. And all served with the sort of assurance and pride you would expect from a big city restaurant with a reputation, but here we were in Madonna, a tiny village in the Langhe hills, where one can only make comparisons and wonder at our own lack of cuisine du terroir, at there being any sort of equivalent, at the fact that the locals' expectations were such that places like La Campana Verde and La Cristina not only existed, they were the norm, and were probably the norm for small villages across Italy.

We ventured into the kitchen to congratulate Massimo and for me to ask him about the torta di nocciola. He pulled a huge tin of pure hazelnut paste from out of his store cupboard to show me what he made the torta with, while I lamented the fact that I wouldn't be able to find any back home. Immediately Massimo scraped some paste from the can into a jar, wrapped up a whole extra torta di nocciola in foil entreating Rob and me to take it on a picnic the following day, and finished with a jar of the mostarda for us to take home.

'On a scale of 1–10,' Rob asked me as he always does about almost every experience, dinner, film, novel, trip, that's rateable, 'what would you give this place?'

In the end some things are off the scale, and the whole experience of La Campagna Verde, of Massimo and Mirella, was one of them.

We had exited via the shop with Mirella our newfound film star in tow, pulling salume out from under the counter and wrapping it in brown paper for Rob and me to take home and cook, so we finally left the restaurant with a complete larder of Langhe ingredients.

I like to think that if the two of us were ever stopped at

customs we could always unpack our bags, unwrap our myriad parcels and bribe the officials with a fantastic three course dinner.

When we'd arrived in Torino a few days earlier we had
driven straight to La Morra, an absurdly beautiful village beneath whose breath-catchingly steep slopes the Barolo vineyards bask, and close enough to travel daily to Bra to the Slow Food Cheese Festival filled with the best of the artisanal cheese makers and affineurs from all over the boot and heel of Italy, with a sprinkling from Ireland, England, France, Switzerland, Spain and Holland. We set off on the most pleasurable part of Rob's job, scenting out the great cheeses that may never have been seen outside their native village or town, certainly never exported to America, and trying to do business with their makers, sound out the possibilities of exporting these rare gems, however small the production, however seasonal, so that his cheese counter at the oldest cheese shop in New York, described by the *FT* as the city's 'only world-class cheese shop', could be filled with their glorious, pungent splendour. Each different cheese is defined by a terroir, its flavour the result of that terroir's grass, its animals, its wild flowers and herbs, its summer and winter pastures, even its chill winds and damp, dank winters, cold earth, decaying leaves and winter feed.

Together we search for the precise opposite of what the supermarket giants search for in their quest for conformity, one size, one shape, one unchanging taste. Each wheel of raw milk cheese made each morning in the same dairy with the same milk from the same cows will taste entirely different each day it is made, unlike its commercially made factory counterpart. It is one of the great wonders of cheese, and one that we should strive, at any cost, to preserve and keep out of the hands of the food police who would pasteurise the cows before they were milked if it were scientifically possible.

First we found a beautiful, fresh, unpasteurised cheese wrapped in a parcel of walnut leaves and fennel by an Italian who rejoiced in the name Eros and looked as though he lived up to it. It is often said by the cheese makers and mongers that cheeses, rather like dogs, reflect the characters and appearance of their owners, and in this case we wanted to believe it. Here was a strong, fragrant, peasant-like, feisty disc of cheese crumbling to a lactic-pasted centre, as raw and earthy as could be. The only problem, as is so often the way, is that its maker had no back-up or infrastructure to export. We would more likely do business with Conrad from Switzerland, an ex-sports teacher turned cheese aficionado, whose booth was stacked with a selection of the most exquisitely buttery, nutty Alpine cheeses like Beaufort, Gruyère and Appenzeller, or Martin from Holland who had some exciting grainy, caramelly, aged cheeses quite unlike the Goudas Rob knew and sold already.

We tasted several hundred cheeses over the three days, attempting somewhat hopelessly to freshen our palates in between each with glugs of water and bites of apple so that each new flavour stood a chance, not easy after the first dozen, or after anything strong like a throaty, salty, full-frontal blue which kills all milder flavours in its path.

To escape the all-embracing clutch of the cheese mongers and their wares, we repaired to the Caffe Converso, a tiny backstreet café where Rob's old acquaintance from previous trips, Federico, served us restorative scoops of hazelnut ice cream with an intravenous hit of espresso. There is no country on earth which makes better ices than Italy and the nutty, quick-melting, milky brilliance of Federico's gelato was enough to assuage tired feet and palates in one.

If you have never eaten the new season's hazelnuts in Piemonte, you have no idea of just how good a hazelnut can taste. Put it on your list of 'things to do before I die' immediately. I remember taking kilos of toasted nuts back to England the first year I discovered them at Slow Food's huge festival for artisan producers, the Salone del Gusto in Torino, and compulsively, until every last nut was roasted, nibbed or ground, baked them into cakes and tarts and tortes with Jersey cream, apricots, raspberries and bitter chocolate.

After this Italian trip, I began dreaming of the perfect hazelnut ice cream, and one day, months later, an idea came to me in a flash. I roasted a pile of nuts until they gave off a toasty smell. I bundled them up tight in a tea towel and rubbed them for all I was worth to slough off their skins – getting rid of the bits is no joke, it's worse than picking parsley out of your teeth. I tried a sieve, upgraded the holes to a colander, but the fragile skins clung like confetti and in the end I had to separate the two by hand. I threw the nuts into the Magimix and carried on blitzing them way after they were ground. Eventually they began to look oily, pasty, sticky, like a nut butter. I put my nose in the bowl and sniffed. Praline! The nuts had started to smell like one of those divine, soft-centred chocolate pralines you find on all the best chocolate counters in northern Italy. I scraped the mixture into a home made vanilla custard, folded in thick Jersey cream and the nutty paste and set it to churn. The result was a match for Federico's and worked beautifully with the pear tarte tatin I made to accompany it, the pastry spiced up with a couple of teaspoons of ground ginger, the pears jewelled with little nuggets of ginger in syrup.

We had spotted a restaurant at the top of the hill in La Morra, the Belvedere, on our preliminary stroll when we'd just arrived. We decided to lunch there the next day. It had the feeling that those respectable, honest, big-hearted local restaurants in Italy have, you feel it as soon as you step inside; in fact earlier, from the exterior where the menu is on view on a podium outside with the pomp and pride of a conductor's score. The doors are large, embracing, cleanly painted, the tables well spaced, substantial, napped with good, well pressed linen cloths and napkins, and the staff seem expectant and eager when you arrive demanding a table for lunch.

Over the next few days we would spot the head waiter, older and more senior than the rest of the waiting staff, taking his slightly flat-footed morning perambulation around the nearby streets with his dog. He exuded that sense that only the seasoned professional of a good, provincial restaurant does, where devotion to the serving of the local, seasonal dishes and understanding their cyclical importance is as much his job as it is the chef's. He had an air of mild, expectant pleasure and excitement about him that I imagined he sported in that same week every year, the week when the first white truffles of the season are discovered and bartered for and the hills are scented and stalked by the men and dogs whose lives depend upon them.

He had probably looked this way for the last 40 to 50 years, over which time he had cultivated the sedate walk around the circle at the top of La Morra to calm the senses that were about to be unleashed in the restaurant when the first whiff of that powerfully seductive tuber permeated and overwhelmed everything and everybody around it.

The first of the white truffles are, like a crime passionelle, probably the most emotive of foods in the culinary lexicon.

Like a high-class whore they are at once secret, clandestine and stratospherically expensive. Battles are fought, won and lost over them, but their beauty is never disputed. You pay richly for your slice of heaven. Dogs die, poisoned by neighbourly skulduggery and inter-familial rivalry; territory is as fiercely guarded and staked out by the opposition as Corleone hide-outs. White truffle terroir is passed down from father to son, from uncle to nephew, and good dogs are rewarded better than the best of wives. My meeting with the local Godfather of hunters and his dog at the truffle fair in Alba one year, where a golden nugget is given to he who has snuffled out and weighed in with the greatest single truffle, told me that when he had dug out the specimen of a lifetime and kissed his dog fiercely and passionately in grateful thanks, his wife remarked that he showed the dog more affection than he ever had her.

I expect there are marriages like that all over the truffle-stashed hills of northern Italy, and I expect one of the reasons is that truffle-hunting dogs are infinitely more receptive to the annual display of over-the-top emotion their overjoyed masters foist on them than their wives, who have probably been usurped by a mistress anyway.

Our lunch at the Belvedere was the first of several meals glorying in the white truffle that we ate over the ten-day stay, augmented by another famous local speciality, a tartare of veal.

The following morning was my birthday. Rob had deceived me elaborately into believing he'd had no time to buy me a birthday present, and only the day before, we had escaped the cheese tents briefly and he'd picked out a chic black pea jacket and some jeans in a back-street shop the like of which no provincial town outside Italy would have. Everything is sexier in Italy, the clothes, the men, the women, the cheese, and in Alba, in the autumn, the smell of tartufo bianco.

I had presumed that was it. However, that morning Rob leapt out of bed, scrabbled inside his bag and returned with a small black box. Inside were the most delicate of modern earrings, a slender stem of gold bamboo from which dripped tiny bird's-eye beads of rubies.

We went downstairs to breakfast in the small, chic dining room of our bed and breakfast, one of those ancient village houses built around a courtyard that had been transformed by daring modernism within.

Two interesting-looking but unfathomable characters were sitting slumped on either side of the dining room in the usual keep-out silence people reserve for early morning coffee and contemplation as the brain unhazes, still cloudy from its sleep. Eventually we intruded and introduced ourselves. Diego Sorba, an Italian, sitting to our left was also staying in La Morra for the cheese festival and was about to open his own cheese shop in Parma. Zoltan Bogathy, a Hungarian sitting on our right, turned out to be there for the same purpose. He had traded journalism for food, opened up a small delicatessen in Budapest and was about to open a huge speciality store selling food and wine from all over the world. Zoltan offered us the singularly horrifying fact that his was one of the few shops to sell real butter in Budapest since communism's impact on Hungary's economy and way of life had been so great that the supermarkets had only stocked margarine for the last few decades.

Diego spoke immaculate English, which I commented upon immediately.

'Well I was a professor of Irish Literature until cheese became my passion,' he replied, as though it were the most normal thing in the world.

It doesn't get much stranger than that surely, but it did.

'How funny,' I said. 'My father was an Irish poet.' I didn't imagine for one minute that Diego would have heard of him.

'I wrote my dissertation on the poets of the 1930s with particular attention to Louis MacNeice,' Diego continued.

I let on that my father and MacNeice had been good friends.

'What was your father's name?'

'C. Day Lewis.'

Diego looked stunned, came to his senses, delivered the coup: 'I have a 1950s recording of your father reading his love poetry. I take it with me everywhere, I have it here in the car, I will go and get it.'

I have only once heard my father's voice since he died in 1972. I had switched on the car radio and been caught unawares. Although his voice is still there in my head over thirty years since his death, actually listening to my father has not been something I've been able to do. And here I was, of all extraordinary coincidences, about to hear him with a group of strangers and with Rob, who had never heard him, and, more portentously, on my birthday.

Sergio, who had designed and ran the b and b, disappeared upstairs to put on the tape, and there began the most extraordinary birthday breakfast I can remember, which the common language of food had set in motion. The small dining room was somehow electrified as my father's love poems were brought back to life by their creator. We sipped our coffee, supped our tea, broke our bread and at the end swapped e-mails and addresses, amazed and excited that we had not one, but two common interests. Rob and I promised Diego and Zoltan that we would visit them on our food travels some time over the coming year, in Parma and Budapest. It wasn't the sort of empty, traveller's promise that one gives knowing that one's paths will never cross again either; we decided instantly that theirs' were destinations, food- and friend-wise, that we would head for.

Not all poets are good at reading poetry, even, curiously, if it is their own. My father was an exception. He had a whisper of an Irish lilt that always seemed more exaggerated when he read out loud; he had musicality, a beautiful timbre to his voice and a sense of rhythm that seemed to make all meaning clear. Diego seemed to be as excited as I was and Rob as moved and fascinated. Sergio made a CD of the tape and Rob and I played it over the next few days as we drove through the hills watching the final throes of the grape harvest and searching out the best local dairies and restaurants.

That night we were due to meet up with Rob's French affineur from Roanne, Hervé Mons, a leonine whippet of a creature with a taut, almost Neanderthal brow, a compelling cheek-to-cheek grin and the looks, body and impatience of a serious athlete bent like a piece of wire in the blocks waiting for the starter gun to go off. Hervé is more driven than the snow, and as intent on the pursuit of perfection and good taste as Rob, whose ageing caves he designed last year for the new Bleecker Street shop. He is one of the top half-dozen affineurs in France, bringing on and ageing the best French cheeses in his ageing caves and understanding exactly what degree of ripeness they should be sent out at, shipped abroad, eaten and enjoyed. He was bringing with him a young goat's cheese maker from Provence called Francois Borel and his wife, whose rare, Roves goats from near Marseilles we had visited a couple of years before and who is the maker of one of the region's many outstanding fresh goat's cheeses.

Rob and I had got lost in the searing heat of the afternoon sun outside Aix-en-Provence on our way to visit Francois's farm, where the goats feed on woodland herbs and organic pastures. Eventually Francois had come out to search for us in the nearby town and led us back to his sun-parched farm and dairy. After we had toured the farm and endured the head-butting attentions of these rare but sociable animals, we went into the cool of the dairy to sample the delicate, wet, white cheeses rolled in sariette, summer savory, which were amongst the best we had ever eaten. No chance of anything like this reaching America though, whose laws determine that all unpasteurised cheeses have to be a minimum of 60 days old before they are considered legal.

We were also meeting up with Rob's wholesale manager Liz, who had been trawling the cheese makers with us and is an ardent formaggiophile, and her boyfriend Adrian, a wine expert and chef. They were staying with us in La Morra and had delighted in the white truffle lunch we took them to at the Belvedere.

I was feeling more than faintly irked, not that I had let on, at my birthday dinner being more of a working party for cheese gurus than a romantic dinner à deux and I was half expecting to be disappointed by the restaurant Hervé had picked in the way one is when one feels unreasonably justified at being pissed off for no good reason.

We drew up at the gaunt, sober-walled Castello di Verduno a little after first dusk. The interior had the institutional refectory feel of a select seminary for religieuses. The high ceilings had an air of looking down on you, and almost ached with tired shabbiness and lack of attention. Difficult not to draw certain instant conclusions about what we were about to receive. The welcome was distinctly uncheery, indeed, no one appeared for some minutes as we stood surveying the formal hall and breathed in its atmosphere, which seemed to suggest that an epicurean experience was not about to be forthcoming.

When we'd finally been ushered downstairs, Hervé suggested we all ate the tasting menu. In normal circumstances I am entirely prejudiced against what I see as a hideously cheffy, showy-offy trick that leaves the diner wilted and bloated and severely out of pocket and the chef smugly believing that he has offered you the experience of a lifetime. It always makes me want to call for meat and two veg, more mashed potato, tomato ketchup, anything rather than the succession of miniature, over-decorated constructions that bear no resemblance to real food that's been cooked to taste of the thing itself. But given that Hervé was our host and that his taste is inarguably as sophisticated and developed as anybody's on the planet, I made a weak attempt at telling him I would be happier with a couple of good dishes before giving up and giving in.

The first dish arrived, and with it, something wonderful and unexpected happened.

It's funny how mood-changing food can be, and how important the where and the when and the who are to the whole equation. It was a small dish of softened yellow and red peppers with a smidgen of anchovy lolling in a good, fruity olive oil, a perfect sweet-salt appetite sharpener, three ingredients, perfectly judged and utterly simple. Of course they didn't really tell us anything about the level of cooking we were about to experience, but they did set the mood.

A plain white plate arrived next, covered entirely with tissue paper thin slices of rosy pink carpaccio of veal. This is another traditional dish which, despite its apparent simplicity, demands the best veal and butchery skills and in this case had been rolled in a salt and pepper crust for a week before being sliced and slicked in a puddle of fruity olive oil scented with rosemary. You could have eaten the meat if you hadn't a tooth in your head it was so soft and the lingering astringence of the rosemary was a brilliant touch.

I began to relax. The '71 Barolo began to work its magic. The plates were cleared, and the next course came, a thin slice of warm calves' tongue, served with a vegetable purée. The purity of each dish so far, unmarred by decoration, or the kind of turret building and paint splashing beloved of so many young chefs, lent a sort of purist air which ran counter and almost anarchically so, to the perfectionism and mastery on each plate, but fitted in completely with the building.

And so it went on. Two perfectly satin-sheened square parcels of tortellini stuffed with pumpkin were trounced by the next course, a risotto balsamico which was one of the bravest and most powerful dishes I have ever seen on a restaurant plate. To dare to serve a hillock of utterly plain white risotto with a puddle of velvety-black, mellow balsamic just poking out underneath it, and to not only pull it off, but make it a dish that everyone who has eaten it who can stir a pot of rice will go home and replicate and enjoy, is some feat. This was a dinner that dared to deconstruct, and in the face of haute cuisine's tired old sense of superiority and its self-parodying excesses, was just what we were looking for.

A dish of vitello tonnato followed, but the rules had been changed. The veal sat alone, at its side a salsa of onion, garlic, capers and anchovies without the tuna, the mayonnaise, or vegetables puréed into the oily, creamy sauce which is the way I learned to make it. It was lighter, sharper, less stuffy.

By this stage I no more wished for a romantic dinner à deux than I did for a three Michelin star restaurant or another five courses, but I was out of luck with the latter. We were each presented with one of those opulently saffron-yolked fried eggs that you only seem to find in Italy. A storm of white truffle was grated over it, and that was it. Truffles are nothing until the heat of a simple egg, the starch of hot strands of fresh pasta or sticky grains of carnaroli rice meet their raw, earthy flesh which then releases its priapic scent and almost overwhelmingly sexy taste. Cook it and it is at once corrupted, dissipated, destroyed; mix it with anything that has more than a background flavour and the truffle is lost, mislaid, ruined.

I would have been happy just to have had this one dish, or the risotto; indeed, I think I would put them on my 'last supper' list of dishes.

After a plate of local cheeses which were, for Rob's taste, a little over-affineured and past their best – the only marginally less than perfect course – came a torta di nocciola with a thin, biscuity base and an intensely nutty, sweet-brittled top, followed by a whole golden poached peach in Muscat and finally a delicate and delicious pale pink fig sorbet with the fruit's characteristic figgy seediness.

You may wonder how on earth anyone who hadn't starved for a week could eat their way through however many courses I have just described, or how it didn't seem like a dreaded tasting menu. I can't really answer either question adequately, but I offer the following observations. Firstly, we were at the table for nearly five hours, so the serving of each dish was staggered in a leisurely, without being annoyingly hiatus-filled, way. There was no sense of being hurried from one course to the next. Neither was there a feeling of ingredients fatigue, the sort you get in chi chi restaurants where each dish is high-piled with the hyperbole of the ambitious chef, too many ingredients, too much decoration and too much built-up food. It is as though you have to eat your way through an alphabet of ingredients and there is no thought as to what does or doesn't work, across the myriad of courses. And then there's the protein overload that is a real killer, meat, meat, fish, fish, eggs, more meat, cheese. The rhythms of a complicated dance-step spring to mind.

When we got up to leave we asked if we could meet the chef, expecting a beefy, wide-girthed Italian of a certain age would emerge gaunt eyed and exhausted from the kitchen. A darkly pretty and delicate small slip of a girl in a crisp long white apron who looked like she should have been doing her homework emerged instead.

'Alessandra,' she said and shook hands.

It was almost impossible to believe she was out of her teens, let alone that she was responsible for this serious kitchen where the cookery skills we had witnessed normally take a couple of decades to perfect, however naturally talented the subject. She had the requisite degree of modesty and shyness that strikes at any male heart and seemed genuinely gratified that we had sprung her from the kitchen, late as it was.

Later in the year when I talked to Andrew Carmellini the chef of the newly opened A Voce in New York about the wonderful dinner I had eaten in the Castello di Verduno, little believing that he would have ever heard tell of the place, he replied immediately with a sort of respectful wistfulness and rue, 'Aah, you mean Alessandra, she is the best. I have eaten there.'

Alessandra, like the white truffle, is one of those 'nearly' secrets, one which the cognoscenti pass on by word of mouth like a Chinese whisper to anyone who they deem worthy of experiencing and guarding their insider knowledge.

It was, without question, the best dinner I had eaten all year, in the best of company and the loveliest of places. It would be difficult if not impossible to beat, it would be stupid to try, and it had happened when I least expected it to, on my birthday, which, however disbelieving of omens one is in one's rational mind, still seemed an auspicious foretaste of the year ahead.

We had Hervé's unerring eye and palate to thank for it, and our initial doubt, my initial bad humour, had been scotched entirely and supplanted by a sense of joy and wonder and anticipation akin to a child's at a birthday party. When the music had stopped I was the one who had unwrapped the final layer of paper and found the hidden treasure within.

I remember my last thought being about the chance meetings that should have brought us all, such a disparate bunch, together that day in that place, ending at the table at the Castello di Verduno and beginning at La Morra, where my father's words had been brought back to me over the breakfast table. Now they were brought back unbidden from the poem he wrote for me when I was a small child, *Getting Warm-Getting Cold* where the last stanza reads:

May she keep this sense of the hidden thing,
The somewhere joy that enthralled her,
When she's uncountable presents older -
Small room left for marvels, and none to say
'You are warmer, now you are colder'.

Peperoni alla Siciliana

SERVES FOUR

This is my version of the peppers
lolling in anchovied olive oil
that Alessandra offered us at the
Castello di Verduno. You may
add or subtract from it as I have.

2 red and 2 yellow organic peppers
1 onion, finely sliced
2 CLOVES of garlic, peeled and sliced
3 TBSP good fruity extra virgin
    olive oil, like Ravida from Sicily
2 TBSP aged balsamic vinegar, and
    by that I mean a mellow, sweet,
    velvety one not a throat
    sharpener
A SMALL BUNCH fresh oregano or
    thyme
18 good black olives, halved and
    pitted
2 salted anchovies, rinsed and
    boned, or 4 anchovy fillets in
    olive oil
1½ TBSP salted capers rinsed under
    a cold tap
sea salt and black pepper

Grill or char your peppers until
    blackened all over in a naked
    flame if possible or, failing that,
    in a hot roasting oven, turning
    them as they blacken. Put them
    immediately into a large bowl,
    cover with clingfilm and leave
them to steam for 20 minutes.
    Peel and seed and cut into long
    thin strips.
While they cool, sweat the onion
    and garlic in hot olive oil in a
    pan over a medium heat, with a
    little salt to release their juices,
    stirring to prevent them from
    sticking and, after five minutes
    or so, covering them with a lid
    and continuing to cook over a
    low heat. Let them soften, with
    the occasional stir, then remove
    the lid and allow them to cook
    a little longer and turn golden
    but not brown.
Add the pepper strips and
    balsamic, with some more oil if
    the pan looks a little dry, and
    the herbs, olives and anchovies,
    which you may crush into the
    onions with a fork.
Continue to cook for a further
    20 minutes. Season.
Cool to warm and serve with
    good bread.

Risotto Balsamico

SERVES TWO

2 TBSP extra virgin olive oil
30G/1OZ unsalted butter
1 SMALL shallot, finely minced
1 STICK of celery, strung and finely
    minced
225G/8OZ Carnaroli rice
A SMALL GLASS of dry white Italian
    wine
UP TO 850ML/1½ PINTS intense
    home made chicken stock
MORE unsalted butter for finishing
    the risotto
freshly grated Parmesan
sea salt and black pepper
best balsamic vinegar

You need the most expensive, velvety, mellow balsamic vinegar for this – mine is a 20 year old. The thin, sharp stuff good enough for a salad dressing just won't do here. It has to be sweetly sticky, viscous and mellow.

Heat the olive oil and butter together in a shallow pan. I have a special Le Creuset cast-iron risotto pan with an enamelled inside; the large surface area helps the rice cook evenly. When the oil and butter begin to bubble, add the finely minced shallot and celery and a little salt and stir them gently until they just begin to soften. Meanwhile heat the wine in a separate pan. Throw in the risotto rice and keep stirring to coat it with the oil and butter, then add the heated white wine. Stir as it bubbles and begins to be absorbed by the rice. Now add the hot chicken stock, a ladle or two at a time. The rice will take around 22 minutes to cook, but the one thing you cannot afford to do is to stop stirring for more than a minute at a time. The stirring is what releases the starch from the rice and gives it the lovely gloopy, starchy texture that a fine risotto should have.

When the risotto is still just al dente, or has bite to it, add a final ladle of stock with a knob of butter, a good handful of grated Parmesan and a scrunch of pepper, white if you are being a purist colour-wise. Put the lid on and remove the pan from the heat. Leave for 5 minutes for all the flavours to mingle and settle before giving the risotto a final stir.

Put a good tablespoon of the best balsamic in the base of each shallow bowl, then carefully heap a mound of white risotto over it. The edges of the puddle should form a black moat around the white mound. Serve with extra cheese in a bowl if you like, though I don't think you need it. Each spoonful of rice and balsamic has the perfect contrast and needs no addition or embellishment. Perhaps serve a salad of pure white, shaved raw fennel afterwards, with an olive oil and lemon dressing, if this is going to be your main course.

Vitello Tonnato Without the Tonnato

SERVES EIGHT

Conventionally speaking, the veal for this dish is poached. I prefer to roast a boned loin and carve it thinly once it has cooled, to retain its juiciness. This is my lighter, more modern version of the classic, re-worked after eating Alessandra's, and includes green olives which go splendidly with veal always. If you miss the mayo and the tuna, put them back in and cloak the meat in the normal way, leaving it to sit under its rich mantle in the fridge for 24 hours.

Preheat the oven to 190°C / 375°F / GAS 5
1.2 KG / 2¾ LB boned loin of veal
1 onion, finely sliced
For the sauce to spread over the veal:
3 TBSP extra virgin olive oil
2 LARGE onions, peeled and finely chopped
3 CLOVES garlic, peeled and sliced
3 TBSP drained, rinsed capers
6 anchovies in olive oil
15–18 good, fruity green olives, halved, pitted and chopped very small
flat leaf parsley
black pepper

Put the sliced onion in the bottom of the roasting pan, plonk the veal on top and roast it for an hour. Leave to cool under foil.

Meanwhile, heat the olive oil in a heavy bottomed pan and add the chopped onion and garlic. Cook over a low heat, stirring from time to time, until softened and golden. Add the chopped capers and anchovies, which you can mash down with a fork, and the well chopped green olives, and just heat through to amalgamate. Season to taste, remembering that anchovies are salt. Add the meat juices and remove from the heat.

Carve the meat very thinly when cold and either pile a little mound of the cooled sauce at the side of each plate of veal, or spread it over the veal on a large serving dish, cover with clingfilm, refrigerate and serve cold but not straight from the fridge.

If you leave the meat in the fridge overnight, take it out an hour before you wish to serve it. Sprinkle with some finely chopped parsley before serving.

White Truffle Pasta

SERVES TWO

If you are lucky enough to have even a walnut-sized fresh white truffle in your hand, don't be tempted to do anything fancy with it. Don't cook it, ever, ever, ever. You just want the breath of heat from the pasta or rice or egg that is the truffle's most esteemed choice of partner to insinuate itself into the truffle, which in turn will infuse its unique and wondrous scent not just over its companion ingredients but over you, the room, the street, the whole village.

Cook *225G/8 oz* good spaghetti according to the instructions on the packet, draining it when al dente, but leaving some of the cooking water clinging to it. Return to the hot pot and throw in a large knob of unsalted butter, preferably the sweet, white Italian kind. Toss a little and scrunch over a little pepper and salt. You may add some good rich Jersey cream or not, depending on how pure and simple you are feeling.

Put into heated bowls and grate over a snowstorm of white truffle as generously as you have truffle.

If you are adding the truffle to a risotto, the same principle applies. Make a plain risotto, and after you have left it for a final few minutes under cover with butter and Parmesan, give it a final stir, dish up and anoint with truffle.

Apple Sponge and Hazelnut Ice Cream

Apples and hazelnuts work so well together, as do sponge and ice cream, hot, sweet sponginess with cold, nutty creaminess, and this is the pudding I came back and made for my daughter Miranda's birthday, inspired by the divine Piedmonte hazelnuts.

Hazelnut Ice Cream

225G/8 oz best hazelnuts toasted in a hot oven until the skins are beginning to go papery but not black, about 5 minutes at 400F/GAS 6

6 LARGE organic egg yolks

140G/5 oz unrefined vanilla caster sugar (keep old, washed and dried pods in jar with sugar)

2 vanilla pods, split down the middle, the seeds scooped out with a teaspoon

500 ML/18 FL oz Jersey milk

570 ML/1 PINT double cream, organic Jersey if possible

Put the hot nuts in a tea towel and roll them around to flake off their skins. Separate the toasted nuts from the skins and place them in the Magimix. And no, there is no point in making this dish with ready-skinned nuts which will have lost a good proportion of their flavour and freshness and won't toast up properly either.

Whizz and whizz and whizz until the nuts go way beyond crumb and start looking sticky and pasty and smell more of praline than nut. Then stop and scrape the paste onto a plate.

Separate the eggs, putting the yolks into a large bowl with the vanilla sugar and the seeds from the pods. Whisk together.

Heat the milk with the two pods until it just reaches scald point then pour it straight over the yolk and sugar mixture, whisking swiftly together.

Return the mixture to the pan over a very gentle heat and continue to whisk, watching carefully to make sure the base doesn't begin to scramble. This process usually takes 10–15 minutes of constant attention.

Once the mixture has thickened you must remove it from the heat and stir in the double cream. Leave to cool. Remove the pods. When barely warm, gently whisk in the praline paste. Churn in an ice cream maker.

Apple Sponge

225G/8 oz unsalted butter (keep 15G/1/2 oz for the apples)

180G/6 oz demarara sugar (keep
  60G/2 oz for the apples)
4 sharp eating apples, peeled, cored
  and chopped into chunks, keep
  from turning brown with a spritz
  of lemon juice
2 LARGE organic eggs
140G/5 oz self-raising flour
ZEST of 1 orange and 1 lemon, both
  organic
2–3 TBSP organic milk

Cream the softened butter and
  sugar together until light and
  pale. Add the eggs and fold
  them in one at a time. Put
  the rest of the butter in a pan
  and melt it before adding the
  chunks of apple and the sugar.
  Cook over a brisk heat for
  5 minutes then remove from
  the heat.
Sift the flour into the butter and
  sugar mixture, and add the
  zests and enough milk to give
  the mixture a soft, dropping
  consistency, about 2 tablespoons.
Throw the just warm apples and
  their buttery, sugary juices into
  the mixture and fold together
  lightly. Scrape into a greased
  23cm/9 in cake tin and bake
  until a skewer comes out clean,
  around 40 minutes, but start
  testing sooner.
Serve hot or warm with dollops
  of the hazelnut ice cream.

2

The Three Muses or How it all Began

I'm pretty sure the first thing Serena taught me how to make was mashed potato with so much unsalted butter and hot milk whipped into it that at first I could only marvel at its extravagance. Mashed potato may not sound like the best or most exciting thing to start with, but if you can't cook good comfort food you are no cook at all.

After my father's death I learned how to cook.

If one were to begin to try to connect the two things, the obviousness with which the one might follow the other, it would most likely be in terms of my wanting to establish my own family, look after and nurture others in a way that was now going to be largely missing from my life, although at eighteen I had no sense of being ready or prepared for the world I had been thrust into.

One thing was for certain, I was out on my own and could boast only the most basic of culinary skills. I had shown neither particular aptitude nor any real enthusiasm for cooking as a child, though I loved good food, but that was all about to change.

I decided to take a year off and model after spending most of the year of my father's final illness at home, and King's College, Cambridge, who had accepted me as one of their first, small intake of women had agreed to keep my place. My grandfather took over certain aspects of my father's role to the extent that anyone in their late seventies who, born in 1896, was essentially a Victorian, could, but then I had a stroke of incredible luck in meeting up with a second cousin I barely knew, while I stayed in Dorset immediately after my father's death.

My cousin, David Shaffer, then a young, gifted child psychiatrist at the Maudsley and subsequently Professor of Child Psychiatry at Columbia University in New York, and a world-renowned expert on child suicide, became a friend and influence immediately, during what was undoubtedly the darkest period of my teenage years, and he has continued to be to the present day.

At the time, he was married to his first wife Serena, a wonderful and inspiring cook, and I became almost an honorary member of David's family, and thus it was I became Serena's kitchen slave and started to learn at her hands. Serena showed me the basics of good home cooking and gave me the confidence to find out the rest for myself. There is really no substitute, no book, that can take the place of watching, trying, testing and tasting, developing your palate and your critical skills, asking and failing, in front of an effortlessly confident and practical cook with a good sense of humour, an even temper and a love and passion for good food made with good ingredients. And, obvious though it may seem, they are few and far between. Being a kitchen slave to someone whose temperament is not suited to teaching is worse than not being taught at all.

I have never had a formal cookery lesson in my life, but have spent time and watched and asked questions of some of the best cooks on the planet, and in my experience the best cooks are invariably generous with their time and their advice if you are keen and hungry to learn. Impatience is the scourge of a good kitchen, and was not an attribute that could be levelled at Serena, always easy going and full of praise.

David and Serena's house in Priory Walk in London had a huge, open kitchen that you stepped into straight off the street, with a table that would seat up to twenty people, a pretty regular occurrence for Sunday lunch at the Shaffers.

David and Serena lived differently. Their kitchen cum dining room cum sitting room was a bold, dramatic statement and one that was entirely new and fascinating to me, liberating, in that there was no separation between the preparing of food and eating it: the kitchen and the dining room. Their kitchen was a room where children played and guests gathered and sat and drank and entertained the cook as she cooked, and the whole pleasure of food was somehow contained yet expanded by putting it in this different context. The kitchen was a theatre of anticipation, and Serena didn't appear to mind people watching her peel and chop and scrub and bake, it was all part of the performance, which entirely took the fear and terror out of entertaining. I learned how to cook in front of people, and as I was just the live-in teenage cousin, the pressure wasn't on me. It *was* a performance, but friends seemed to like it and find it relaxing, it cut through all the bullshit of the hostess behind the green baize door missing the party as she struggled, hot, resentful and drinkless in her pinny with the soufflé, not even getting to talk to the friends she'd invited to lunch or dinner.

Serena and David's friends were frightening and wonderful at the same time. Serena was a dress designer, had been at St Martin's College of Art, and her friends, who never missed a Sunday lunch – indeed, I'm sure they ate no home-cooked food for the rest of the week – included the elegant and delightful Manolo Blahnik, who spoke as rapidly and excitedly as machine-gun fire and had just opened his first shop, Zapata, in Kensington Old Church Street. Serena lived in his impossibly glamorous high purple wedges, patent ankle-strapped stilettos and movie-star style mules and I was an instant convert, spending everything I ever earned modelling on my feet. There was always a certain cachet in not spilling hot fat or olive oil on a pair of Manolos, there still is, and it certainly taught you to be a more careful, less messy cook.

There was the waspish, sartorial oracle Michael Roberts, then fashion editor of the *Sunday Times*, now fashion director of *Vanity Fair*, who used to hoot with laughter at dressing a male model on his Sunday page as a dosser from cardboard city in a dirty raincoat tied with string, and finding kids on the King's Road wearing the look the following week. There were photographers like Eric Boman and his boyfriend Peter Schlesinger, both outrageously beautiful, the former blond and blue-eyed, Peter famously immortalised in the Hockney swimming pool picture;

magazine editors like *Time Out*'s Tony Elliott and fashion designer/activist Katherine Hamnett; and then David's friends who were writers, painters, journalists.

It was a different world to the older, establishment world of my parents, the writers, poets, painters, actors and musicians who had peopled my childhood, but were seen and not heard. Typically for a child of my day, I had been secluded from the world of the grown-ups in the nursery upstairs. I viewed every-thing from the top of the stairs, where I sat secretly in my nightie as my parents' dinner parties carried on below, and the guests talked, sang and played the piano in the formal, first-floor drawing room.

David and Serena's coterie of friends were in their twenties and thirties, so had grown up in the 1960s. As the outsider, the teenage observer, I was worried as to whether I would ever find such a world – indeed any world – to fit into. However, even the impossibly cool, successful, people who graced David and Serena's table seemed to be relieved to be in a proper home, eat-ing a proper Sunday lunch, sitting round the table and partaking of the solid, tangible, family things that perhaps they were unable to re-create in their new, enviably chic and independent lives.

David is the only person I know whose social ease was such that he used to leave his own lunches or dinners before the guests, without ever seeming rude, expecting, encouraging the party to go on without him. He would head upstairs to write a paper, think about a case, go to sleep, before going back to work, and quite often reappear hours later to find no one had left, but we had just moved on to the next meal, supper. Or he would disappear up to his study with whichever guest sought his advice, as everyone did, and still does, whatever their age, which was delivered with the utmost calm, kind, considered reasoning. It was always indisputable, honest and disarmingly unjudgmental and David gave it in the most acceptable way he felt the recipient could take it and act upon it.

Sunday lunch was the high point of the week both in London and at David and Serena's house in Dorset. Once I became a semi-permanent resident, and made it obvious that I was there to learn, Serena began to pass on the secrets that she had only begun to learn herself in the few years since she had left home and married young, at eighteen.

I learned how to spike the sacrificial sized legs of lamb with slivers of garlic – which was anathema to David – and stubs of fresh rosemary, which Serena cooked at nuclear temperatures until pink, and rested under silver foil and tea towels until the juices penetrated back through the meat. I whisked the batter for the Yorkshires, then left it covered under a damp cloth, became acquainted with the starchy sweetness of roast parsnips that we had never had at home, and which she always par-boiled with the roast potatoes. I wrote down notes for her buttery purée of mashed swede and carrot and her more soigné carrots Vichy; for gravy flavoured with some sliced onion on which Serena always bedded the joint down before roasting it, which caramelised and blackened in the pan; for a perfectly sharp, light lemon mousse that was, at the time, à la mode. I whisked egg whites and grated cheese and learned that the secret of a good cheese soufflé, any soufflé, was just not to be frightened of making it. Serena never told me there was any danger of a soufflé not rising, so, armed with the right technique I just did as I was told and expected it to work.

I sliced apples and rolled out sheets of her home made pastry for the apple pies, the chilled butter grated straight into the Magimix from the fridge or even the freezer if she'd forgotten to take it out in time, and watched as Serena speedily assembled and swirled up the flour, butter, sugar and nibbed almonds for her fruit crumbles which were cooked in industrial-sized earthenware dishes, the fruit erupting and breaking through the crumble, branding its colours onto it in a bubbling, sticky goo.

She did everything speedily, apparently effortlessly, and that was an eye-opener, something I wanted to emulate, the idea that a faultlessly delicious lunch could be effected with such consummate ease in front of the guests.

I learned by osmosis, by the repetition that becomes, eventually, second nature; by watching Serena as she cooked willingly and happily for her family and friends without, apparently, ever having to consult a recipe. She was happy cooking, and she kept a happy kitchen. Serena was good at looking after David in what may very well be considered the old-fashioned way, but it didn't appear old fashioned, since she still ran her business designing clothes, brought up their two small sons and was never seen in the kitchen without her Manolos, a slick of sexy crimson lipstick and smudgy brown eye shadow, a flawless complexion and an enviable cleavage. Being motherly and sexy was new to me, but the truth is, Serena was the original domestic goddess; women's lib was in its infancy, but Serena was in her prime, emancipated, not enslaved, by the things she loved doing best, and if one of them was cooking in her kitchen, looking after her husband, her children, her friends, then that was her choice and no women's libbers were going to subjugate her with their dialectic!

I'm pretty sure the first thing Serena taught me how to make was mashed potato with so much unsalted butter and hot milk whipped into it that at first I could only marvel at its extravagance. Mashed potato may not sound like the best or most exciting thing to start with, but if you can't cook good comfort food you are no cook at all.

Next, she taught me how to make the best beef stew, a classic carbonnade made with chuck steak and a pint and a half of Guinness. It was the dish I made for my very first dinner party. I browned the onions, the celery, the carrots then the garlic. I made a little bundle of a bouquet with rosemary, thyme, bay leaves and parsley with a couple of strips of orange peel tied into it. I reintroduced the browned beef to the pot, plunged the bouquet into its heart, then began pouring the fizzing black Liffey water into it until the bubbles began to tremble with heat, not just fizz, and the juices to mingle, thicken, coalesce. I brought the pot to a lazy simmer, covered the ingredients with a circle of greaseproof and the heavy, Le Creuset lid and slid it into the oven for one and a half hours.

When cooked, the peculiar bitterness of the stout had been ameliorated by the scented sweetness of the orange and the carrots and the meat was braised to gluey tenderness. It was one of those 'first moments' when one realises the extraordinary power heat has to transform the taste and texture of raw ingredients into something completely different. It was a rite of passage and a dish of pure pleasure that will always reflect back to the time it came into my life and became a sort of lifeline. Not a winter goes past without my cooking it at least once.

Helping Serena cook started off as a way of thanking her and David for taking me into what was the most relaxed and undemanding household I had ever been in. And given the pressures over the previous year and a half since I had begun to think my father was not going to get better, to the time of his death, and on to the next huge step I was about to take out into the world at Cambridge, it was the most lucky and fortunate bridge that could have been thrown down for me to cross.

However, it was no bolt from the blue that I should suddenly take up culinary cudgels and decide to learn to cook. If it hadn't happened when the opportunity with David and Serena presented itself I suspect it would have happened at Cambridge where eventually, armed with a basic repertoire, I read and fed my fellow students from the collected works of Jane Grigson and Elizabeth David, cooking their books from cover to cover. It was just a matter of time; after all, I come from a long line of greedy women, all of them unashamed gourmands, some of whom could cook and others of whom just knew a lot about good food and eating.

The earliest influence of all, the one who, if I think about it, had the greatest influence on my palate, was my maternal grandmother. She never cooked. She probably didn't know how to boil an egg. She married at 17 and always had a cook. She would order the day's food from her bedroom every morning, where she would be sitting in front of her dressing table perfecting the immaculate hair and make-up that was her trademark, and discussing the dishes and how they should be prepared in such fine detail with the cook that you would imagine she was a professional chef. She knew exactly how food should taste and be prepared, understood the mysteries of most of the techniques you would find in *Larousse Gastronomique*, but when it came to actually doing it, it didn't enter into her list of accomplishments. She was an armchair cook.

Famously, when she first married my grandfather and was untutored in the art of house-keeping, my grandmother called her butcher and ordered 18 pounds of steak: a pound for each of the guests who was coming to dinner that night. She only made that mistake once. She did, however, always provide a table as sumptuous and generous as you could ever imagine. Every meal was like the last supper, and she clearly harboured a secret fear of ever being caught out with not enough to eat for at least double the number of people who were expected. I suspect this is part of my genetic inheritance.

My grandmother was elegant in the way that ladies who had all the time and inclination in the world to be elegant were in those days, dressing in the best couture, her wrists and ankles bird-like even when she put on weight in middle age, and with never a hair out of place. As a child I assumed her strawberry blonde, waist-length hair which she coiled into a pleated chignon as I watched, was her own colour, and always felt cheated that I hadn't inherited it, but I eventually realised that it was pretty unlikely to have kept its colour well into her seventies.

My grandmother was never cross. I never remember her raising her voice when Dan and I went to stay, which we did every school holiday, though I'm sure she could be stubborn and intransigent if it suited her. The thing was, it didn't. She led what seemed to me to be the perfect life between the large, beautiful house called Upper Parrock, with its gardens, kitchen garden and over two hundred acres of land and woodland in East Sussex, and a small flat in Mayfair, from where we would go on our frequent holiday and half-term sorties to 'the little grocer's down the road', which is how she saw Fortnum and Mason. Every member of staff would almost genuflect as they said 'Good morning m'lady,' to the tiny figure striding regally but somehow always filled with amusement and delight, through the food halls, stopping off for us to marvel over the ants in chocolate and the bees in honey before sweeping us upstairs to the dining room for lunch or to the Fountain for our favourite tea. Chocolate sacher-torte, fresh orange juice and blackcurrant ice cream was as immutable as the shop itself, and Dan and I would never have varied the menu. Breaking with tradition was simply unthinkable. That's what tea at Fortnum's meant.

My grandparents had what I believed, and still do, was the happiest of marriages. 'Car', as I always knew my grandmother, looked after my grandfather and made sure the table at Upper Parrock was the best in the land and that he never wished for anything. The deal was, nor did she, and it seemed to work at all levels for the 52 years of their marriage. A not inconsiderable achievement.

Nothing tasted as good as the food at my grandmother's house, particularly the 'great barons' of roast beef on a Sunday and the roast potatoes cooked to black in the dripping, and nobody else's roast potatoes ever have tasted so good. Food memories from childhood play these sorts of tricks on you and are largely to do with that first incredible explosion on the tongue when you try something new. After that you yearn for what is essentially an unrepeatable, visceral experience, as emotive and thrilling as the feelings you have when you first fall in love and all your senses are on red alert.

That penetrating scent of the Sunday roast cooking wafted through the dining room, where the great eighteenth-century oak refectory table was already set with Georgian silver and the herd of silver cow creamers that my grandmother collected; it wafted in from the kitchen and on into the huge drawing room where the great, grey oak logs crackled and spat constantly in the huge open fireplace they were fed into summer through autumn, autumn through winter and spring, giving that sense of changelessness that only the seasons outside disputed.

In my father's autobiography, *The Buried Day*, he opens the first chapter with his memory of frying bacon, indeed, it is his first memory. Memories of childhood are inevitably sensory, inevitably about a smell and its association with place, the two of which are inextricably bound. My three children are in total agreement over the scents that speak to them of home and child-hood, and are the most evocative and enduring. There is bread baking and its hot, damp, yeasty scent permeating the kitchen as it cools; there is the scent of a cake at the point at which it smells ready; there is the Sunday roast which is Miranda's favourite, particularly if it is lamb underscored with rosemary and garlic. Harry loves the pungent scent of fresh basil with its particular, fragrant, almost aniseedy notes, its reminder of warm climes and a Mediterranean sun; Charissa loves tomatoes from the green-house. There is fresh coffee brewing and the bacon my father wrote of which we all feel is the most powerful of them all.

But it is oak, mingled with the scent of the roast, which always hit you as you walked in through my grandparents front door, that is the smell I remember most from my childhood, other than the first scent of turf smoke that we looked out for as we crossed Ireland each summer to the west.

How eagerly after we'd arrived at my grandparents' did we wait to be called to the table, to follow the roast with one of Rhoda, my grandmother's cook's, many traditional puddings: lemon chiffon pie, apple, Bakewell or treacle tart with thick cream from the farm dairy, chocolate sponge spiked like a hedgehog with whole almonds and drowning in bitter chocolate sauce, crumble made with Victoria plums straight from the tree.

Breakfasts were equally magical, from the occasional treat of a crisply fried wild salmon fishcake which was my grandfather's favourite, to kippers jugged to smoky-wet juiciness with a melt-ing knob of farm butter slipping down their backbones. There were softly cooked skeins of perfect scrambled eggs from my grandmother's hens sprinkled with chopped parsley and halves of grilled tomato from the greenhouse. Sometimes we would simply indulge in the unimaginable luxury of cornflakes with ivory clots of double cream, Demerara sugar and bananas. The cold cream clung to the crunchy flakes and the gritty sugar to the cream. It was decadent and utterly delicious.

Afternoon tea was as much of an event as lunch, though maybe a comma rather than a full-stop. A trolley was wheeled into the dining or drawing room with perfect brown egg and cress sandwiches and white sandwiches full of Shippams crab paste which we always had something of a love/hate relationship with. It was sort of compulsive but a bit like cat-food. Then there would be Fuller's fancies, tiny iced and butter-creamed cakes which my tooth was not quite sweet enough to wholly like, and sometimes their coffee cake with walnuts set at intervals on the top. I preferred the triple-decker Victoria sponge made by Mrs Pollard, the gardener's wife, with home made strawberry jam and cream spilling from its twin midriffs. There was always a faint dusting of sieved icing sugar and the grid patterned memory of cake rack still etched on its sandy, buttery crumbed top. It felt frightfully grown-up to be given a cake fork to eat it with and a bone china cup and saucer of real China tea, which I pretended to like for years before I really did. But the greatest treat was the cylinder of chocolate Bath Oliver biscuits which we were allowed to plunder and spread with lashings of thick farm cream.

My grandmother made us feel part of a grown-up world, a world where good food and good taste went together and could be discussed and enthused over in a way which was more frowned on than fashionable at the time.

Every morning we would wake to birdsong in the creeper that

covered the ancient house, and the distant scent of toast toasting and coffee brewing. How little those smells and tastes meant then. How little did I dream that in years to come, when the great house had gone, and both my grandparents with it, memories of those tastes and smells would convey the most intense sensations. I would taste past happiness in its most potent form of loss and regret.

Usually the cousins would come over to our mutual grandparents for Sunday lunch – a ritual which my oldest cousin, Deborah, an exemplary cook and partner in greed, and I, have carried on throughout our respective children's childhoods – and we five children would sit at our own table being as subversive and noisy as we dared, since we weren't being kept in check by our respective parents at the big table. However, the presence of our grandfather loomed large, his dynastic, disciplinarian mien permeated the house and if we went too far, weren't impeccably mannered, showed signs of disrespect, he pounced. It was enough to know he would. I also observed, from an early age, that whilst he kept an immaculate table and was the most generous host, he never ate much himself. We ate the puddings, poured on lashings of cream, while he had a small piece of cheese, an apple or just cracked a few Brazil nuts which were always laid out on the sideboard on a glass dish with walnuts and hazelnuts and a pair of nutcrackers.

My grandmother's love and appreciation of the finest ingredients, of simple, good things being grown and picked and cooked within yards of the kitchen, and allowed to speak for themselves, were all things that I didn't know were special then, but have come to value as the most special of all. Helping Pollard the gardener pick the tiniest ripe tomatoes from the greenhouse, or peas for a dish of petits pois cooked with mint, butter, cream and the heart of a lettuce; simple asparagus cut and cooked straight out of the earth, tiny new potatoes with flecks of mint and butter, carrots still sweet from the ground and raspberries still warm from the cage, were all part of the legacy which my grandmother didn't so much teach or preach as show and suggest. They became, and are still, my guiding principles.

Without realising it, I had acquired a sophisticated and discriminating palate, and all without being able to cook anything other than an omelette, but when I went off to boarding school it stood me in bad odour rather than in good. I simply wasn't prepared to eat food that looked and tasted as dismal as it did at Bedales. These being the days before school canteens, we sat on tables of ten in the dining room, the food was dished up by a sixth former at the head and there was no choice. If you didn't like the million-ways-with-mince and soggy cabbage and the dead man's arm with lumpy custard, too bad. You ate it or starved, or in my case survived on Mars Bars from the school tuck shop and Quaker macaroni cooked in a pan then drowned in Heinz tomato soup and grated Cheddar cheese that I made on an illicit primus stove I kept in my dorm. Amazing that I was neither caught nor expelled for risking the girls' boarding house to the flames.

Once a term my grandmother sent emergency rations, the most esoteric and wonderful hampers from Fortnum's stuffed with cooked ducks, tins of lychees and raspberries, Schloer apple juice and chocolate Bath Olivers. Not forgetting the Malvern Water bottle she would fill with vodka. We would fall upon the food with the usual ravening maw of teenage hunger and demolish the lot at a sitting.

Finally I led a hunger strike at school against the appalling standard of the food but hadn't, as yet, begun to relate the quality of the cooking to the raw ingredients. Naturally the strike had no effect whatsoever on the staff or the chef, who served it all up again at supper, but from then on I decided to espouse a singularly unpleasant, near macrobiotic diet, despite the fact that I loved food and adored meat.

The word 'organic' may have had a completely different dictionary definition then and had certainly not passed into common currency, but I had managed to cotton on to the fact that 'wholefood' was better for you and that we were all on the way to ruination and disease if we lived on marge and Mighty White, white pasta and rice, too much red meat, too many tinned and processed foods, boiled to death vegetables, white sugar and golden syrup, which just about summed up the complete culinary lexicon at school.

It was the beginnings of the bran revolution and school food was the enemy. I started to take my own muesli and wheat germ into breakfast in a back-pack with some live yoghurt. My friends saw this as fully-fledged eccentricity bordering on insanity, particularly since I've always hated yoghurt and don't like milk. I forced it down, telling myself it was good for me, that I would lead a longer and healthier life. I bought Tamari sauce and tofu, bean sprouts and bottles of Biotta beetroot juice which was the colour and viscosity of offal blood and had a sickening, earthily sweet taste and which I sipped by the thimbleful.

Never again, after a few months of it, did I ever eat or drink something purely because it was good for me. The notion of food and pleasure became sacrosanct, you couldn't, shouldn't, divorce the one from the other.

The vegetarian option at school was equally grim. Hard-boiled eggs in a sorry, lumpen white sauce flecked with Green Giant sweetcorn; tweedy vege-burgers like corrugated cardboard; a slop of putrid, khaki-coloured curried vegetables and rice. You either starved or ate, greedily, pleasurelessly.

At home there were no concessions made to my new vegetarian regime. My father had just been diagnosed diabetic on the way to our discovering that the underlying cause was really cancer of the pancreas, so my mother was already catering for one special diet. She was not about to entertain my newfound notions of what we should all be eating and start buying brown rice, millet and tofu-burgers. I didn't know how to cook so I just lived on vegetables, cheese and eggs.

Monotony is a great destroyer of ideals.

Before I went up to Cambridge, my father's health deteriorated to the point at which it was obvious to me he must be dying. It was unspoken until the day I got the results awarding me a place as one of the first girls at King's College the year they went co-educational. The overwhelming and surprising news was instantly vitiated by the fact that I was then sat down and told by my mother that my long-term suspicions were correct and my father was dying, so I shouldn't go away that Christmas as it would be his last, and that we were on no account to let on to my father that he was dying. That the doctor had said we mustn't take hope away from him.

This was not just a difficult concept to adjust to, the pretence that he would get better, but the whole deception and charade that we as a family were being forced to embark upon and which, apparently, was common at the time. No degree of rationalising or imagining made it comprehensible to me at just eighteen and in hindsight hasn't since, but that was the way it was. The house we lived in at the bottom of Crooms Hill in Greenwich quickly seemed to take on the air of the place where my father was going to die, it no longer seemed the same home. I remember my father's praising the lamb my mother had cooked for supper one night only to be told that it was veal. Perhaps his taste-buds had been blighted by the illness, or perhaps it was the pills whose label said, nauseatingly, that the ingredients were concocted from pigs' pancreas. Alongside this he was losing weight so fast that, despite dressing as immaculately as ever, his clothes hung scarecrow-like from his coat-hanger frame and he was permanently cold.

My godmother Jane, the writer Elizabeth Jane Howard, came to lunch. She took me aside afterwards and suggested that my father should not be allowed to die in the changed atmosphere of this tall, gloomy house and without the care and attention of a fully trained nurse, whom she had had installed at that time at her home on Hadley Common in Hertfordshire for her mother Kit. Married to Kingsley Amis and with her brother Monkey and painter friend Sargy Mann also living there, and step-children Martin, Phil and Sally showing up as and when they felt like it, it was a full house, but Jane asked if I could help persuade my mother that we should move up there as a family; that my father should be told he was going there to convalesce. We were like fellow conspirators in the plan, which made me feel the situation was not quite so beyond all our control as it had seemed until then.

When we arrived at Lemmons, Jane and Kingsley's huge and beautiful house with a garden more like a grand, country house garden than one of the outer suburbs of London at the end of the Northern Line at High Barnet, there was a brief period when I almost believed a miracle had happened and my father was going to get better. The new company and stimulation were something that my father, always a stoic, seemed able to play along with and enjoy in a way he hadn't had to at home with just us, and, not wanting to disappoint in the social sense, or to disappoint himself as far as his standards of good behaviour were concerned, appearances were kept up at all times by him, and, consequently, by all of us. If there was to be no chink in my father's private armour against pain, then how could we possibly show him that we could see what he wasn't prepared to show us?

The joint charade, which I believed it to be, didn't make it any easier though. Every time I went into my father's room to see him and talk or just keep him company while he attempted to eat lunch or supper, I was aware of the short distance between what I was saying and what I was really thinking and wanted to say. The fact was, I couldn't tell him that I knew he was dying, that I loved him, that I didn't want him to die and was much angrier about it than he appeared to be, because of the rules of this endgame that didn't make sense.

'I know you're dying, why are we deceiving each other about something so important, so final?' I wanted to say, believing it would be a relief, and that if ever faced with something similar, I would insist on honesty. It had to be easier. But I just sat there.

I wonder if my father ever saw it in my eyes or whether he gave clues away that I didn't pick up on, but I think he probably didn't until the very end a few months later.

In the meanwhile, with such a houseful, every mealtime felt like an occasion; there were never less than a dozen people at the table and often nearer twenty. I was Jane's jobber and chopper, and I think she was quite pleased to finally have a female ally in a house that, up until then, relied entirely, domestically speaking, upon her. My unskilled labour meant I couldn't ruin or be responsible for anything but I could help, and I could begin to learn a little about cooking and budgeting for an ever-shifting population of people with huge and, in Kingsley's case, eclectic appetites. I could learn, like Jane had, how to take it in my stride; how not to think of it as anything to complain about, after all, it might mean that I too could establish and live with a commune of writers, painters and inventors some time in the future, and gather them around a circular table thrice daily for a delicious feast.

The kitchen lent itself to these huge, impromptu performances and it was a chance for me, still awkward in adult company, to spend more time with Jane who, quite apart from being my godmother, had become one of the first grown-ups to become a friend without being judgemental or parent-like. And I sensed she was sympathetic to my plight, which I was, in a funny way, almost unaware of, and not just to that of my mother, my brother and, of course, my father. I think I was sympathetic to hers too, knowing that she had had an affair with my father years before and feeling that she loved him still, though probably in a different way now, and wanted him to die gracefully in an environment that would give him all the things he loved and needed most. We became, somehow, a little unit outside the main protagonists though we never discussed it at the time.

The attention I got from Jane and the time spent with her in the kitchen also meant that my mother had more time to cope with the impending horror of losing my father and of becoming a widow rather than a wife.

Jane loved food and loved cooking but, married to Kingsley who saw food as more of a time consuming nuisance and a waste of valuable drinking time than anything else, she was sorely tested. Kingsley would start drinking at around 11 am, often making a jug of Bloody Mary so lethal that he had felt it more accurate to re-christen his version a Fucking Mary.

Fucking Marys were served not long after Kingsley's breakfast fry up and part-way through the morning's writing, as an incentive, like school break, to get you through to lunch time. Kingsley would shuffle hung-over and be-slippered but fully functioning to the stove in his Beethoven sweatshirt, despite, usually, having crawled up the stairs to bed on all fours a few hours earlier, and would fry himself a pan full of banana and potato fritters with whatever he felt like in the more mundane eggs and bacon line, and wash the whole lot down with a tankard of ginger beer. I secretly believed this was the only time Kingsley enjoyed eating, not least because it was an unveiled insult to Jane and her extremely good cooking.

At the time, potato and banana fritters seemed like a normal, grown-up breakfast habit, albeit disgusting and funny, but not essentially weird, as so many grown-up habits were, though looking back on it later it was both bizarre *and* disgusting and deeply weird.

Every meal was convivial, which was its whole point in Kingsley's eyes, in that he was unmoved by and uninterested in food, but loved an audience, was a generous and amusing host, so amusing, that jokes and impersonations that he performed at breakfast, lunch and dinner left one in stitches, yet always worrying that one could never amuse Kingsley as well as he would amuse everyone else. It doesn't occur to you, ill-prepared for the grown-ups table and with all the absence of eloquence of a gawky teenager, that you are there precisely because you are the best and most receptive audience. And because you are new, haven't heard all the jokes yet, you will laugh longer and harder. Right down to Kingsley's party piece of being able to complete the whole alphabet perfectly intelligibly during the course of a single burp, which Dan and I spent years practising afterwards but never managed to pull off.

My father, pretty soon confined to his bedroom, missed these uproarious mealtimes, though Kingsley used to appear in papa's room every morning with his music catalogue and select exactly what my father wanted to listen to that day. It was extraordinary that the process of dying could be made so palatable; could sometimes be almost forgotten; that there was always laughter despite Kingsley's lack of interest in or repudiation of almost all Jane's culinary offerings.

At lunch time Kingsley simply went to the enormously well-stocked pantry and opened up a jar of the most heinous tasting pickled mussels or clams, or seized a pickled egg or onion to accompany his bread and cheese, which he would wash down with whatever alcohol he was being paid to write about for that month's *Playboy*. Jane and I would have made a cauldron of something like minestrone, which everyone else would fall upon, followed by a huge salad and some bread and cheese, but secretly I sort of envied Kingers his insult to good taste and his single-minded approach to controlling what he ate and when.

It was, in a way, no different to my father's past regime, his daily, unchanging lunch of a bowl of cornflakes, a Penguin biscuit and an apple. I believe now, though I didn't know it then, that writers, perhaps any artists, starved of the norm in their profes-sional lives, seek the comfort of sameness, of routine rituals, wherever they can, and food is the place where they can thought-lessly, mid-stream, stop off and indulge in the most primitive of eating habits in preparation for the afternoon ahead.

In the deep-freeze next door to the kitchen there were gallon tubs of all the best ice creams from Marine Ices at Chalk Farm — chocolate, vanilla, pistachio, coffee, strawberry, banana — which Monkey, Jane's brother, was in charge of. He bought industrial-sized packets of ice cream cones and squeezy bottles of chocolate, raspberry and fudge sauces; Cadbury's flakes, packets of hundreds and thousands and sprinkles of nutty crunch. He delighted in being responsible for the garish, fairground vulgarity of the one, the utmost good taste of the other, and the perverse marriage of the two. It was an adult's-eye view of childhood paradise revisited, with no holds barred, and after every meal we would head for the freezer and Monkey would delightedly push double and triple scoops down into our cones for us to festoon as indiscriminately as no ice cream van or Italian restaurant would ever dream of with a cornucopia of extras. If Mart and Phil and Dan were back for the weekend, we'd take our spangled cornets into the library and play Monopoly so competitively and aggressively that we would still be at it seven hours later when Jane called dinner.

At dinner time Kingsley would eat what we were eating, dishes like belly of pork and beans which was a delicious, poor man's rib-sticker of a cassoulet, shepherd's pie, spaghetti Bolognese and kedgeree, and, despite never praising their merits, would at least consume, very slowly and deliberately, the small plateful that all serious drinkers manage to choke down to at least line their stomachs before the evening's boozing carries on in earnest. While my father's hearty appetite waned, Kingsley's lack of appetite never faltered.

If Papa ever voiced a desire for something, ice cream and chocolate sauce more often than not, since his sweet tooth was legendary, we would all be thrilled and set to work immediately, as happened on the day when, out of the blue, he suddenly said he felt like some profiteroles.

It was a weekend. I had been sent back to Bedales for the day where my brother was still at school, and on returning home, found the atmosphere in the house somewhat different to how I had left it. My father had apparently enjoyed a plate of home made profiteroles but had subsequently been in so much pain that Tess, the nurse, had immediately decided to administer morphine. When I arrived back from Hampshire, my mother wondered why I hadn't brought Dan back from school with me, but it hadn't occurred to me, since when I had left there had been no question of my father's being so close to the end that we should have all been gathered around him.

I was sent in to see Papa. He had not yet been knocked out by the injection.

He managed a smile; a pained smile but a smile, and made it clear he was listening as I told him about my trip to see my brother.

I said goodnight.

He said 'Goodbye.'

That was the only time the mask dropped, or appeared to drop.

No one uses language more precisely than a poet; each word in each sentence has its place, could not be replaced by an alternative. Whether the drugs were working already I don't know, but his 'Goodbye' was the last thing he ever said to me, in fact the last words he spoke. I have thought about it ever since and never felt less than sure that it was the tacit understanding that I had been searching for but unable, forbidden, to ask, and that 'Goodbye' was, as far as Papa was concerned, enough. That it should be enough for me, was all that he could give, that I had had the rest and would now have to be on my way as he was on his. Alone.

I didn't tell anyone what he had said.

That night I was allowed to spend the night next door to my father's room in Kingsley's library on his peacock-coloured velvet Victorian sofa. I did not sleep. My mother, Jane, Tess the nurse, Ursula Vaughan-Williams – Ralph's widow, an old family friend and Dan's godmother – kept a vigil next door, which, despite my protestations, I was excluded from. In the morning I was told to ring school and have my brother catch a train home to Lemmons. I woke George, the housemaster, who was momentarily confused and cross until he remembered the situation. I rang Sean, my half-brother who lived in London. I went back to my father's bedroom where he was still breathing in short, shallow breaths.

It was more peaceful than alarming, this final few hours, after knowing how much pain he'd attempted to conceal from us over the last year. The transition from life to death was almost imperceptible, and so unlike that first transition that brings us into the world, announcing, rather than denying our presence. It meant peace, pain-free peace. It didn't seem to me as though anything had happened. It felt as though my father were still there, so the tears didn't come.

An hour or so later Jane and I seemed unsure as to what to do next, as to how life should go on. Was thinking about breakfast or about being hungry blasphemous, obscene? I have no idea, but we were both afflicted by a sudden storm of hunger and drove into Barnet in the rain to the baker's shop. We bought a bag of doughnuts which we somehow had to eat there and then and not bring back into the house. We ate the whole bagful, scratchy sugared, abruptly trickling a hidden stash of viscous red jam, all six of them gone in minutes as we sat staring sightlessly out of the front windscreen through the rain.

Perfect Scrambled Eggs

Without a perfect egg you won't get a perfect scramble. I favour brown speckledy Maran hens', Cotswold Legbars or Mabel Pearman's Burford Browns – the last two available from good supermarkets – or any freshly laid free-ranger with a truly golden yolk. In May I buy turkey eggs in the Taunton farmers' market, a pound a throw, and it only takes one each to make the best scrambled eggs in the universe. They don't have quite the richness of duck eggs but they make up for that with their colour and softness of texture. If you are using hens' eggs, you need three per person, whisked with a little slug of creamy Jersey milk or even cream if you're feeling extravagant, which will make for a creamier, smoother scramble. Don't add any salt when you add a good scrunch of pepper to the whisked eggs and milk – it will make the eggs watery – wait until the end.

Melt a generous 30g / 1 oz of best unsalted butter for a three egger or a little more for a six in a pan over a gentle heat. Add the egg mixture and pull off the heat to begin the stirring of the curds. Keep the heat to a minimum, the slower you cook the eggs, the better they will be. Keep putting them back on the heat for a couple of minutes and stirring, then removing them for 30 seconds and continuing to stir. Eventually they will begin to set loosely right through.

Remove from the heat and stir in another 15–30g or so of butter in small bits. Finish on the heat but leave the eggs sloppily set. They will continue to cook as you spoon them onto warmed plates.

I favour hot buttered granary toast on the side, like The American, so it doesn't sog, a small pinch of finely chopped parsley on top of the eggs and a sprinkle of Maldon salt once they're on the plate and grilled tomatoes on the side.

Carbonnade of Beef

SERVES SIX–EIGHT

So here it is, the dish I cooked for my first dinner party, which I would perfectly happily cook for my last. Both my daughters, Miranda and Charissa, love and make it. I get my beef from Richard Vaughan, his aged for 33 days longhorn, the stuff of legends.

2 TBSP olive oil
1.5KG / 3 ¼ LB chuck steak, cut into
    large cubes and trimmed
1 large onion, chopped
450G / 1LB carrots, cut into fingers
6 CLOVES of garlic, peeled but left
    whole
2 TBSP plain flour
1 TBSP tomato pureé
700ML / 1 ¼ pints of Guinness
1 bouquet garni with 3 bay leaves,
    2 sprigs rosemary, thyme and
    parsley and 3 strips of orange
    peel, tied together with string
salt and pepper

Preheat the oven to 150°C / 300°F / GAS 2.

Heat the oil in a heavy-bottomed casserole and seal the meat briefly on all sides. Remove with a slotted spoon and put to one side. Add the onion, carrots and garlic and let them begin to colour before sprinkling them with the flour. Add the tomato purée, stir and then return the meat to the casserole. Pour in the liquid and bring to boiling point. Season, cover with a sheet of greaseproof paper and a lid, and put in the oven for 1½ hours.
When the meat is tender, remove and discard the bouquet garni and serve hot, with mashed potato or colcannon.

Short Rib of Beef and Borlotti Bean Casserole

SERVES SIX

Hearty peasant fare which I have cooked since my student days, having originally eaten this dish at my godmother Elizabeth Jane Howard's kitchen table. This is my version. If you can get Geoff Sayer's Well Hung Meat Company Toulouse sausages sent to you, bury a few of them in the pot and you will have a poor man's cassoulet.

450G/1LB *borlotti beans, soaked overnight*
2–3 TBSP *olive oil*
1 LARGE *onion, or 8 or 9 shallots*
6–8 CLOVES *of garlic, peeled and whole*
THE HEART *of a head of celery with its leaves, chopped*
675G–900G/1½–2LBS *beef short ribs*
2 × 400G/13 OZ TINS *organic peeled tomatoes*
1 JAR *organic passata*
3 *bay leaves,* A BUNCH *of thyme and parsley stalks tied together, and* A LARGE HANDFUL *of fresh, flat-leaf parsley black pepper and salt*
EXTRA *flat-leaf parsley*
6 *Toulouse sausages*

Boil the borlotti beans in plenty of water, removing the scum and boiling fast for 10 minutes. Then slow to a simmer and put the lid on for 40 minutes. Drain the beans (which will be undercooked at this stage) and reserve their liquid. Heat the oil in a large, heavy-bottomed pan and sauté the chopped onion or whole shallots, with the garlic and chopped celery until softened and translucent. Add the short ribs, placing them in the bottom of the pan. Brown them on both sides. Next add the passata, the tins of tomatoes, the herbs and the beans. Season.

Make sure that the stew has an inch (2cm) of liquid covering it – if it hasn't, then add a little of the reserved bean liquid.

Tuck the Toulouse sausages into the bottom of the pan, bring to the boil, reduce heat to a gentle simmer, put on the lid and leave to cook for 1–1½ hours. Once you are happy that the beans are thoroughly cooked, remove from the heat, put a quarter of the beans through the coarse disc of a mouli, sprinkle with flat-leaf parsley and serve – my favourite accompaniment is mashed potato made with un-salted butter and hot, creamy milk.

Lemon Chiffon Pie

SERVES SIX-EIGHT

Isn't the name enough to conjure up a sort of silky rapture of a pie, its scent of lemon wafting through the kitchen. I have no idea how Rhoda made hers, but this is how I make it, and it adapts well to chocolate and coffee versions.

Preheat oven to 190°C/375°F/ GAS 5

For the short crust pastry:
180G/6 OZ flour and 90G/3 OZ unsalted butter baked blind for 20 minutes, washed with a little egg white, spiked with the tines of a fork and finished off in the oven as the centre is not cooked inside the tart shell.

For the filling:
2 organic eggs, separated
90G/3 OZ unrefined vanilla caster sugar
JUICE OF 1–2 organic lemons and the zest of one
1 TSP gelatine powder dissolved in 1 TBSP warm water
150ML/5 FL OZ double Jersey cream

Beat the egg yolks with 60g/2oz of the sugar thoroughly then add the juice of the lemons.

If they are small and not very juicy, two not one. Cook this mixture in a double boiler or in a bowl over a pan of simmering water, the base not touching the water, until it has thickened, whisking it all the time.

Remove from the hot water and add the zest and gelatine, continuing to whisk it off the heat until it has fluffed up and is on the point of setting.

Whisk the egg whites until they reach firm peak stage, then whisk in the rest of the sugar until they are satiny.

Whisk the cream until softly holding, not too firm or it will go rigid and grainy.

Fold both egg whites and cream into the lemon mixture. When the mixture has set so that it will hold its shape, but not before, scrape it into the cold tart shell. Serve cold.

NOTE: You may prefer to make a slightly sweet tart shell with a tablespoon of unrefined icing sugar sieved in with the flour and an egg yolk added before a little less cold water to enrich and bind the pastry.

Profiteroles

The last pudding my father ate.
His love of puddings is part
of my genetic inheritance and
seems to have continued on
down the line to my children.

Choux paste
85G/3OZ unsalted butter
A PINCH of salt
270ML/9 FL OZ water
*140G/5 OZ plain flour, sifted into
    a bowl*
*4 organic eggs, three kept whole,
    one whisked*

For the filling
*300ML/10⁶ OZ double cream, Jersey
    if possible*

Chocolate sauce
*200G/7OZ bar good dark chocolate,
    Valrhona 64% cocoa solids*
55G/2OZ butter
4 TSP golden syrup
3 TBSP Jersey cream

Preheat the oven to 200°C/400°F/
GAS 6.

Line a baking tray with silicon
paper and set aside. To make
the choux paste, put the butter,
salt and water in a pan and
bring to the boil. Just as it
comes to the boil, remove the
pan from the heat and quickly
add the flour. Stir with a
wooden spoon until it coheres,
then return to a low heat and
cook for a minute until it comes
away from the side of the pan.
Remove from the heat again and
leave to cool for a couple of
minutes – you don't want the
eggs to cook when you add
them. Break the first egg into
the pan and whisk it vigorously
in with a fork.
Add the next 2 eggs one at a
time. Then, depending on how
resistant the mixture is, slowly
add the final whisked egg a bit
at a time until the mixture is a
little easier to work and looks
glossy.
Choux will solidify if you leave it,
so immediately place teaspoons
of the mixture on the baking
tray and bake in the preheated
oven for 15 minutes. Reduce
the temperature to 150°C/
300°F/GAS 2 and cook for a
further 15–20 minutes or until
crisp and brown.
Remove from the oven and pierce
the side of each profiterole to
let out the steam. Cool on a
rack.
Whisk the Jersey cream for the
filling until slackly stiffened.
Just before you are ready to

serve the profiteroles, slit them, add a good spoonful of cream to the middles, re-splice and then pour over the warm chocolate sauce, as thickly as you dare.

CHOCOLATE SAUCE

Melt the chocolate in a double boiler with the butter, golden syrup and the Jersey cream. At no stage should the top pan or bowl touch the water, nor should the water boil, or your cocoa solids will separate. You can make the sauce in advance and reheat it.

3

You Say Tomato: *Cooking for the American*

I had to break him in gently.
My beef stew became a *carbonnade*
suffused with the bitter undertow
of a pint and a half of Guinness
and some strips of orange peel
and herbs. The oxtail was really
queue de boeuf des vigneronnes,
gluey with bone-sticky juices,
flecks of oak-smoked bacon
and crushed seedless grapes.
Most importantly, I knew how
to make chicken soup…

It's time to tell you how it all began, this life of to-ing and fro-ing, of crossing the Atlantic as though it were the Bristol Channel, of leading a double life between the racing city pulse of New York and the slow, somnolent heartbeat of the depths of the Somerset hills.

It all started five years ago on a trip Rob made to Ireland in the April of 2002. His first ever trip to Ireland. Up until then I had been flying solo, exploring the world of food wherever it led me for my weekly food column for *The Daily Telegraph* and numerous other food magazines. This time, Bord Bia, the Irish food board, had invited me to speak at an international food symposium in Kinsale, County Cork, and for once I was unable to get out of doing something that my better instincts told me not to do.

Kinsale is a magical corner of Ireland, and inarguably the best larder in the land, but public speaking is something I studiously avoid. In retrospect it was one of the luckiest day of my life; in reality it was a nightmare of nerves and weeks of build-up, wondering why I had accepted in the first place.

Rob was part of the mob of American heavyweights from the international food world who had come to check out all things Irish, which in his case, as a first timer, included the famous washed-rind cheeses of the Beara Peninsula which he was planning on visiting with Neal's Yard's founding father Randolph Hodgson after the conference.

Somewhat presumptuously, within a couple of hours of meeting me, Rob asked if I wanted to go with him, but I had to turn him down as I was heading back to England the following day. My brother Daniel was coming over on one of his all too rare visits to Somerset from Ireland to spend the weekend with me and the children.

Rob had strolled brazenly and late straight up to the front row of the marquee where five hundred people were sitting waiting for the Irish Minister for Food and Agriculture to make his speech before I made mine, and had sat down directly in my eye-line so that when I marched up to the podium I had to avert my gaze. I was uncomfortably aware that I might lose my place otherwise, which was all peculiarly disturbing. Crazy though it may seem, I remember thinking one, just one, irrational thought, 'My life has changed', as he sauntered up the aisle, apparently fixing his mega-watt stare full beam on me.

Or perhaps I was just suffering from an advanced case of *deludia gravis*.

I also remember noticing how incredibly white his teeth were and how out of season brown he was.

He could only be an American.

After the speeches Rob emerged from the back of the queue that was waiting to meet me and introduced himself. We appeared to be wearing identical mossy green V-neck cashmere jerseys. His eyes were the colour of early summer gooseberries close up, his grin wide and unapologetically boyish.

'You said all the things people want to hear but nobody ever dares say,' he said. And, handing me his card, 'It was a passionate and brilliant speech and I'd like to buy you dinner on the strength of it. Do you ever come to New York?'

Despite his 'not being backward in coming forward', as my family would say, he also, though I don't know quite why, seemed irresistibly shy.

And no, I am not flattery resistant, particularly if the flatterer is irresistible.

We bumped into each other again an hour or so later when the delegates were milling around in the hotel foyer, which is where Rob collared me with the invitation to head off to the misty-fingered peninsula where a handful of Ireland's best cheese makers have their small dairies.

An hour later we ran into each other at Kinsale's renowned café restaurant Fishy Fishy, just a step from the water, but both of us were lunching with other people. Rob asked me about my plans for dinner, which were cast-iron unbreakable: I was guest of honour at a Bord Bia dinner with a group of chefs, so I tried my best to get him invited. Carolyn Cavele handles the PR for Bord Bia and it was she who had twisted both my arms and sat on me to get me to give a speech. The least she could do was offer Rob a seat at the dinner. But she wasn't biting. In fact she didn't seem to register the tones of entreaty I had adopted, or if she did, she ignored them, telling me that every seat was taken. As Richard Corrigan, my favourite Irish chef, hadn't been seen since the previous night's festivities and for all we knew was still holed up in a snug intravenusing poteen, I had thought Rob could come in his stead. Carolyn thought otherwise and said she had already filled the empty chair with a journalist from Dublin.

As he left the café after finishing his lunch, Rob called me over and asked if he could give me a hug, simultaneously asking where I came from as there was something faintly familiar about me.

'I'm Irish,' I replied definitively. 'My father was born in County Laois and left Ireland when he was a tiny boy when his mother died, but we always came back for the summer and I've always thought of Ireland as home.'

'Have you got any Jewish blood in you?' he asked.

'Yes, my mother.'

His face lit up instantly as though I had just tripped the right switch and confirmed something important. With that, we went our separate ways for the remainder of the afternoon, only bumping into each other briefly in the farmers' market where I was busy investigating the dark and bloody secrets of Ireland's black pudding makers in the mizzle that is endemic to the Green Country and where the commingling of the words 'mist' and 'drizzle' best describe the climactic perma-damp. 'It's a soft day,' we say to each other, more in hope than certainty that the pissing rain will be blown away into a skein of fine Irish mist and perhaps, even, to the glimpse of a tepidly grudging Celtic sun.

Rob had covered up and was wearing the kind of heavy-duty green anorak that Americans seem to buy specially, like they buy Burberrys for London, when they are going on a trip to Ireland or the English countryside, as though they will then blend in with the locals. The locals, meanwhile, are dressed in damp wool, old, unravelling tweed jackets or ancient Barbours whose oiled cloth has long since dried out and cracked and smells of sheepy lanolin, beer-and-baccy and pub carpets.

That night, after driving back from dinner via an altercation with a stone wall, the drunken chefs I had dined with and I spilled out of our charabanc, our roisterous singing session still in progress, onto the hotel forecourt to find that, as is the Irish way, things were only just beginning to come to the boil at 1.00 am. The smoky tent was heaving with a crowd so thick you could barely cut a swathe through it, let alone see from one side to the other through the fug. There is nothing anywhere in the world like a mob of stociously drunk Irishmen if you're not used to it, which the bewildered-looking first-timers from abroad clearly weren't.

There was no sign of Rob as I ploughed my way through, and no sign of him in the hotel bar where the hard-core drinkers who didn't 'slither on the boards' (a great Irishism for dancing) were propping up the bar.

I found out the following week, when we finally spoke again, that Rob had never heard the word 'ceilidh', so had snuck off to bed none the wiser about the nocturnal hoolying that is the very fabric of Irish life.

Three days later, I flew to New York for my 'mother-out-of-law's' memorial service. When my brother Daniel married Rebecca Miller, another major plus was that it brought her father and mother, Arthur Miller and Inge Morath into my life.

Inge was an intrepid and talented Magnum photographer, with a spirit and youth so captivating and contagious, even into her seventies, that one couldn't help but be touched and infected by it. I thought of her as my mother-out-of-law almost from the moment I first met her, so had decided I couldn't possibly miss the occasion to celebrate her life.

On arriving in New York, I headed straight for my cousin David's house in Greenwich Village where I always stay, and asked him if he'd ever heard of Murray's and if he had a clue where it was.

'Sure, it's just round the corner, less than a minute away,' David said.

So the next morning I headed up Bleecker Street. Perhaps I could take up Rob's dinner invitation rather sooner than he would have expected.

I stepped into Murray's for the first time.

Murray's in full swing is not like any other shop I have ever been in. The redcoats who man the counter are a highly knowl-edgeable, eclectic bunch of fromageophiles, who have found themselves, without quite realising it, taking part in the daily drama of the Murray's reality food show. You can almost smell their enthusiasm as you check in to the shop to be greeted by Cielo from the Dominican Republic, Rob's longest-serving, loyalist staffer, complete with bottle-blond goatee and bobble hat, as he shrieks and whoops a couple of octaves higher than the general hubbub of the shop-floor to grab the attention of his customers. They are very much *his* customers too, he knows their taste, their troubles, their inside leg measurements and when disaster strikes, as it did recently when Cielo's father died, a beautiful bouquet arrived the next day from Whoopi Goldberg whom he has looked after for years.

It is said that Cielo has sold more cheese than any other counterman in America, and if you were to watch him in action, you wouldn't doubt it.

The shop-floor is pure theatre, the customers known by name, offered tidbits to taste, informed, pampered and indulged, the counter and windows stacked with a glorious panoply of cheeses so high, so wide, so deep and so pungent that there is a sort of cheesy haze or smog hanging over the lactic landscape before your eyes.

There's the hard and the soft; the fruity, stinky, carnally-scented depths of the washed rinds and the fragrant, lemony, milky mildness of the raw young freshers. There are the crusty, crumbly, whiffy, ochre hard rinds and the aged, larded, cloth-bound beauties of the great, golden farmhouse Cheddar wheels. There are acres of pasty, salty, creamy blues and miniature drums of aged goat nudging shoulders with younger ivory-soft discs. The display encompasses all the great regions and cheeses of the world, and there are never fewer than around 300 of them poking their heads out of the tops of the display cases with rampantly descriptive labels that render them as feisty, sensual and ripe for the plucking as a Dorset milkmaid.

At the counter I enquired after the owner and his whereabouts. I was met with a Berlin Wall of resistance. This was clearly a business that closed like a clam when anyone tried to break its sacred seal of privacy. I was not about to be offered their boss's telephone number, it was more than enough that I'd wheedled out of them the fact that he was still in Ireland and not expected back to work until the end of the following weekend. Who on earth was I to presume, even when I presented my *Daily Telegraph* trump card and said I wanted to interview their esteemed owner for my weekly food column, that that should possibly be construed as a credential or a calling card?

So I asked them to track Rob down on his mobile, and marched through to the tiny corridor at the back where Frankie, as I now know him, got on the telephone to warn Rob that there was a serious nutter in the shop who wasn't about to leave until she had spoken to him. I came to the telephone and was greeted with the legendary line: 'What the fuck are you doing in my shop?'

'What the fuck are you doing in my country just a county away from my house in Mayo?' I rejoined, having ascertained that Rob was in the middle of having his car pulled out of a ditch somewhere in the continuing damp and misty mizzle of County Galway where he'd headed up to after Kinsale.

Typical American, I thought, they can never get the hang of the Irish roads or the fact that when a sheepdog runs out in front of you, you have to sink the welly — Mayo-speak for drive faster — since sheepdogs will only run alongside you for as long as they can keep up, probably thinking they're just rounding up another errant sheep. I made a mental note of his driving skills and clocked the fact that he'd also managed to contract food poisoning on his travels up the west coast, so was living on live yoghurt at the time of finding himself up to his mudguards in the bog.

Pretty apposite for a dairy man, I thought secretly. It didn't, however, seem to have dampened one thing, his falling in love with Ireland, which I also noted as a very good sign. I offered him my house in Mayo to recover in, but his immediate riposte was, 'I wouldn't want to go there if you weren't there.'

We talked for about 40 minutes, then discovered our planes would be crossing somewhere over the Atlantic Ocean that weekend as we both left each other's shores for home.

'I guess we're destined just to be ships that just pass and all that,' he finished, clearly not wanting to conclude the cliché.

But how wrong he was, that was not what happened at all.

Insuperable? A 'GI' romance, as in 'geographically impossible'?

Since our first encounter the morning of the speech, me from the platform from which I was addressing the five hundred, he from the audience, from where he had first staked me out, Rob and I have crossed the Atlantic too many times to count the passport stamps, and in the intervening years we have slowly got to know and got involved in each other's respective food cultures and businesses as well as starting a life together.

It was a slow process. That summer Rob began educating me in the ways of the greatest culinary melting-pot of them all, New York. Little did I know that what brought and bound us together — food — would become a cause of deep division. Indeed, when I look back on our first meals together I can see that we were suspicious, sceptical, snobby, disdainful, deprecatory. In fact we held each other's country's eating habits in such low esteem that there was little room for compromise. We each began a covert operation to make the other see the error of their ways.

In my case I was convinced my credentials were pure platinum, while Rob's were subject to a variety of interpretations. He had been voted New York's leading cheese monger by *Time Out*, but had been starved of home cooking for over a decade; indeed, the nearest he got to it was a twice or thrice weekly take-home rotis-serie chicken whose lineage is best left untraced. His Manhattan life was about restaurants, takeaways and home deliveries; about Danish pastries and doughnuts. He had a serious palate, knew every good chef in town — sold cheese to the best of them — but the sum total of his cookery skills was cremating slabs of meat on a barbecue, making lox and bagels for Sunday brunch and eating yesterday's sour cream apple pie straight from the box for breakfast or slices of crunchy, sugary, cinnamon topped sour cream coffee cake, which, by the way, hasn't a whiff of coffee to its name since it is actually a cake to eat while you drink your coffee. How American. Can you imagine strawberry ice cream but hold the strawberries?

As for apple pie for breakfast, there were clearly going to be some cultural boundaries that could never be breached. That is, until we came back from The Little Pie Company's shop one evening and the following morning he spooned the remaining slice of sour cream apple pie cold from the box into my mouth before I had a nano-second to protest at his unquestionable audacity. The cream clung coldly, sharply, insolently to the apples and the crumbly, cinnamon scented, sugary top and it tasted even better than it had the night before, though that could have been partly to do with the whiff of debauchery about the whole experience; the fact that he dared to push the spoon into my mouth and there being no question of my being able to resist.

Rob saw himself as something of a food prodigy, which of course he is, undeniably, but my belief was that he hadn't quite managed to distance himself from his suspect past as president of a supermarket chain before he converted to what the Yanks call 'specialty foods'.

My first trip to see him after our initial meeting in Kinsale that spring, in the June of 2002, began the long road to disabuse me of my prejudices and he of his. I was taken to a famous soul-food restaurant called The Pink Tea Cup in the West Village for brunch which included hominy grits (coarsely ground corn), pancakes with maple syrup — tooth-achingly sweet — and a dish made with black-eyed peas served with a biscuit. A biscuit to us is what Americans call a cookie, while an American biscuit is, in fact, a scone. Their scone is a savoury lump of risen dough rather than the sweet version, which the Americans associate with our arcane English ritual called 'tea', where it is served with clotted cream and home made strawberry jam and accompanied by a pot of proper old-fashioned leaf tea. Let's not get into the cream debate, other than to say there is no such thing as real cream in America, be it clotted so thick the proverbial spoon stands to attention in it, or the rich, ivory-hued Jersey sort that has never been subjected to that vile American process, ultra-pasteurisation.

It was at The Pink Tea Cup that I learnt that one seminal food influence of Rob's life had been the old family cook Cora who came from the Deep South. Rob's mother Florence had tried to teach Cora the rudiments of their family cuisine, which we shall call Jewish suburban American, notable for such dishes as chopped liver, chicken soup, standing rib roast and corn-beef hash. But Cora had introduced a few dishes of her own, such as southern fried chicken, which Rob described to me as the pinnacle of cuisine: 'Crisp and peppery fried chicken that's been dredged in flour, deep fried, but never greasy although probably fried in Crisco, served with home made French fries and biscuits with honey.'

It brought to mind the Southern Spanish/North African style turkey cooked in cinnamon and honey that I ate on a trip to the bodegas of Jerez during the Vendimia — the grape harvest — one year, where a ten course feast at a wonderful restaurant called La Mesa Redonda — The Round Table — cooked by the great bodega owner, Migueol Valdespino's chef brother, paired a different sherry from the bodega with each course.

A little startled at the sweet, musky, spiced dish on my plate — I had not eaten the famous Moroccan pastillas filled with the likes of pigeon, icing sugar and raisins at that stage — I experienced the palate shock which no imagination can prepare your taste-buds or taste memory for. You just have to remain open-minded. It was not at all how I had anticipated and it was absolutely delicious, but by God it seemed strange eating such sweet meat, the veritable baklava of meat, drenched, as it was, in the sweetest substance on earth.

Gradually I began to understand what I was dealing with. I could relate to the blueberry pies Cora made with that forbidden ingredient, lard, in the crust, but the land of Crisco was a geographical unknown. This, after all, is the stuff the Americans have banished from their diet for the last few decades, replacing it with olive oil, egg-white omelettes and statins.

The day after the Southern food initiation, Rob took me to Russ and Daughters, a Lower East Side Jewish 'appetiser' shop, where his friend Mark introduced me to tubs of herring in cream sauce, chopped liver made with chicken fat, wild Baltic smoked salmon, baked salmon salad, white fish salad, cream cheese spreads, sable, all of which I cast a cold eye upon; how could it possibly be as good as the London Cure of wild smoked salmon I buy from London's oldest smoke house, run by Lance Forman's family for four generations, or as delicately, richly delicious as crêpes Parmentier served with a chunk of Michael Brown's Somerset smoked eel, a dollop of home made horseradish and sour cream sauce and a sprinkling of chives?

We went back home and Rob prepared the classic lox and bagels, spreading a slick of Ben's cream cheese from his shop onto toasted onion bagels — he never ever uses butter and cheese together on bread or biscuits — adding a generous seam of smoked salmon, a paper-thin slice of raw onion and a juicy slice of ripe tomato. This was sacrilege. Why ruin the classic combination of smoked salmon and cream cheese? He explained that the onion cut through the rich smokiness, that the sweet-sharp tomato contrasted with the creamy clagginess of the cheese, that all in all this was the best way to serve this most classic of brunch dishes, that a flavour short was a flavour lost.

I had to concede he was right.

There were clearly some things that Rob knew that I didn't but, I insisted, America had to bow down to the superiority of our ingredients: to Middle White pigs with a thick scarf of fat to help them taste how pork tasted before the industrial, lean-meated fast breeds took over our tables and deprived us of ever tasting anything properly piggy. Then there are the Longhorn cattle with buttercup-yellow fat reared by my friend Richard Vaughan in Herefordshire and hung for 33 days. British game, hung to rich, tender, opulently fruity gamey-ness.

Further proof, back in Greenwich Village, at my favourite Manhattan butcher Ottomanelli on Bleecker Street just above the corner where Murray's is, was Jerry informing me that the Americans don't release their pheasants into the wild like we do after they've been reared in pens; what's more, it's illegal to sell game with shot in it, so the birds are killed like chickens and never hung until they taste gamey. Not even guinea fowl gamey.

Thus a ball of lead shot that would probably come out in the wash if you happened to swallow it, is considered more dangerous than eating American beef, two-thirds of which has been raised on a diet of hormones and growth promoters.

I don't know about you, but I would rather rattle with shot than develop secondary characteristics. You'd have to spend years living like Parson Woodforde and feasting on trios of wood-cock, snipe and grouse for breakfast and game pies and puddings for supper to be in any danger whatsoever of contracting lead poisoning I would have thought.

And then there are our unparalleled soft cane fruits and berries, our ancient orchards, our unpasteurised, unhomogenised milk and cream, our cold-water fish and fine river fish.

All this for The American to discover and delight in, and for me to delight in showing him.

The first time I sent Rob out to my kitchen garden to pick the carrots for supper he couldn't find them, didn't know they grew frondy tops above ground. He didn't know a bay leaf from a briar. It could be my life's work, I mused, just to get him to recognise the dozen herbs I cook with most frequently. As for digging up my pink fir apples for supper, he'd probably head for the trees in the orchard. He had to swap Sunday brunch for traditional English Sunday lunch; learn to sit down to every meal rather than lean at counter-tops or believe the TV dinner was the ultimate dining experience; practise having a conversation round the table, though even now, if he comes home tired from work he will say: 'Do we have to talk at dinner or can we read our books?'

I'm afraid I always insist. We were brought up to believe that you only read while you sat at the breakfast table, but Rob appeared to believe that it was fine to join a silent order of monks at every meal time and engross himself equally with plate and papers or book, anything, so long as the relationship between fork and page wasn't inadvertently broken by the cook or anyone else daring to suppose that meals and conversation went together like mustard and a sausage.

When he came over to my house he had to get used to everything being home made, home grown and hand picked as and when it was needed. And the fact that the words 'food' and 'convenience' were never used together in the same sentence, though his talent at fridge raiding and building the best triple decker sandwiches from leftover scraps, with either an instantly concocted Russian dressing of squeezy tube tomato paste and Hellmans or his Dijon and mayo combo shot through with the heat of chilli jelly and peppery watercress, soon became a regular fixture whenever we were walking the hills or picnicking on our flight from Bristol to Newark which Continental had the good sense to begin three years into our relationship.

In turn, I taught Rob how to carve English-style: where we slice our beef thinly, the Americans have standing ribs which they carve in great tranches like steak; we serve ours with puffed up Yorkshire pudding flooded with gravy, the batter having been ladled first into the spitting hot dripping and cooked above the beef, but Rob remained unmoved, as he did with the bread sauce I invariably serve with roast chicken and turkey and which he thought was some strange peasant aberration. Apple sauce, on the other hand, they seem to serve with everything, even chicken.

He was terrified of the sort of 'John Bull', 'Olde Englande' dishes that he assumed everyone lived on here, the likes of steak and kidney pie, stewed oxtail, bangers and mash, toad in the hole, bubble and squeak, spotted Dick and custard, trifle, rice pudding, bread and butter pudding.

I had to break him in gently. My beef stew became a carbon-nade suffused with the bitter undertow of a pint and a half of Guinness and some strips of orange peel and herbs. The oxtail was really queue de boeuf des vigneronnes, gluey with bone-sticky juices, flecks of oak-smoked bacon and crushed seedless grapes. Most importantly, I knew how to make chicken soup, the 'Jewish penicillin' on which he had been reared as a child and which seems to be the drug of choice when any American is languishing or gripped by anything from a fever to just plain feeling sorry for themselves.

The first time Rob demanded chicken soup I knew I could deliver. The best, free range, organic hen was poached in water, white wine, herbs and vegetables. It was cooled, the fat skimmed, the bird stripped of meat and the carcass simmered with more fresh vegetables with a few morels soaked and added to the intense stock. Finally the bird's breast was pulled into succulent strips, a few more fresh leeks and slithers of celery and carrot added and the soup was ready to serve.

'It doesn't taste like my mother's,' Rob said.

We would clearly have to come to some sort of an accommo-dation. Whilst known for speaking their mind, it is often difficult to detect the level of irony or sarcasm or plain provocation that makes up the everyday diet of New York Jewish-speak and attitude. It wasn't a compliment or a criticism; actually it was most likely a veiled compliment, and I was probably supposed to take it that way. After all, how could something even so lovingly, tenderly nurtured, simmered, skimmed possibly approximate to his mother's, to the version he remembers first tasting decades before, that would not have had the time, the care, the patience, the quality of ingredients and certainly not the morels cooked into it, but would still always be best because it was his mother's and the one he'd grown up with?

Illness is not a time to get competitive or to inspire divided loyalty in a Jewish household, and this was lesson number one.

In fact there was one dish alone that clinched my reputation, or that is the way I like to see it, a dish which I have been careful not to blunt the impact of with overkill. My chicken Savoyarde, a gently poached chicken, stripped from its bones and anointed in a satin cloak of white wine, cream and stock, scented with an absurd amount of tarragon, Gruyère, and then gratinéed in the oven under a breadcrumb and Parmesan crust until molten and bubbling, provoked a reaction which, to begin with, sounded worse than damning with faint praise. I didn't begin to understand Rob's apparently understated, critical opinion of the dish I knew would seduce the palate of an anorexic, wheatgrass-eating vegetarian.

'It's quite tasty,' he remarked.

We may speak the same language, but it is as alien and different in its nuances as our food. It was a revelation to me that 'quite' meaning 'not very' this side of the Atlantic is a superlative to an American, and, paired with 'tasty', a damning-with-faint-praise sort of a word to a Brit, is a paean of praise to a Yank.

I got over my sulk and we accommodated and took note accordingly.

Cooking in New York meant getting used to its food shops and markets, cuts and kitchens. Rob rented a series of apartments during the early stages of our romance, and we went through a string of kitchens which seemed to be equipped for everything but cooking. Not a chopping board or grater, a sharp knife or decent pot or pan. Cupboards filled with jars of herbs as dusty and musty and sneezy as snuff or stacked with ancient appliances gathering dust in the gloom of a top shelf way beyond reach.

'How do New Yorkers live?' I enquired. They seemed like an alien species. It transpired that some bachelors never even breakfasted at home, couldn't make themselves a cup of coffee, yet, peculiarly, even the smallest, most ill-equipped of kitchens sported giant microwaves and fridges the size of walk-in morgues. Empty, of course.

The result was that we went out a lot. We tried the great and the good, the starred and the new and discovered immediately that we were both inverted snobs when it came to modish, fussy food. We preferred the small, unpretentious, ethnic neighbourhood places: late-night falafel pushed hot and crisp into steaming envelopes of pitta bread and salad at the hole in the wall called Mamoun's on MacDougal Street. Cinnamon scented slabs of French toast with sugar-bled berries and maple syrup at Home on Cornelia St for a late and lazy weekend breakfast. Lobster rolls and fried oysters at Pearl, pastrami and latkes at Katz's Jewish Deli. It is said that eating latkes has killed more people than the Nazis; as far as I am concerned the maxim 'everything in moderation' should apply to everything but latkes, which should carry a government health warning.

And finally we got round to the best fried chicken I have ever eaten, at Blue Ribbon on Sullivan Street. It may not come up to the legendary Cora's mark, but then nothing is ever as intense as the things we remember and dream about from our childhood. The Blue Ribbon serves the maize-coloured parcels of insanely crisp, hot, spicy, battered chicken with buttery mash, collard greens and the infamous bowl of runny honey to dip your chicken into. Strange, but it's just the thing to order hot off the plane from England when the time clock is playing havoc and you need pots of comfort food and sleep. Their blackened, fried catfish with mash and greens is another simple and perfectly executed dish that is what the best American food is all about.

I am in danger of a full conversion, no, worse, of proselytising, so I'd better stop and get on with the story.

One summer I found myself at 50 Carmine, Greenwich Village, eating Sarah Jenkins' peerless, slow-braised porchetta stuffed with fennel and Tuscan fennel pollen that she had gathered that summer. By the following summer she had upped spoons and left to cook on Long Island and our favourite neighbourhood joint had passed, as so many do, into short-lived restaurant history. When Sarah took over the kitchen at Bread on Tribeca a few months ago, a collective sigh of salivation and expectation arose from Rob and me and many other quarters, and we hot-footed it down to Church Street that very night. We were greeted with a glass of Prosecco and tiny, powder-puff soft brioche buns filled with flakes of aged Pecorino and truffle butter and by a menu with the best of the old and the seasonal new on it – that night's salad had tiny shelled green almonds lurking in it and there was a dish with soft curds of raw ricotta, tiny tomatoes and basil turned into Sarah's buttery, al dente home made pasta.

Time stood still, all was well with the fast-moving restaurant world again, it had spun on its axis and, like a roulette ball, dropped safely back to earth. Until it spun once again a few weeks ago and Sarah left Bread, is having a baby, and is looking for a restaurant of her own.

New York is the first city of restaurant openings, to which the food fraternity whirl like dervishes from the *New York Times'* Wednesday reviews, using every contact to get a table while the joint is still buzzing, then bitching and bragging, berating and bemoaning and occasionally praising their findings before doing the same all over again the following week. The 'Have you been to…' there is the equivalent of our 'Did you see…' TV culture over here.

What Rob and I look for is a neighbourhood restaurant that you can walk straight into off the street without a booking, and get fed by a fine cook with barely a glance at the menu. We like chefs who we know well enough, and who know our taste well enough, to say, 'Shall we just bring you food?' and are eager to try their latest dish on us or seduce us with the thing that's inspired them most at that morning's market. It's surprising just how grateful we are, when we are tired after work, to let someone else make even the apparently simple decision of what to eat for us.

There are things that I thought I would never order again in a restaurant, or even go to the sort of restaurant that served them in the first place: steak, hamburgers, French fries, pizzas. Engrained snobbery of the English sort I know, but that was all swiftly kicked into touch when I met Rob.

I don't think the steakhouse ever died in America, nor did it ever become infra dig even in the eyes of the serious gourmands, but I was pretty resistant to its charms when he suggested, early in our relationship, that we should go and eat at the New York Strip House. I was unaware of its being the home of 'strip', as in strip steak, rather than as in stripper, but felt the correlation couldn't be entirely linguistic, and I was right. There is no doubt that this is the sort of food you want to eat when you've just got physical. It's one of the few times girls really crave red meat, though they can't quite make the cut in terms of quantity that boys can even when they're baying for it. So Rob confounded my prejudices again, walked me a few blocks uptown and turned me on to man's food, to thick hefts of charcoal grilled Porterhouse and New York strip steak the length of a size 18 boot, which are cut into juicy pink wedges on wooden boards at your table, the skillet-striped meat as hot as a branding iron, its charred, aged flesh served with whole heads of garlic that you pop out of their soft skins as easily as wobbly teeth, potatoes cooked in goose fat and stand-on-the-spoon béarnaise.

I tackled the soft, red, charcoal-edged flesh with the abandon of a lion to its prey, or should I say lioness?

I still, however, hard as I try, cannot ever, ever finish my American steak house steak; always end up passing Rob the final triangle of meat that has defeated me. But I am now convinced, as convinced as any red-blooded American, that the steak house will live for ever and deserves to, that its charms are not only obvious and appealing to red-necks and truckers, teamsters and captains of industry, they are also appealing to me.

These days I am equally as happy with a prime burger cooked medium rare, preferably with cheese deliquescing from its middle, a hit of piquant gherkin, a blob of ketchup and a soft sesame bun. Something of a palate makeover, I admit, but imagine never changing your mind about food? If anything or anyone was guaranteed to quell my native snobbery about American food, no one could have made a more thorough, more convincing job of it.

What have I done in return, you may ask?

It's simple really. I took on a man in more need of a home-cooked dinner than anyone I'd ever met, though who am I to say which of the two quickest ways to a man's heart is ultimately the winner. Having left a marriage where take-outs, home deliveries and restaurants were a way of life, and the perfectly designed kitchen of his beautiful house looked like it had barely been christened, the first thing I did was sit Rob down to a slow-braised breast of Somerset lamb, stewed at a mere murmur in wine and herbs: thyme, bay, rosemary and parsley with vegetables from my garden, shallots, celery, garlic, slim fingers of new carrots and served with a snowy hillock of silken mashed potato into which I'd lobbed thick slices of melted butter with the hot creamy milk.

I have been cooking for him ever since, he seeing the continuing performance of this nightly act as part and parcel of the myth of falling in love which would, he believed, in its turn, be rescinded and supplanted by an empty store cupboard, a microwave, fast food, an insistence on dining out and who knows what other abominations once familiarity had set in. But then he's a cynical New Yorker and I'm an unreconstructed romantic who loves to cook, particularly for the ones I love.

So far he has been proved wrong, and for my part that has meant the good fortune of never being taken for granted.

Finally, divorced and with his lovely Greenwich Village townhouse sold, Rob bought his new apartment. We, or should I say he, agonised over his 'bachelor kitchen' where the surfaces and stove were priceless and included a handmade butcher's block work-top that had to be craned the 5 floors up to the apartment, and an all singing, all-dancing, Wolf oven with built-in griddle top. But what did he need cooking equipment for, after all he was never going to cook more than a chop, a baked potato with sour cream and a twig of broccoli? That, he insisted, is what bachelors do, or, in reality, much more than most New York bachelors do, with sheaves full of take-out menus lurking like trousseaus in their bottom drawer.

I gradually insinuated the odd crucial gadget onto the pristine surfaces, though Rob had a tendency to put each one away like a redundant suitcase each time I'd used it. I have never trusted the cook who has to find her Magimix at the back of an out of reach cupboard, her blenders and Kitchen Aid in a hidden drawer. Why hide the tools you work with every day? He wouldn't hide his cheese cutters, I wouldn't hide my pen. It was almost impossible getting him to allow me to have a kitchen drawer stocked with spatulas and spoons, a masher, a grater, a sieve; with measuring spoons and peelers, yet his sub-zero walk-in morgue was ordered with the kitchen, pre-dated any cutlery or serving dishes and is permanently empty until I arrive back in town, but for a packet of fresh ground coffee beans from the coffee shop on Bleecker Street and a bottle of the only farm milk you can find that hasn't been homogenised.

Back in New York, my first mission is to see that the fridge is filled to the gunnels, and slowly, very slowly, the 'bachelor apartment' comes back to life, becomes more of a place to call home. Never more so than when Rob comes back from the shop and sniffs the air, sees the table laid, the linen napkins poised on the dining table, inhales the scent of buttery, Indian-spiced chicken; ribs braised with fresh turmeric and ginger root, molasses and Tamari; a simple daube or stew of wild boar and morels or osso bucco; chicken soup, poulet Basquaise, it doesn't matter what really, a slice of toast and a scrambling egg or a cake baking will do as long as the fundamental rules of civilisation have been observed and the best ingredients have been turned with the minimum of fuss into the perfect end to the day: a simple and delicious supper.

Once the kitchen was up and running we were all set for the next stage, the thing that confounds and excites and amazes

Americans more than anything else I have experienced: an invitation to dinner.

Is there ever such a test of compatibility and taste as entertaining? It's not that either of us are novices either, past marriages and ways of life have seen to that, but our ways are different, so I had to adjust the dial to an alien culture where the latest thing is a cheese course served with drinks before dinner, and where salad is served as a starter.

And I had to remember that Rob was entering this more European way of life late, where people turn up to supper, to lunch, to stay, with the ease and familiarity that eschews the proving of anything. That Brits come to the table to relax, to gossip, to hang out, to eat and to drink, as Rob observed and pointed out, not necessarily to talk politics, success, money, or prove with staff, champagne and caviar that they are masters of the universe.

Rob's past life had been different, the portals of his house had been somewhat sacred and closed to outsiders and they had never entertained. He took to the new like a small boy to Lego, fitting the bits together, deciding who would work with whom, composing more of his eternal lists of possible guests, and always asking me what I was going to cook.

He was as nervous as a kitten the first few times, as anxious for people to leave as for them to arrive on time, and mindful and critical of whatever I was cooking.

After the first few successes and post mortems, he seemed far more at ease, and knew he could ring me at three in the afternoon and say there were an extra four people for dinner. And knew that I'd still be speaking to him when he came home.

He began to realise that friendship is cemented by good food, by the act of giving friends even the simplest of dinners if you have cooked it yourself, and I began to understand that New Yorkers are genuinely thrilled at getting invited to your home for dinner in a way we are all too familiar with to see as exceptional. In New York, people rarely seem to cook or eat at home after work, so the novelty of it almost overwhelms them. Make them an English pudding and you have a devoted friend and admirer for life. It's nearly that easy!

We had met through food, and food had been central to the blossoming of our relationship and our life together. How much else we learned about each other, too, through our mutual passion.

Yet in the early stages there were still times, apart in our respective homes, when each other's ways of life seemed as alien and far away as the moon, not just the Atlantic that separated us.

New York Spicy Spare Ribs

SERVES TWO

The first time I found little saffron coloured gnarly fingers of fresh turmeric in the local health food shop, Lifethyme, on 6th Avenue I was gripped, and used them in everything I cooked for weeks. The earthy, deep under-scoring they gave each dish was so different to the powdered form and naturally, the healing properties advertised were addictive. If you are unable to buy the real McCoy at a nearby Asian store, back to the jar for the powder, I'm afraid.

Preheat oven to 150°C/300°F/GAS 2

2 IN/1CM *fresh turmeric root or*
  1 TSP *dried powdered turmeric*
2 IN/1CM *green ginger root*
6 CLOVES *garlic*
2 TBSP *blackstrap molasses*
1 TBSP *chestnut honey*
1 TBSP *tomato paste*
4 TBSP *Tamari sauce*
1 TSP EACH *cinnamon,*
  allspice and ginger
⅓ TSP *cayenne*
1 TBSP *cider vinegar*
90–120 ML/3–4 FL OZ *dry cider*
A RACK *of organic pork spare ribs to*
  allow six to eight per person

NOTE: *If you are cooking for four or more people, don't just double up the sauce quantity, a little extra will do nicely with a slug of cider.*

Peel and grate the turmeric and ginger roots and put them in a bowl. Peel and crush the garlic cloves with a little sea salt under the large blade of a knife. Throw them into the bowl. Add all the other ingredients and stir together.

Slice the ribs so they are single if the butcher hasn't done it for you and turn them in the spicy brew. Leave for 30 minutes.

Put them in a roasting tin and cover tightly with foil. Cook for an hour. Remove the foil and turn the heat up to 180°C/350°F/GAS 4. Continue to cook, turning the ribs every 15 minutes, until the sauce has gone gloopy brown and thickened a little and begun to cling to the ribs. This could be any time up to an hour, depending on how thin or thick or intense you like the taste.

Serve with rice into which you have thrown some cooked peas or broad beans, and any other vegetable you feel like on the side.

Spiced Leg of Lamb with Tahini Sauce and Ratatouille

SERVES SIX

Ottomanelli's on Bleecker Street, down the road from Murray's, and Florence Meat Market on Jones Street round the corner became my favourite New York butchers in a trice. If you can, think ahead and make this ratatouille a couple of days in advance for the flavours to marry, then serve it warm or cool on the night, and marinade the lamb in the fridge overnight too, then most of your work is done. I know it may seem quite a cross-cultural combination but it works superbly. I served this dish at a Sullivan Street dinner with brown rice and some carrots roasted with fennel pollen which my chef friend Sarah Harmon Jenkins had given me a stash of as a present from Tuscany.

1 leg of lamb
For the marinade:
1 TBSP coriander seeds and 1 tbsp cumin seeds toasted in a pan for a minute and crushed in a mortar
½ TBSP cardamom seeds, crushed with the above
2 IN/4CM EACH grated turmeric and green ginger root
1 TSP EACH cinnamon, allspice, ginger
½ TSP cayenne
1 SMALL CARTON sheep's yoghurt
1 BUNCH fresh coriander
olive oil
sea salt and black pepper

Put all the ingredients for the marinade into a bowl with the chopped coriander and a table-spoon or two of olive oil and stir together.

Make some slashes in the meat right through the fat so that you can spread the marinade all over the meat and into the slashes. It helps to do this on the clingfilm you're then going to wrap the meat in to keep it sealed tight in the fridge over-night. The paste will spice and tenderize the meat ready to cook.

Roast in the normal way in a hot oven. I put my joint on a layer of sliced onions and cook it until pink. For a joint around the 2kg/4lb mark I suggest about 1½ hours at 200°C/400°F/ GAS 6.

Leave the joint to rest for 20 minutes but I do think lamb needs to be served hot rather than warm, due to the congeal-ing properties of the fat.

Carve the meat and put the slices on top of the brown rice and roasted carrots on a warmed serving dish, pouring the spicy juices over the dish.

Tahini Sauce

I use the organic dark tahini which is made from toasted sesame seeds, a more intense flavour than the untoasted. Sesame is not only delicious, it is high in calcium.

3 CLOVES *garlic, peeled*
4 TBSPS *dark tahini*
JUICE OF *1½ lemons*
sea salt and black pepper

Put the garlic cloves in the mortar with a little sea salt and crush them to a wet paste then whisk in the tahini. Thin the paste with lemon juice. Carry on whisking and add water until the sauce has the consistency of double cream. Season, taste and adjust the lemon juice if you need to.

Serve in a bowl to pass around with the meat. You may add a little sprinkle of crushed, toasted cumin to the bowl if you like. The simplest sauce in the world. Also great with lamb kebabs.

Ratatouille

1 LARGE *organic aubergine, cut in slices, not cubed*
2 *red peppers*
2 *yellow peppers*
3 MEDIUM *courgettes, yellow and green for colour if you can find both*
2 *red onions*
6 CLOVES *garlic*
1 LARGE 750g/1LB 10 OZ *tin tomatoes*
1 TBSP *or* A LARGE SQUIRT *tomato paste*
A FEW SPRIGS EACH *of fresh thyme and rosemary*
extra virgin olive oil
A SMALL BUNCH *of fresh basil, purple if possible*
sea salt and black pepper

Brush the slices of aubergine with olive oil on both sides and put them in the hot oven on a roasting tray for 15 minutes or until cooked to nearly soft.
At the same time, roast the peppers in the oven, turning them each time a side has blackened, or cook them on a naked flame until black all over before putting them in a bowl covered with clingfilm and letting them steam to release

the skins for 20–30 minutes. Peel, seed and slice into strips.

Meanwhile, slice the courgettes into thickish discs and sauté them in olive oil until al dente, and peel and slice the onions and garlic and sauté them together with the chopped thyme and rosemary in a large, heavy-bottomed pan until softened and translucent. Keep the heat gentle so that they don't brown.

The point of cooking all the vegetables separately at this stage is so that they retain their individual flavours. Cubing the aubergines is more traditional, but I favour the brushed with oil method as they don't absorb oil like sponges this way yet still stay rubbery, they actually soften and don't taste oily.

Add the tinned whole tomatoes and a tablespoon of tomato paste to the onions and continue to cook, chopping the tomatoes down into the onion.

After 10–15 minutes, when the watery juices have evaporated and the sauce thickened, add the other vegetables, stir gently to amalgamate but not so that the vegetables break up, season to taste and cool.

Now put the ratatouille in the fridge, covered, until you need it.

Either take the ratatouille out of the fridge an hour before you need it and serve it cool, or heat it through very gently to warm and serve it straight from the pan. Taste and adjust the seasoning again and tear some purple or green basil leaves over it.

For extra tomato texture and depth, add a dozen cooled, stove-dried tomatoes to the warm ratatouille before serving. For the Stove-Dried Tomato recipe, see *Tamasin's Kitchen Bible*, page 162.

Vitello Piccante

SERVES THREE

You can buy wonderful veal in
New York; in England it is more
difficult, though lovely Heale
Farm in Devon, the first people
to rear it blamelessly rather than
intensively, will send it to you
by overnight carrier. This is a
gorgeous dish I first cooked in
Sullivan Street with the Ligurian
mixed green and black olives
Murray's sells.

3 thickly cut, about 1 in / 2cm,
  veal chops on the bone
For the marinade:
a fruity, extra virgin olive oil
sea salt and black pepper
1 SPRIG rosemary (1 DSRTSP),
  finely chopped

Massage the meat on both sides
with the olive oil and season
both sides with salt, pepper
and the rosemary. Leave on
a plate for an hour at room
temperature, not in the fridge.

1 TBSP purple basil (green if you
  can't get it), chopped
2 TBSP flat leaf parsley, finely
  chopped
1 TBSP caperberries, finely chopped
2 TBSPS mixed green and black
  olives, Ligurian or Nyons if
  possible, pitted/chopped weight

1 CLOVE garlic, peeled, crushed with
  a little salt and finely chopped
ZEST of an organic lemon
JUICE OF ½ lemon
unsalted butter for frying

Simply put all the dry ingredients
into a bowl, adding the lemon
juice and enough olive oil to
make a thick, but slightly sloppy
sauce when stirred together.
Leave out for 30 minutes while
you prepare and cook dinner
as you want all the flavours to
mingle.

Put a knob of butter in a heavy
pan and melt gently. Add the
chops and cook over a medium
heat until you can see the
colour has changed from pink
to creamy white to about half
way through the chops' thick-
ness. Turn over and repeat.
This takes roughly 10 minutes
a side depending on the heat.
The chops should be slightly
bouncy when pushed with your
fingers, not resistant.

Remove to warmed plates and
immediately spoon over a
couple of tablespoons of the
sauce over each.

Serve with braised endives to
add a bitter note, or some broad
beans and carrots and with
small new potatoes roasted
whole in the oven with garlic
and rosemary in olive oil.

§4   *'Don't Feed me Paws'*

I surveyed the creature's lean, pointy
face with its fearsomely powerful,
hinge-like jaw that never drops
anything it picks up and is impossible
to dislocate. Wouldn't want to get
your arm caught in that. It might
prove a trifle tricky to carve, too…

For the first few years of our relationship our life had been dominated not just by food and the thrill of the next flight across the Atlantic, but by lengthy, cross-continental telephone conversations when we were apart. BT had almost as much to be happy about as we did. Virtually all these conversations, if I think back, included blow by blow accounts of what I happened to be cooking, who I was entertaining, what recipe I was testing or cooking on camera for the next book or television programme. Rob would be there in New York in his rented apartment with his take-away Thai, I would be here in Somerset or Ireland with a house full of children, their friends, my friends, my best and greediest cooking conspirators, talking food porn over the airwaves to him.

'Well, the ice cream has bashed up pralinéed almonds and membrillo melted into it... I slugged the praline with a hit of Fino... raw Jersey cream and ten egg yolks in the custard... I might make honey madeleines to go with it... I'm trying out an almond cake with a blood orange and Clementine syrup poured down skewer holes in the top... the colour of a Safari sunset... I'm making what you'd call chicken pot pie with leeks from the garden. Paul and Marigold are coming over so I've got to think of a good pudding for Paul. I've got to live up to the burnt orange ice cream he wrote up in *The Spectator*. He said it was the best he had ever eaten... I picked a pheasant up off the road this morning on my run, I thought I'd plunge it head-first into Julian Temperley's Somerset cider brandy, set fire to it and cook it with barley, juniper, apples and onions...'

Normally Rob's response was predictable: 'It all sounds so... well... civilised,' which is precisely how he perceives English country life: as a sort of Jane Austen-like place where all American preconceptions come true, a wonderland of smart

dinner parties and scintillating conversation; where people stay
for weekend house parties, trysts and affairs are begun, engaged
upon and ended cordially over the pre-prandial sherry, and
people play croquet, tennis, the piano; hunt, shoot, make music
and love and stay up late for charades and port, all this interspersed with endless meals taken leisurely over hours at ancient
oak tables in chilly, baronial-sized dining rooms.

I suppose it comes from all the English novelists his mother
Florence handed to him as a child and which clearly came to life
in his head in a way that even present day reality won't quite
excise.

However, this time I must have taken it a dinner too far.

'Could you stop talking about food and what you're cooking,'
Rob said peevishly.

'You have no idea what it's like sitting in my apartment
with another disgusting, greasy take-away after ten nights of
restaurant dinners on my own with a newspaper and *no* dinner
or weekend invitations. And by the way, it's totally unhygienic to
pick stuff up off the road and cook it, it's absolutely disgusting,
you don't know if it's diseased or what was wrong with it, how it
died or what's been eating it.'

'I only pick up road-kill if it's still warm and nothing's pecked
out the eyes,' I said deliberately, realising before I had even
started that not only was this not a debate, but that I should
never have got into it. It could only make things worse. The
Americans are obsessed with their food hygiene, their homogenised milk; they keep eggs and tomatoes in the fridge, the latter
going squishy without ever ripening – they are, after all, a semi-
tropical fruit. And if the American attitude to sex is as hands off
as their attitude in the kitchen, where many of the restaurant
cooks put on rubber gloves even to toss a salad and don't seem

too enamoured at the idea that food needs to be felt, touched and caressed as much as it needs to be smelled and tasted, well, therein lies the rub.

I stopped the nightly résumé immediately. That is, until the event that I am going to tell you about. We were spending too much time apart and it was one way of Rob telling me how much he missed me. Well, how much he missed my cooking, at least. Men always tend to offer compliments elliptically. In fact I managed to stick to the enforced abstinence quite successfully for some time, I've got plenty of greedy girlfriends to talk to whenever I need to talk about the latest creation or discuss whether something is likely to work.

I stuck to it religiously until I had a telephone call that I couldn't resist telling Rob about, it was, I was convinced, way beyond the realms of normal food porn or anything in his orbit. Or mine for that matter.

I have never cooked badger, and, to my – almost – certain knowledge I have never eaten it, though I am something of a veteran road-kill cook. Mugged pheasants are ubiquitous round here, as are rabbits, and if I am in the west of Ireland around mad March hare time, when the ritual mating season seems to turn the brains of these beautiful creatures and they throw themselves in front of passing cars, I scoop them up, sling them over the handle-bars of my bike, hang them with a bag tied round their heads to catch the blood, paunch them and jug them à l'ancienne.

Hare blood, in case you are uninitiated, is a great delicacy added to a garlicky aillade, with the liver and heart, red wine and red wine vinegar, towards the end of cooking time of a classic civet de lièvre or hare stew.

It had never occurred to me, however, that badger might be edible, particularly since badgers became a protected species in 1992. Squirrel, hedgehog cooked in clay so the spines part company with the flesh and stick to the cooking pot, blackbird and rook pies – my Irish chef friend Richard Corrigan believes rooks are given to the beaters on shoots because the landowners know they are inedible – and the velvet shed from the deer's antlers, are all the boast of those who see country lore as a kind of look-what-I've-chowed-down gastro-contest.

Whilst I'm prepared to try anything that isn't still alive as in alive and kicking – oysters don't twitch on the half-shell – the very thought of the maleficent Brock was too *Wind in the Willows*-ish by half.

I had taken a telephone call from a man called Arthur who had seen me on the local ITV news programme extolling the joys of road-kill and professing my distaste for the ignorant, squeamish townies who happily munch barely born poussin and cruelly industrially produced meats while criticising our way of life. If they see a bone they appear offended, indeed, they seem most happy with tasteless, skinless chicken breasts. The sight of a head, a beak, a crop or a trotter and they'd go into anaphylactic shock.

Arthur had been interviewed for the same news item and treated as though he were a deranged weirdo for surviving on what he could scrape off the black-top. I suspect I was chosen as a well-known local food writer who might offer some sense and balance on the subject, though I don't think the newsroom got quite what they'd bargained for. I was asked what I felt about eating dog, the usual newshound sort of trick question that might panic someone not used to television interviews. Arthur had already told me about the canine residing in his deep freeze after meeting with a bumper and told me he'd tried bat and otter as well. 'It would be fine by me,' I told the newshound, 'as long as it doesn't involve running over the family pet'.

A few days later I got the call.

'I've got a couple of badgers,' Arthur began. 'I thought perhaps I could bring them up from Cornwall and you might like to cook them.'

Not the typical free food offer I usually get from the PR bosses of the major supermarket chains, this was irresistible in the extreme.

The following day Arthur arrived on the doorstep with two large, dark-fleshed creatures wrapped and swinging like small corpses in plastic sacks over his shoulders. I had never realised quite how big badgers were. He slapped them down on my work top and the first gouts of fuchsia-coloured blood dripped in thick patters like red rain onto the flags. Something about him made me feel uneasy although I couldn't quite put my finger on it. It was February. He was dressed in shorts and sandals like some scarily sadistic gung-ho games instructor.

'This one has hung for three and a half weeks,' he continued, turning the creature's nether regions sufficiently in my direction for me to see they were tinged with green. The smell alone was as rank as a commanding officer.

'This one has been in my garage two and a half weeks,' he said showing me the second limp creature which looked and smelt decidedly gamey.

'I only need that one,' I said pointedly, suggesting that Arthur returned the green-arsed specimen to his boot.

Arthur got back into his car and I stood staring at the creature in the bag for some time, wondering quite how I always seemed to get into this sort of fix. It would be easier to cook the beast than bury it, I supposed.

I checked all the cookery books that might have had recipes for braised badger, roast badger any kind of badger in their index, but even the game cookery books eschewed the subject of *Meles meles.*

I checked the internet, as a recent debate had been raging on bovine tuberculosis, and one of the schools of thought, which was that TB was passed to cattle by badgers, had prompted a call for a total cull across England. Given that a survey of road-killed badgers had only found one in seven of them infected, and that a massive cull would never completely eradicate TB anyway, and the additional fact that some scientists believe that the disease is passed from cattle to badgers rather than the other way round, I decided that it would be perfectly safe to put the Brock in the Aga and cook it.

I *had* to ring Rob to let him know, and to tell him that I'd decided to invite Nigel, a nearby cattle-farming friend over with his wife Gladys who had been nanny to my three children, to try it.

'Don't *ever* feed me paws,' he remonstrated immediately. 'I can't believe you're going to cook a badger and eat it, no one would do that sort of thing over here, it's the most disgusting thing I've ever heard of.'

I surveyed the creature's lean, pointy face with its fearsomely powerful, hinge-like jaw that never drops anything it picks up and is impossible to dislocate. Wouldn't want to get your arm caught in that. It might prove a trifle tricky to carve, too. Arthur had left the creature whole, so the next job was to remove it from the undertaker's plastic sheet and set about butchering it with my completely inadequate tools. What I really needed was a circular saw.

I decided to cook the hams, or back legs; to roast them slowly with a little juniper and some Marsala, and to bag up the bits and deal with them later.

'No *way* am I going to eat that,' my younger daughter Charissa said vehemently when I told her what was for Sunday lunch. So I also roasted a precautionary loin of Middle White pork.

Nigel has what can only be described as deeply traditional farmer's taste in food. His idea of a good night out is to go to a pub and order a mixed grill you can barely see over the top of it's piled so high with meat. Steak, gammon, sausages, liver, bacon, chops, enough meat on the plate to feed a family for a week is his idea of a proper mixed grill. He'll eat the two veg, chips and peas, and the gravy, but anything that looks or sounds like a sauce is verboten and rice and pasta are right off the Richter scale. 'That were alright' and 'I'd eat that again' are as good as you get from Nigel, the equivalent of Rob's 'quite tasty', but you have to know what to cook him to get showered with that sort of praise. Surprisingly acquiescent when I asked him over for a badger roast, it turned out badger was a dish he remembered local farmers and country people eating years ago, and one that his father and grandfather used to eat in the days before farmers stopped living entirely off their animals and the land. Gladys is always up for anything, and thought the whole idea was a hoot.

Handling raw badger is not altogether pleasant, and I speak as someone unsqueamish about handling anything from raw offal to fish, alive or dead, sticky or slimy. I'll gut and paunch and scale and skin with the best of them. The thing about this badger, however, was not the feel of it, it was the rank muskiness of it. The flesh was the colour of a deep, dark garnet and as high as any wild venison or snipe, grouse or woodcock I've ever plucked and gutted.

The muskiness didn't abate in the oven either.

As the hams cooked I began to wish I'd just fed them to Ruby Tuesday my Irish setter, given her the dog's dinner of a lifetime, bottled out completely and stuck with the pork, or ordered a take-away like Rob would have done if I'd dared to serve him a badger roast.

I set the hams down on my carving board, the ruby juices leaking like a flesh-wound as I attempted to carve. The lack of fat didn't help, nor did the fact that I hadn't marinaded the meat for a few days and broken down the taut muscle. The wretched leg seemed to be cocked like a dog's in rigor mortis on the carving board.

How to describe the taste? Well, it was higher and ranker than venison and far more difficult to chew. It was not like anything I'd ever eaten, game- or meat-wise. We tackled it manfully before we all decided that we'd done our duty and now it was time for pleasure, for the succulent loin of pork and apple sauce, the tender white meat with its brittle shell of salt crackling, caramelised sweet roast parsnips and crunchy roast potatoes, the things that a good old-fashioned Sunday lunch are really all about. And a boozily Somerset cider brandy laden apple cake for pudding which I knew would be on Nigel's approved list, even though he would try to stop Gladys from thwacking clotted cream off the spoon onto the still warm, appley cake crumb in the sort of soft scoop size normally reserved for ice cream. He'd fail, of course, and she would chuckle at the very notion of controlling calories at Sunday lunch.

'Diets always start on Monday' is Gladys's philosophy, and she's dead right.

Will I cook badger again? Would I add it to my road-kill shopping list? Only if I was starving, baying for flesh because I'd just spent a year on a desert island surviving on coconuts, yams, breadfruit, witchetty grubs and salted fish and the only other meat left on earth was spam.

After lunch I pulled the bags of frozen badger bits out of the chill of the freezer and consigned them to the bin without a second thought about waste: enough was enough, and in this case badger brawn, stewed paws and roast saddle would be far, far too much.

§5 *If You're Going*
to San Francisco

It started out with a few loony
visionaries, people like Bill Niman
and Alice Waters of the legendary
restaurant Chez Panisse, who
got going in the 1960s and 1970s
alongside a sprinkling of drop-out,
hippy vegetable and fruit growers
to make a little patch of Utopia away
from what most of industrialised
food production in America
had become.

In March we headed west. There were two good
reasons to go to San Francisco on St Patrick's Day, although I'm
sure we would still have gone had there just been one, the food.
I think Rob saw it as part of my further education programme,
a rite of passage into the heart, soul and gizzard of American
food culture, though from what he had told me, San Francisco
is another country. It is not like the rest of America, culinarily
speaking, any more than Manhattan is.

Be that as it may, my son Harry was about to tour the west
coast of America with his Oxford University a cappella group
Out of the Blue, having toured the east coast the previous year
in the Easter holidays. He was cutting it somewhat fine with
revision for his finals, but ever since he had heard the group at
the end of his first year, and rehearsed secretly all summer for
the auditions at the start of the Michaelmas term in October,
singing had become an all-consuming passion.

The 13 undergraduates write all their own harmonies, choreo-
graph every song, busk the streets, cut CDs, sing at the Oxford and
Cambridge May Balls, do private gigs, perform at the Edinburgh
Festival, and every summer term they take a night at the New
Theatre in Oxford which 1500 students, parents and devotees
come to. It is their biggest gig of the year.

To see the boy who hadn't opened his mouth since he headed
for Eton at 13 and refused to sing even when playing the guitar,
sing the solo to Coldplay's *Fix You* in front of a rapt audience of
over a thousand, was one of the great surprises and shocks of my
life, and, I guess, of his. To say that one is always surprised, or at
least prepared to be, by ones children is somewhat obvious, but
when the thing that is least likely to happen in your own mind
happens: the shy, self-conscious, modest boy who wouldn't court
attention let alone hold an audience to ransom is suddenly up

there on stage, looking for all the world as though that's just where he's supposed to be, well, it gives you more than pause for thought.

He looked, as my American friend Cynthia Zarin put it when she saw him last year at the Knickerbocker in Greenwich Village, a restaurant cum jazz venue where Rob had got them a gig in exchange for a good dinner, '…just like Cary Grant, he's a matinée idol, he's just like his uncle', as Harry stood there, his spare, 6 foot 4 inch frame elegant and spider-like in the pencil-slim, dark blue Paul Smith suit, holding an almost private, intimate audience with those he was singing to, and with the kind of stage presence that only attends those who have no notion they have it.

And my brother Daniel *was* in the audience hearing Harry for the first time that night, with his wife Rebecca.

If I hadn't already heard the group several times before and known exactly what I was in for, I would have had that awful feeling that parents have when they know they are about to suspend their honest judgement in order to judge their children as their children. As it was, there was now another family member whose judgment would be even more ruthless and professionally so, and who I didn't think would suspend it even for his favourite nephew.

They sang their opening songs. Harry began to sing his solo. Dan shot me a look of startled surprise a few bars in, the kind of look that intimated he was then switching judgement to professional mode. He raised two thumbs up in my direction as the song drew to a close, and I knew they'd done it. They'd impressed him on equal terms.

There is something about the level of energy, passion, commitment and the sheer hope of the young at the start of their discovery of themselves and what they may be able to do as artists, that is its own reward. It fills the heart and it stills the room. And it's magical for the parents and friends who know and care about them.

So Rob and I decided we would follow the Out of the Blue tour of the west coast of America like oldster groupies, check out the famous food scene of San Francisco, and spend a weekend with one of America's campaigning food gurus, Bill Niman. His cattle ranch lies sprawled across 1000 acres of prime Bolinas land on the edge of the ocean – if you can call anything prime that sits quakily, queasily close to the San Andreas fault and might, I presume be swallowed up by it or spat high into the sea in the not too distant future.

Bill had been offering to take us to some of the food landmarks inside and outside the city for ages and to introduce us to some of the local heroes of their food world, the artisan growers and restaurateurs who have helped catapult San Francisco into the premiership league.

Rob and Bill are similar sorts of oddballs. They would admit to being quirky, to being a pair of old-style hipsters turned pioneers, who have boldly dared to go where no one else was even dreaming of going in the Dark Ages of industrial food manufacturing that they came into straight from university in the 1960s.

Bill abandoned teaching construction for the land and became a Californian cattle rancher and meat producer. His Niman Ranch meat is the standard-bearer for the best animal husbandry and meat that America has to offer. Rob left the family supermarket business and the specialty food stores he had run for the world of cheese when he bought Murray's;

immersed himself in the liquid-gold glories of curds and whey, learned about the art of affinage, the ripening and ageing of cheeses in specially designed temperature-controlled caves and studied the age-old, farmhouse, raw milk methods of making it that have been practised the world over since the first milk sat unused in the pail and soured overnight with the warmth from the fire.

San Francisco is the acknowledged Mother Earth of the new American food movement, although it would be fair to say that, 40 years or so on, it may not appear as pioneering as it must have seemed when it all first took root.

It started out with a few loony visionaries, people like Bill Niman and Alice Waters of the legendary restaurant Chez Panisse, who got going in the 1960s and 1970s alongside a sprinkling of drop-out, hippy vegetable and fruit growers to make a little patch of Utopia away from what most of industrialised food production in America had become.

In our small world everyone knows everyone, or has at least heard of everyone, so eventually Rob's and Bill's paths collided, they got stuck into each other's food and they discovered just how similar their New Jersey backgrounds were: both of them sons of immigrants, both with fathers and grandfathers who had become butchers, grocers, food retailers, and linked not just by a childhood spent in the same place, but by both being childless, divorced twice and having struck out on their own and left their roots some way behind them.

I think I first became aware of Bill's bacon when one of his sales assistants brought some charcuterie into the old, small Murray's opposite the new store a couple of years ago for the staff to try and I turned my nose up at it in my food snobby way, since Rob was doing one of his typical, lambaste-the-Britscrappy-food tirades about how inferior our bacon was and how it didn't match up to Niman Ranch. Comparisons aside, if you haven't savoured Bill's apple-wood smoked rashers cured without nitrates, and frazzled to strips of snappy crispness, you have no right to think the Americans can't make a bacon sarnie taste as good as one of your own, with the fat leaking hotly and wetly down through the wad of white bread and melting the goodly thick unsalted buttering that is the only other ingredient of the real McCoy. We use Bill's Niman rashers in many of the dishes that I produce for the Murray's ready-made food section, which I got up and running a couple of years ago, and includes a classic quiche Lorraine made with the three ingredients that make it classic: eggs, cream and smoked bacon. Aside from the little snippings I stir into the cream and eggs, are the two long, crisped strips I perch on the wobbly filling when it has just cooked beyond the stage where they would sink straight into it like quicksand, so when the quiche is ready, the rashers are curled in a crisp cross on top to provide contrast to the satin-smooth middle. Once I had tried Niman Ranch rashers I literally ate my words, and realised I had no right to think that the Americans only manufacture super-sized, hormone-plumped, chemically smoked factory hog.

We left Manhattan on a cold Friday night, the streets filled with everyone celebrating St Paddy's Day as hard as if they were really Irish, for the city I have only ever seen in the movies. To me, San Francisco is Clint Eastwood car chase city, where beat up cars from homicide take off into the air at ski-jump junctions before they smack shuddering and screeching down onto the tarmac below and no one is ever seen eating anything other than burgers bleeding red sauce and dirty green gherkin, and puffs of deep-fried, sugar-gritted doughnuts, be it breakfast time, lunch time or midnight.

I was looking forward to comparing the ingredients, the markets and the restaurant food of the Big Apple's melting-pot cuisine with that of this patch of the West Coast that seems to own the moral high ground, has pioneered the principles of good eating ahead of anywhere else in America.

I was wondering whether the pioneering mentality of the 1960s and 1970s had atrophied or whether SF was still putting up new shoots, green shoots, from its radical roots and managing to stay at the forefront of the food scene. And I was looking forward to catching the few glimpses of Harry on a foreign stage that would be all I would see of him until the summer.

We arrived in San Francisco ragged and ravenous. The time difference meant that Bill had booked the four us a table for the equivalent of 1 am. so St Patrick's Day was as well past its prime as we were. Delfina is on 18th Street and Bill and his wife Nicolette had told us of its reputation as a neighbourhood restaurant that has taken its local producers and growers to heart. There was Fulton Valley chicken, Dungeness crab and Delta asparagus; there were Wolfe Ranch quail and Tofino Inlet salmon all of whom would clearly be proud to know that their hometown was considered as important as they were.

The provenance thing is as annoying as it is a justified badge of pride. We should cheer rather than jeer, though it does tend to turn every menu into a full essay rather than the mouth-wateringly delicious vignette that is all a hungry diner really wants before the dish appears. I mean, when we go out we want to be surprised, not to read a Waitrose shopping list of ingredients, a full statement of cooking methods, and a geographical study of all the places the poor artichoke or chop ever visited in its past life. I had to cheer when I saw Niman Ranch flatiron steak and French fries on the menu. In present company I could hardly switch ranches and eat quail. In fact quail is almost a dirty bird in America at the moment, for obvious reasons.

It is also a sign of the way that the indigenous San Francisco food culture has developed to see a cheese course featured, though despite the localness of the rest of the menu, there isn't a single local or American cheese to be found. There's a Robiola and a Blu della Alpi from Piemonte; Parmigiano Reggiano; Brescianella all'acquavite, which is a cow's milk cheese from the Lombardy and a black truffle moliterno from Basilicata.

The restaurant, industrial canteen-sized and styled, is noisy, thronging with a weekend crowd, obviously a hot, hip favourite.

What I see in this recent obsession with provenance, is clearly part of the Alice Waters legacy but should not be confused with good or even great cooking skills. Herein lies the problem at the heart of it: that we should be lulled into believing that because what we eat comes from an impeccable source, that that alone constitutes good cooking, and is good for us to boot. For better or worse it is also about the hands that cook and the brain that creates the dish.

Some of Delfina's dishes disappoint despite their impeccable sourcing. The bagna caoda bears no resemblance to this most classic of dishes, with none of its stinging, buttery, anchovied intensity; the insalata del campo with its bitter greens, pancetta, walnuts and Parmigiano is ordinary, bland, not resplendent with the grassy, peppery tones of an intensely flavoured olive oil to bind and harmonise the flavours: the nuttiness, the bitterness, the salt. Rob's Tuscan-style spareribs with cannellini beans fail to ignite the palate and my Niman Ranch steak is over-cooked and lacking in succulence and flavour. The Americans seem to like softer meat that doesn't have real bite and muscle, and they don't go for the gamier, meatier taste that we who like traditionally bred beasts get so excited about. I'm sure it has a lot to do with the way they grain finish their animals too, rather than keeping them grass fed to the end. Nothing is quite as gutsy or as tasty as it should be.

The real revelation is the crisp, blackly crusted sourdough bread with its slightly damp, spongy-smooth crumb. I have never eaten San Francisco sourdough in San Francisco before and would have been happy to eat nothing but bread all evening if there had been a zinging olive oil to dunk it into. I collared our waitress and discovered it came from a famous city bakery called Tartine which Rob and I decided we would have to pay a trip to after our respite on the ranch. One good food find is enough to fire us up and start us, like explorers heading up-river, on a trail back to the source.

We switchback at what, by now, must be around 4am our time, for what seems several eternities. Up an interminably windy roaded hill and down a further sequence of bends corkscrewed like a telephone cord, the road finally flattening out until we turn up a wooded track to Bill's ranch. It's too dark to get any sense of the place when we finally arrive, but that the house is a single-storey log cabin, built by Bill himself and heated by nothing other than the wood fire he burns in the sitting room.

The fire is out.

We get dressed and climb up into the old brass bed, socked, knickered and jerseyed against the surprising spring chill. It is one of those places where the dark and the quiet are so intense that you almost feel you are being buried alive. We must be in the middle of nowhere. We shiver all night.

In the morning a wan sun tries to slice through the chill and the mist, but its cold lemon heart doesn't stand a chance.

The house is surrounded by a lush valley garden and by clumps of beautiful, straight-limbed hardwood trees reaching high into the sky like tall ships' masts. After breakfast Bill and I sit down to talk about the mission he set out on 35 years ago when he abandoned his first career teaching construction and took on his first litter of pigs. He describes it as '...the turning point. I had always wanted to do it full-time.' Originally Bill had bought the ranch and taken on a huge mortgage, but in 1984 the Federal Government agreed to buy the property and the land from him and preserve it, and he became a lifetime tenant '...on December 4th, my birthday. I got the cheque and was free to do what I really wanted to do which was to raise cattle to feed people, and enjoy the creation of the animals, of converting grass and forage into something for human consumption. It's like a miracle, it's such a perfect system.'

The people who became Bill's mentors to begin with were his neighbouring farmers: 'Solid, traditional ranchers. They were still doing it right round here and adhering to the conventional wisdom. There were no hormonal implants and they understood that there are economic imperatives for treating your animals well.

'The genesis was to feed our family, then our extended family and like-minded people, to take responsibility for our lives. Our small, extended township had quite a few bright people from entrepreneurial backgrounds. I view the world as a business opportunity so I really loved that, it turned me on. I had no grand vision at that stage.' That was to come later.

In the afternoon we drive out in the pick-up with bales of hay to the great spit of seaward land where Bill has his 200 head of cattle. We feed, count and check them. We saw no one in two hours on the empty, thousand-acre expanse of pasture where cliff-top meets Pacific Ocean, save for a bizarre couple walking a pair of wolves on chains, the man as vulpine looking as the two pale, mangy-furred creatures with their killer-cold, topaz blue eyes.

'They're locals,' Bill told us, referring, presumably, to the humans.

As to the sanity of walking the creatures amongst a herd of cattle, where we had spent over an hour side-stepping and run-ning away from the locked-horn fight for supremacy between the old king of the bulls and his apparent successor, Bill shrugged and shook his head disbelievingly. It would be a pretty cruel and bloody outcome if the cattle decided they felt threatened or the wolves slipped their chains.

There is a growing problem as a new generation of cooks, so distanced from the food they eat and its original state, eschews the pleasures of the flesh if it actually bares any real resemblance to flesh and bone, and point-blank refuses even to acknowledge the existence of the grisly, gristly bits that those of us who are into hard core drool over: the sweetbreads and brains, the tongues and tails, the snouts and trotters, the cheeks and ears. Has it never occurred to them that their hamburgers and franks, their faggots and pies are filled with the bits they'd sooner starve than buy from their butchers?

Bill, as he had stated, is primarily a businessman. He may have his ideals, but he still has to find a customer for every part of the beast: the bones, the trim, the tails, the feet, the marrow. He produces grain-finished prime beef and refuses to compromise its quality. And nothing would have induced him to change his farming methods or grow leaner animals because some food faddists — or should I say fattists — were obsessing about animal fat.

'I grow for good eating, for tenderness and for tasty meat,' he says unequivocally.

Since 1971 he has grown the business gradually, one ranch at a time, moving to different climates like Idaho and Oregon where he has found other like-minded farmers to rear for him, so that he has beef to sell all the year round.

'We've 75 cattle ranchers in the far west where it's open range, cheap grassland unsuitable for other crops; 500 pig farmers in 10 states, mostly in the corn-belt, almost all free range. We have 10 sheep ranches, several in California and 3 in Utah which each have 10,000 sheep on millions of acres of public land.'

Big business it may be, but it doesn't exist just to cater for an élite, well-heeled market. That's not what Bill's philosophy is about at all.

'I'd really like to say our farmers have fed one million people a day from every walk of life. And more important even than that, is our influence over the rural landscape; everything we do is about educating people about that.'

Feeding a million people a day, even at the level of a really decent burger in a diner or restaurant, or a meat pie filled with all the extremities that so many of us disdain but that tastes like a meat pie should taste, that's a vision, an accomplishment, and one made in the knowledge that the meat Bill is selling has come from animals who have been properly fed, loved and sheltered. In fact Bill has pioneered the use of shelters for shade in the Central Valley of California, in the vast feed lots where he has 100,000 cattle. 'Animals will perform better if they're treated well, but unfortunately there are a lot of farmers around who see animal welfare as bullshit.'

The following day we head back into San Francisco for the famous Saturday Ferry Plaza Farmers Market. There are bundles of local green and fat white asparagus with tightly furled tips and pale violet stems, heaps of spiky leaved artichokes, tiny Chinese lantern globes of turnip and early salad greens. There are wonderful local sourdough breads at the Acme Bread Co. whose founder, Steve Sullivan, started making bread in his dorm at University College Berkeley following Elizabeth David's recipes from her seminal book, *English Bread and Yeast Cookery*. Over 20 years later he is still at it, albeit with 168 people working for him, making handmade loaves and pastries, all with organic flour.

At the back of a van, a couple of chefs are working a couple of heavyweight, cast-iron skillets, sloshing a liquid, primrose-coloured heap of scrambling egg into shape in the one and a wild mushroom omelette in the other. Hog Island Oysters is busy shucking oysters and selling clams from the pristine estuary of Tomales Bay around 50 miles away. You can buy doughnut muffins from the Downtown Bakery and day-glo stemmed chard from Dirty Girl Produce, who sell Early Girl tomatoes and fresh canellini and cranberry beans in season. The Cowgirl Creamery from Point Reyes is hawking splendiferous 'clabbered' cottage cheese and fresh and aged cheeses like Red Hawk, St Pat and Me Tam. Cow girls, dirty girls, early girls, what on earth is going on here? Could this be the earthiest place on earth?

It is just warm enough to strip to T-shirts and pretend summer is a breath away across the Golden Gate Bridge. We arrive at the Frog Hollow Farm stand owned by orchard fruit grower Al

Courchesne who likes to be known as Farmer Al. Farmer Al looks like the definition of a nursery rhyme farmer who has tied a scarlet bandana round his neck but forgotten to bring his hoe. He towers above us in his old dungarees and is nothing short of a local landmark. In fact he's better than the Statue of Liberty and just as statuesque. I didn't know sane, consenting adults still wore bibbed and braced Osh Koshes. He owns apricot and peach orchards and makes Frog Hollow jams, sorry, jellies as the Americans insist on calling them. God knows how or even whether they differentiate between the two. Cherry, apricot, nectarine, plum, peach and pear, marmalades and chutneys, Farmer Al's stall is a jammy paradise, though I have to confess to my usual element of Euro-sceptery and snobbery when I arrive. Could some arriviste of a Californian orchardier actually turn his fruit into anything as intensely flavoured as the best French jam? Could the local orchards rival those at Nîmes where I have plucked colic-inducing 'apricocks' from the tree like Elizabeth the First until the damage was done? I doubt it. And have you ever tasted peach jam that actually tasted of those perfect, fragrant, scented summer peaches from Nîmes or Italy? Well I haven't. Theirs is a fragrance that resists bottling.

Al offers us some tasters. The apricot jam has held its own in the pot, it hasn't been reduced to amorphous, gloopy sweetness through over-cooking. And it is as intensely apricot coloured as I have ever seen. Apricots are a fruit I have always preferred cooked, turned into a thickly syruped compote or tart with sugared, black-scorched skin or buried under an almond spiked crumble. The jam has brilliant hued halves of fruit that slop out onto the bread and the taste is so intense, so perfect, it is almost unbearable. The agony of the apricot, its rush of pain and saliva to the jaw. I am cajoled into tasting the peach jam. I can't remember ever eating two jams that are so reminiscent of the summer, of the boughs they have been picked from, of the high summer ripeness they tell of, and, apart from buying as many pots as I can carry, I tell Rob we must stock them in the shop if Farmer Al will do business with New York. It takes six months, Farmer Al, fittingly enough, prefers the orchard to the e-mail, but they did finally arrive at Murray's!

So the next big decision of the day is where to have lunch. Always the most exciting decision one has to make on days like this. Bill has suggested any number of restaurants in the city, but we follow our noses to one of those wonderful boys' toys of a rotisserie van, the kind you see in every French outdoor market – Rob has a secret desire to own one, a fully equipped cheese van which we could roar across America in, starring in our own road-foodie movie in the ultimate culinary Winnebago packed to the gunnels with raw milk cheese, and converting middle America as we went.

We are greeted by a sight and scent that would awaken the taste buds of the dead. Whole organic and free-range birds are trussed and turning in orderly rows, their skins crisping to the colour of Marmite, their fatty juices dribbling onto a tray of perfect pebbles of waxy new potatoes below. There are racks of Bill's Niman Ranch ribs, thick-cut pork chops on the bone, and lush pink racks of lamb. Other than a simple herb mix and good sea salt and olive oil, there are no other ingredients except the lemon quarters and seasoning sitting on the counter for the customers to shake and squeeze. Who needs a restaurant?

We get talking to the Roli Roti Gourmet Rotisserie owner Thomas Odermatt, who is from Switzerland, then decide we can wait no longer, and watch him skilfully sharpen his knives, then tuck a blade so adeptly around the bones to separate them that they dare not but part company with the cage of carcass they have been attached to instantly. He carves our lunch from all the different meats, scoops up a rake of potatoes slipping and skating in their hot fat and serves it all up for us to eat outside, watching the bay life sail by.

What it is about this kind of food that gives me so much pleasure is simple. First, the joy of finding 'fast food' that is really slow food. The best food. Then it is about discussing it with its creator and finding his ideals and expertise are thrillingly spot on. Then there is the element of surprise. You think you are going to end up in one place, but are diverted by another. You are in good company, feeling hungry and you are not disappointed by anything, the taste, the smell, the price. You have found value for money and someone doing an honest job with the zeal you have yourself, and in this case, taught by their butcher father in Switzerland, so passing on the tradition, and in this case, transferring it to another place that will recognise it for what it is.

Sitting tearing chunks of warm meat and crackling from the bone as the water laps next to us, dipping it into the oily juices, picking up the slippery, lemon and thyme spritzed potatoes from the same paper plate, is as satisfying as anything on earth. Rob is never happier than when a Fred Flintstone sized piece of charcoaled or roasted meat is wafted under his nose and he can tackle it like a barber with a Number 1 cut, right down to the last follicle.

This is, without doubt, the best meal we eat in San Francisco, and fuels me with such a protein-rush that I lose all sense of inhibition and find myself dancing an Irish jig in front of a tram queue as my feet just can't stop when I hear an old black musician playing blues harmonica as we pass by. There is a spontaneous ripple of applause at the end and Rob looks on with a kind of disbelieving pride — he knows I am a watcher from the wings, not a performer. I maintain that it is the harmonica player the bus queue is clapping anyway.

That night, Bill has managed to get the Out of the Blue boys a gig at the Onema Inn, miles out in the country, a two-hour ride from San Francisco, and though they have only just flown in, they have been promised dinner, so are game for it. Bill leads us out there with a group of his friends and we arrive to find the boys tucking into an early pasta supper. There is that strange sense of seeing people removed from their normal context. Here is my son in professional mode, in his other life, far from home and family and university, meeting me with the sort of pleased yet polite formality that is natural in the company of his peers.

They had arrived looking like hillbillies and been ushered upstairs to change, Harry says, adding that the management had appeared somewhat nervous as to exactly what they had taken on. It is clear, however, that they, the management, have been charmed in the only way a group of 13 now impeccably groomed and mannered Oxford boys can charm Americans into realising that everything they ever heard about Oxford boys is true. The manager comes up to me later and has clearly been seduced by the complete baker's dozen. 'They're so charming and *so* polite. We weren't quite sure when they arrived, but they cleaned up and came downstairs and I'd have them all to stay. They keep on thanking me, and their *accents*…'!

Niman Ranch meat is all across the menu and Bill is treated with the reverence due a priest, as he has been wherever we've been with him. As the food arrives, the boys begin to sing to the full house from the bar and ante-room beyond. Every knife and fork stops clacking and mouthfuls are suspended mid-chew. If the Americans thought a bunch of English boys couldn't do a cappella like they can, they're in no doubt now. There are cheers between each song and gradually more and more people leave their tables to group around the edge of the room and get up close. Rob comes up to stand behind me, as proud of Harry's singing his solo as any parent. It has been a complicated but rewarding transition for him to make, not having his own children, but effectively having three surrogates, and knowing that my three are what my life has been about for the last 20 something years and will continue to be about for the duration. But I know we would not be listening to tonight's performance had it not been for Rob edging Harry into doing the one thing he was so loath yet so desperate to do: stand up and sing. I am reminded of it every time we hear Harry, and each time I am convinced anew it has been the making of him.

When the boys head off into the night towards their next gig, Harry having filched most of the steak from my plate in a post-nerves, post-singing, hunger attack, we turn back to conversation, everyone enlivened and released by the combination of that triplicate of things that feeds the soul and the heart like so few others can so well: good food, fine wine and song.

America's food identity comes from this place, Rob reminds me again later, worried that perhaps I will not do justice to, or understand, quite how important a movement it has been in goading and chiding the rest of America for all these years. It is, he feels, still best and more advanced here, still unique, a region where wine, goat's cheese, Niman Ranch meat, ice creams and cool fast foods and the first of the country's small producers like Farmer Al all flourish and grace shops, markets and tables from the smallest of cafés to the smartest of restaurants, and where places like Zuni Café and Chez Panisse are the yardsticks by which all others are still measured. San Francisco stands alone and has dared to be different, and, whether it still has the culinary edge or not, which we are not about to find out definitively in such a short trip, is still doing it with conviction and panache.

We leave Bill's ranch to spend a couple of nights in The Huntington Hotel at the top of the ludicrously P.G.Wodehouse sounding Nob Hill, a hill so steep that I am reminded of the fairy tale of the glass mountain, and almost feel if I were pushed from the top, I would slip off its edge and end up in the bay. It is a hotel whose veneer of splendour is, for once, more than epidermis deep. Every member of staff we speak to seems to have worked in the hotel for 34 years. They do not, however, give the feeling of being poached, pickled or preserved in aspic. Every guest seems to be as regular or permanent a fixture as the staff. The two greet each other like long-standing friends whose habits and foibles are known and discreetly accepted, and the pictures and furniture look like they haven't shifted an inch over decades. It is so un-American. I love it.

We decide almost immediately to make it our hotel whenever we come here, a thing we do wherever we are, even if we know we'll never come back. If you were as spoilt and fussy as all-get-out, you would still be pushed to find fault. Just finding a place where service is seen as a goal and a given rather than as something quaintly servile and of the past is unusual, and, in this case, the staff seem to have been picked for their character rather than their absence of it, which is more often the modern way in so many places that are not family run. No young Turks with earpieces dressed in menacing black and looking cooler than their customers here. At the Huntington you *know* there is no question that hasn't been asked and satisfactorily answered before, there is nothing left on the list to shock or refuse, and the smoothly oiled wheels of courtesy and kindliness and watchfulness and attention to comfort, are at once spoiling, without inducing that sense of being cynically guest-watched that is as undesirable as inattention.

Rob has decided we can't do SF without doing Berkeley, so we drive over for lunch, pretty sure that we can talk our way into Chez Panisse when we get there since we had bumped into Alice Waters in The Tasting Room, a charming small restaurant in the East Village, some weeks previously, and Alice had said just to use her name.

I think I had expected a sort of huge, campus-like, more metropolitan feel to Berkeley: spacious, leafy, open, sophisticated, so am surprised by the somewhat suburban, dowdy main street with its faded, shabby shop fronts and series of small cafés, delis, coffee shops, and the odd hippy leftover of a vegetarian café selling wholefood not dissimilar in feel to Totnes in Devon, from a menu that doesn't appear to have changed in 30 years. And it doesn't appear to have changed its clientele, any more than does Peet's Coffee Shop where we stop off. There are three fat, unshaven, rheumy-eyed derelicts talking very loudly over the canned Mozart and lattes and appraising us, as we walk in, as suspicious outsiders. Close up they are clearly not real derelicts, they are kings of the campus, probably senior professors, glorifying in their well-honed intellectual dishevelment and its implied superiority. They must have heard me order the coffee, for, in unconcealed tones, one turns to the other and remarks, 'The English don't speak to you.' It is not clear whether he is expecting and hoping for a reaction or too deaf to realise he can be heard.

'No,' I offer equally loudly. 'An English gentleman always waits to be introduced.'

The three escapees, carbon copies of the old buffers in Kingsley Amis' *Ending Up*, don't appear remotely embarrassed; indeed, they appear as bullish as if they had been confronted by a stranger seated on their bar stool in their local, and start asking the nosiest of questions. Before I can say anything else rather ruder than I have, a woman with two small, ugly, square-faced children, 'so ugly you would give them away', I say to Rob, since the derelicts have put me in a mind to shock, steam noisily up to the counter between us and the oldsters, and Rob drags me out quickly, saying, 'Berkeley was the epicentre of the free speech movement of the 1960s. It was the first radical campus, the Black Panthers came out of Oakland and I think there has to be some relation between this very left culture and the food.' The radicals are certainly pretty free with their language here, if a little more gnarled and rooty than they would have been in the 1960s. But the only counter culture I want in a coffee shop is friendly service and great coffee. The place feels more and more like a time warp as we continue on down the main street checking out the locals, in the way that only university campuses can, with their enclosed exclusivity, their clubbiness, their rarified community that even gets to look like it has a look, a type, a code of dress and where outsiders are not permitted to walk on the proverbial grass.

We walk upstairs into the restaurant at Chez Panisse, and yet again I am taken aback by how refreshingly un-modern it is, with its threadbare carpet and its 1960s, all wood look; how untouched and unlike a chic, sleek, modern city restaurant. It reminds me more of the first Cranks in Marshall Street in Soho in the 1970s where pale, whey faced but pretty girls in floral sprigged Laura

Ashley who looked so unhealthy they could only be vegetarians, served leek and mushroom croustades, vegetable and millet stews and homity pies made with heavy, whole-wheat pastry, and where, for the first time, you could see the cooks cooking and there was no barrier between you, the customer and the kitchen.

At one counter a young, intent head is bent over the assemblage of a kumquat, avocado and beet salad, at another a Meyer lemon tart sits awaiting its first taker, and, though it is not yet one o'clock, the restaurant is fully booked and we would have to wait a considerable time to get seated and fed. Not for us the 'hand-cut pasta alla Bolognese with English peas' which reads so eccentrically but compellingly.

It is rather like getting to the altar but realising you're not going to be able to pay your respects and take Holy Communion. I have heard about Chez Panisse for as long as I have been cooking hot dinners, met Alice several times in several different cities from Torino to New York, but still I haven't got to eat in Alice's restaurant.

Back down Shattuck Avenue we turn into a small mall, pretentiously named Epicurious Garden, which is in the throes of opening up a few specialist food stalls. There is a soup kitchen named Soop, whose menu states that they named it thus after our great, indigenous and near earliest of cook book writers, Robert May, who wrote *The Accomplished Cook* in 1660. I have a facsimile edition of it at home. The name may be pseudo-Shakespearean, but the message is fashionable, melting-pot cuisine; a tableau of different ethnic street and home comforters making modern soup-speak of ancient tradition. The owners are busy cooking a test-run before they open and the kitchen is steaming with vats of wonderful, organic vegetable soups like wild mushroom and barley, Tuscan white bean, Indian red lentil,

butternut squash and pear, and some meaty, stewy ones like
Italian wedding soup with pasta, meatballs and Parmesan;
a classic chicken noodle soup and chicken hominy with lime,
vegetables, thyme, oregano, epazote and chipotle.

Opposite there is an artisan chocolate shop, and down the
aisle we spot Taste, whose opening week menu is like the best
school lunch box you never had. There is a flatbread sandwich
stuffed with roast asparagus, yellowfoot chanterelles, goat's
cheese, red spring onion and tapenade; a baguette deep in
Serrano ham, dry-cured Niman Ranch ham, Tuscan Pecorino,
parsley pesto, aioli and endive; assorted salads, Valrhona
brownies studded with sour cherries and hazelnuts – you get
the picture.

Suddenly, at the back of the mall, I spot some ovens flaming
and a group of harassed-looking chefs and servers trying
frenziedly to cope with the line of people waiting to order. The
Socca Oven is run by a Frenchman, and today is their opening
day. He tells me that 'socca' is a Provençal pancake that goes back
to the mid-eighteenth century, when the socca sellers sold their
ware at markets and work sites and were the favourite meal
of the workers. Made with chick peas, I have cooked them to
accompany soups before, but here they are being spread like
a thin-crust pizza, with delicious combinations of the sorts of
vegetables you associate with those inimitable Provençal markets
like Carpentras, Apt and Cavaillon.

Apparently the socca sellers used special wagons with built-in
charcoal ovens to keep their pancakes hot while they shouted
out their wares. Originally the socca were made on a large, round,
copper pie tin called a plaque and cooked in an intensely hot
oven for about six minutes. The copper spreads the heat evenly.

They look irresistible. We order a sautéed green and yellow

zucchini and vine tomato socca with harissa and one with caramelised onion, anchovy and black olive, and sit outside in the
sun on a warm wall, sharing the perfect lunch. True to their
native origin, there is a salt cod and tapenade version and a slow-
roast pork socca with a mushroom duxelle and truffle oil, but
each socca is workman sized and a second would be unthinkable
even if you happened to carry a hod for a living.

It is beginning to strike me that the current renaissance in San
Franciscan cuisine, is about turning the superb produce that has
become accepted as the very fabric of the place into a sophisticated, upmarket, but staying-true-to-its-roots version of what
is really only street food, global fast food. All the new small
businesses seem to be about a single concept, be it a soup, a
sandwich, a socca, a rotisserie organic chicken or an ice cream.
The same is happening in New York, where you can find single
dish restaurants and retail all over town, from risotto restaurants
to cup cake emporia, like the teen haunt-of-choice's Magnolia
Bakery up from Rob's shop on Bleecker Street where the queues
stretch until late into the night; from falafel shops to, believe it
or not, a rice pudding restaurant.

Browsing the bookshops of Berkeley in the late afternoon,
we spot a tiny ice cream parlour called Sketch which is about as
unlike the ubiquitous American chains as you could find. We
get talking to the slight, pretty Asian girl serving, who is called
Ruthie. She and her husband Eric have been pastry chefs at
Aqua, a high-end restaurant we had lunched in the previous day
in San Francisco. This was their first small venture together. The
ice creams were unsurpassed even by any I've tasted in Florence,
the gelato capital of the universe in my book. We tasted them all:
red bean, candied ginger, dark chocolate, Earl Grey tea, ruby
grapefruit granita, burnt caramel, organic coffee, blood orange

sherbert, spiced apple sorbet. This is as near an earthly paradise as Rob, who sees no dinner as complete without ice cream to follow, could have imagined in his wildest dreams. If he could have persuaded Ruthie to open a parlour opposite the flat in New York, he would have attained the state of Nirvana rather earlier than planned.

We head out along the coast to Half Moon Bay, where the Out of the Blue boys are going to be singing at Sea Crest School. It is dark when we arrive in the deserted parking lot in a back street of this small town, the most unlikely of venues, and there are only two people in the school gymnasium. It's not exactly a sell-out by the look of things.

Twenty minutes or so before the boys are due to start, the crowds begin to arrive, whole families with their children – we are the only outsiders – and pretty soon the place is so full there are rows of small children sitting in front of us cross-legged on the floor.

Whatever misgivings we had about the boys capturing and keeping the attention of the children was entirely misplaced. They are spellbound, shrieking with laughter at the comic songs and not moving a muscle when Harry begins his haunting solo.

At the end the screams for encores carry on for three extra songs, and then the boys come down to talk to the children to whom they had already delivered a master-class in the morning, and the parents, some of whom have been housing them and looking after them royally. The children start autograph-hunting, and Rob remarks that it is a bit like how it must have been for the Beatles back in their early days, with the teenage girls proffering arms, scraps of paper and in some cases backs and fronts of t-shirts for the boys to sign. They are mobbed for 40 minutes.

We old groupies drive back over the Golden Gate Bridge and up to Nob Hill for our last night of luxury. The boys had recently won the Western European collegiate a cappella championships and this tour is something of a warm-up act for their return trip in May, when they have to sing in the finals in New York, the first group outside America ever to have made it this far. It will be something they, and we both, will always remember, and the thirteen boys are touchingly, modestly unaware of the impact they are having at their gigs right down the West Coast, and at the local semi-final where they have made a guest appearance and been uncomfortably alerted to just how good some of the opposition is. As far as they are concerned, just getting to sing in the Lincoln Center in New York is more than any of them ever dreamed of, and they know they are the underdogs up against the pick of the American a cappella groups whose tradition, after all, it is.

Though the ubiquitous mist has barely lifted during our stay, San Francisco has etched a pretty potent impression. It is like an off-shore colony or outpost, a mere distant relation to the mainland, it thinks and feels and is animated differently. I don't warm to the climate and its obfuscatory veil that keeps everything suspended in a sort of narcotic half-light, and the underlying sense that its occupants are permanently braced for a seismic shift that could erase the last century's footprint entirely, but I do warm to the fact that they are making their mark no matter what. That they, like Rob and Bill, have dared to be different, to stand out against the received wisdom of the day, gone on embracing the counter-culture until their little bit of it has grown from alternative to mainstream.

'San Francisco was about the 1960s,' Rob says. 'We were hopeful, we were political, we believed in free speech and we were anti-war. Politics spilled over into all elements of life, into food and sex and music, especially music. Then those dreams died and we got old. Now the country is run by Republicans and fundamentalists, here and in England, both from our generation.'

'It is easy to parody that and be cynical,' I say. 'But when you see Harry and the boys you realise that that's part of life's renewal. Those boys still have the same sense of excitement and discovery you had.'

'There's no point in believing Utopia is a pebble skim across the bay,' I continue. 'But there has been a seismic shift, and one of the places it's happened is in the food world, your and my world. It has made us question the worst offenders, begin to exercise a degree of control, and adopt a healthy cynicism and mistrust of the supermarket chains and agri-business' world domination.'

'Coming back to San Francisco reminds me of when things changed, and of my earliest memories of food,' Rob muses. 'Things didn't work out as we'd hoped, the liberation from the constraints of society, from what we once had, but Harry and the kids don't know that. We can re-live our hope through them now.'

It was a decade later, in the early 1970s, when food began to change my life, and when I really had to grow up. Our conversation reminds me of that, too.

Black-Eyed Pea Salad

This is an almost-Greek salad with a little more body and spice than the classic. Soak the black eyes overnight first.

450G/1LB *black-eyed peas*
2 *bay leaves,* A STICK *of celery,*
    2 *onions in their skins studded*
    with A COUPLE *of cloves each,*
    A COUPLE *of carrots to cook with*
    the peas
1 *red onion*
2 CLOVES *garlic*
1 LARGE *carrot*
1 *sweet red pepper*
24 *black Nyons olives*
180G/6 OZ *sheep's milk feta*
2 TBSP *parsley*
1 TBSP *dill*
2 TSP *cumin seeds tempered in a hot*
    pan for a minute and crushed in
    a mortar
6 TBSP *extra virgin olive oil*
1–2 *lemons*
sea salt and black pepper

Cook the peas by covering them with water to 2 cm above them in a heavy-bottomed pan and adding the cooking vegetables but no salt which would toughen them at this stage. Boil for 10 minutes, scum and then simmer until cooked. Drain. In the meanwhile, peel and slice the red onion and garlic finely and peel and grate the large carrot on a coarse grater. Seed and slice the red pepper into very fine strips. Chop the herbs. As soon as the peas are drained, season them, lash on the olive oil and lemon juice and toss in the vegetables, pitted olives, cumin and herbs, turning everything with your fingers to amalgamate. Assemble in a large mound on a serving plate. Crumble the feta over the top and add some more olive oil and lemon juice to taste before serving warm or at room temperature.

Quiche Lorraine with a Crisp Bacon Top

SERVES SIX

Such an under-rated and bastardised classic this, which should consist of three and three ingredients alone: cream, eggs and smoked bacon. And these have to be the very best of their kind for the dish to sing. Putting slips of crisped smoky rashers on top of the unctuous custard doesn't change the principle a jot, but does add another dimension texture-wise and make the old classic look inspired anew.

Preheat oven to 200°C/400°F/ GAS 6

For the pastry:
180G/6OZ organic plain flour
85G/3OZ unsalted chilled butter cut into cubes

12 RASHERS smoked streaky bacon, the rinds snipped off
¾–1 PINT/340–450 ML Jersey cream
2 organic eggs and 4 yolks
black pepper

Bake the pastry blind in the usual way and dry out it in the oven for a further 5 minutes, pricked with the tines of a fork.

Meanwhile, snip 6 of the rashers into bits and cook them in a frying pan with no additional fat. They should remain soft, not crisped. Drain on kitchen paper and cool.

Whisk together the cream, egg yolks and whole eggs with the pepper and get ready to pour from a jug into the tart shell. Place the bits of bacon on the bottom of the tart and pour in the custard quickly, returning the tart to the oven at 180°C/ 350°F/GAS 4.

Fry the other six rashers without their rind until crisp and drain.

After the tart has been cooking for 20–25 minutes and is very nearly set, but still wobbling, perch the strips of bacon on top so that they sit and don't sink and continue to cook until the tart is golden and just trembling faintly in the middle. It will carry on cooking outside the oven.

Cool on a rack for 15 minutes before serving. Tarts are never to be eaten hot hot, they don't taste.

Apricot Tart

SERVES EIGHT

Californian apricots ripen way before our French and Spanish ones, so this is an earlier treat in New York than it is at home in Somerset in June and July. They go extremely well after lamb too, as well as they go with it in Moroccan cooking. I have made creme fraiche custard apricot tarts before, but here is a made before dinner cold tart that has been burnished under the grill, the apricots standing to attention rather than peaking out through a cooked custard.

Preheat the oven to 180°C/375°F/ GAS 4

For the sweetcrust pastry:
180G/6OZ organic plain flour
85G/3OZ unsalted butter
1 HEAPED TBSP unrefined icing sugar
1 egg yolk

Sift flour and icing sugar into Magimix or bowl and add the fridge cold butter in small cubes. Blitz or work briefly before adding the egg yolk and a scant tablespoon of ice cold water. Bring to a dough by blitzing again briefly or working by hand and the moment it coheres, wrap it in clingfilm and refrigerate for 30 minutes. Roll out and line a greased tart tin with a removeable base. Bake blind for 15–20 minutes until the sides have gone a pale biscuit colour. Remove the beans and prick with the tines of a fork all over.

Return to the oven until crisp, about another 5–7 minutes, but don't let the base brown or bubble. Remove to a rack to cool.

340 ML/12 FL OZ Jersey milk
150 ML/5 FL OZ double cream
1 vanilla pod, split lengthwise, the seeds scooped out with a teaspoon
1 LARGE organic egg
3 LARGE egg yolks
75G/2½OZ vanilla caster sugar
45G/1½OZ cornflour
12–15 apricots, halved and stoned
muscovado or unrefined granulated sugar
½ JAR good apricot jam
1 TBSP Cointreau

Pour the milk and cream into a pan with the pod and seeds and heat to scald point. Meanwhile, whisk the egg, egg yolks and sugar together until pale and creamy. Sift a little of the cornflour into the bowl and whisk in until no longer lumpy and repeat until it is all whisked in.

Remove the pod from the hot milk and pour a third of the milk over the egg and sugar mixture. Whisk well and return this mixture to the milk in the pan. Whisk continuously over a gentle heat until the custard thickens, then keep beating out the lumps and cooking it down to rid it of its floury taste for another 5 minutes. Pour into a bowl to cool, whisking every so often so that a skin doesn't form on top. When tepid, you can scrape the creme patissiere into the tart case and spread it out evenly.

Now place the halved apricots in radiating lines from the outside in to the middle, upright and touching each other. Sprinkle a little sugar over the tops as carefully as you can so that it doesn't all fall to the bottom of the fruit and put the tart tin, the pastry edge protected by a strip of foil, under a hot grill until the sugar has melted and turned brown, or aim your blow torch at the sugar and effect the same. A singed, slightly bruléed edge is what you are after, but don't get carried away. Heat the jam with the Cointreau in a small pan, then brush the glaze over the tart top. The orange scent from the Cointreau is lovely with the tart apricot.

Remove the tart base from the sides and place the tart on a large, flat white plate to serve. No cream necessary.

§6   *Waiting for Venice*

I nurse a *Don't Look Now* vision
of shadowy canals and spectral
white bridges, of gliding past its
chiaroscuro corners eaten away
by angrily rising water, of tourists
sweeping down like starlings and
consuming the place, of its being
both beautiful and damned,
condemned as a city of dreams,
gnawed, eaten away, destroyed…

Of the major omissions in my life – too many to
name, too little time to remedy most – none have I felt so keenly
as Venice. Not to have been to Venice is like being denied one
of life's must-have experiences, and though there is no logical
reason as to why I haven't just easyJetted my generally under-
deprived self there and put a stop to this silly nonsense once and
for all, there has always been an uneasy feeling in the back of
my mind that when the right time comes I'll know it and it will
happen.

Unlike any of the places I have travelled to throughout my
life so far, Venice has had a strange, irrational hold on me even
without my going there; and it is the only place on earth I have
determined I shall only go to when I have the right person to go
with. Until then it will wait for me, and I guess I will wait for it.
That in itself has become my justification for not going, and it
has worn so thin, I have become so shabbily, openly resentful,
that it is in danger of cracking. I have said this to Rob so many
times now that the hint is in danger of becoming more of a threat
than a pleasure – to him that is – and naturally he has already
been there with his ex-wife. Who hasn't?

The corollary to all this is glaringly obvious, I tell myself:
suppose I don't like Venice? Suppose, in some fundamental way,
its having been built, like a castle in the air, into such a stratospherically unrealisable fantasy place, it disappoints and doesn't
live up to expectations? Worse still, suppose I go to the city of
dreams with the man of my dreams and a hideously Thomas
Mannish event takes place – let's face it, one cannot protect
against fate and one is often unable to see where it's leading one
even when one has virtually arrived – and we row brutally and
terminally, or the whole romance of the place fails to ignite and
we realise that that must mean it's all over. If Venice is unable to

work its magic on us, surely it *must* be all over?

I nurse a *Don't Look Now* vision of shadowy canals and spectral white bridges, of gliding past its chiaroscuro corners eaten away by angrily rising water, of tourists sweeping down like starlings and consuming the place, of its being both beautiful and damned, condemned as a city of dreams, gnawed, eaten away, destroyed, turned into the theme park on the lagoon unable to escape its glorious past yet hijacked by its tourist-infested present, its miraculous pictures and painted ceilings admired not with the silent awe and wonder befitting its Renaissance past, but accompanied by the banal commentaries and cameras of the crowds clustering in the sinking city and somehow desecrating the brilliant dream and light and mist and glow that the place once was.

There. I have said it all. Perhaps I should just never go to Venice.

17.10 pm, Wednesday 4th October 2006. easyJet flight 6173 heads off on time from Bristol for Venice and we are on it. Rob had promised, after my epic birthday dinner at Castello di Verduno, Piemonte, last year, to return to Italy for this year's birthday and for us finally to spend it in Venice together.

The trouble was, every room in every decent hotel we had been recommended had been booked months before. Venice may be for lovers, but not for spur of the minute, even two months ahead impulsive ones. It is for forward planners.

So Rob booked up for his birthday instead, telling me to imagine that it was mine, and I have bought the plane tickets. I have also been appointed CEO in charge of finding all the places to eat in over the four days and of masterminding the itinerary. No pressure, other, that is, than the fact that Rob happens to be the most exacting of travellers on the planet. By that, I don't mean if it isn't a five-star spa with a personal butler he won't check in. He is more a value for money tyro, be it a topnotch, best hotels of the world, cover-girl of a place or an unassuming, full-fry, polyester sheeted b and b miles off the unbeaten track of a west of Ireland island.

And then there is the perceived wisdom that the food in Venice is universally expensive and the worst in Italy, though knowing Italy that mightn't be so bad. It isn't Kazakhstan after all.

So, it is my duty and my pleasure to winkle out the best and most interesting local restaurants serving as near authentic Venetian food as the word 'authentic' means these days, and book us in. I also have to pick and mix what sights we are going to see, in what order, and with what culture-free zones in between that won't induce a sense of middle-brow guilt and shirkery or a sense of great work of art fatigue. This is, after all, a mere toe in the murky waters of Venice; only a four-day trip; if we get the balance right, it will become a place I imagine we'll always come back to, where we could return a hundred times and still feel a sense of awe and wonder and discovery.

I also happen to have a secret weapon in the shape of my editor, Susan Haynes, who left it later even than I to take her first trip to Venice last Christmas, and who has subsequently, with her well-tested and annotated copy of *The Osterias of Venice,* become my gustatorial ready reckoner.

It is Rob's birthday on our last night in Venice, a Saturday, his fifty-ninth, so somehow the food has got to sweep to a crescendo of excellence on his natal night and I have to be mindful of the fact that it will be exactly a year before his sixtieth birthday, more relevant than might be immediately apparent.

It is not that Rob is claiming a somewhat late-flowering mid-life crisis, more that he has an acute sense of his own mortality and this year seems to be as much the turning point as next. He is already anticipating what it means to turn sixty. He is taking stock. His new business is up and running and growing exponentially, but does he want to be working harder and harder at his age? He is conducting an inter-continental relationship with a mother of three. He is childless and twice divorced. What and where is the future going to take him? He worries about his health in ways that I can't even conceive of worrying about – well, anything. And Venice is a city that is built on the very mortar of mortality, its timelessness a constant reminder of time itself.

And it is the turn of the year. At the cusp of autumn when fecundity and fruitfulness are being thrown at us like rotten apples, we are aware that the cycle of life and death is at its zenith before it hastens back to earth, to decay and rot and darkness and rebirth.

Is anyone in later years *not* aware that each turn of the year is about a little death, about returning to the ground; that the damp, chill air and earth, the low sun, the watercolour sky, the logs sparking and spitting in the grate are a reminder of how short the day is, are somehow all metaphors for the long night ahead?

It strikes me as I write this, that food writing and travel writing commonly tend to compartmentalise the experience being written about, despite its being personal, a critical journey, and often, with breathtaking ease, skim the surface of it. If you tell the story of a journey without context, I guess that is inevitable, but in writing about our trip to Venice I cannot talk of the one without the other, the context is part of the experience. It may only be a four-day break from Bristol, but this trip is a kind of reckoning. I am as nervous of that as I am of Venice itself, and the power it might exert over me, over us.

We arrive in the dark. Unable to make out even the best known landmarks of the city beyond us seems, curiously, to amplify its impact. We are here, but until we awaken tomorrow, it is still a dream. The water taxi whisks us over the black lagoon towards the faraway lights, jumping the water, slicing through it like a steel, banging back down, sending a shock of spray up and over us until we are sent cowering into the cabin.

We moor at The Metropole's private Watergate – the word has been reclaimed by the Venetians – and enter another world. It was here, in this building, indeed, in what is now the dining room, once the conservatory chapel of the Pieta church, that Vivaldi was concert master from 1703–40, writing his most famous works where the guests are now enjoying their Michelin-starred dinner. The décor is a combination of haute deco, Baroque and boudoir red plush velvet, with antique mirrors recording every glance, every swag, every tassel and tail, and perfumed candles glimmering under the over-ornate Venetian chandeliers and Fortuny lamps.

There is clutter everywhere, displays of sculptural twigs and flowers, glass cases brimming with extraordinary collections: nineteenth-century visiting cards, belle epoque evening bags, corkscrews and nutcrackers, fans and an enormous and somewhat maudlin collection of Italian crucifixes. It is a Miss Havisham of a place; its ambience insistent that no corporate ownership or chain could possibly be responsible for it. It is saying, defiantly, we are family owned and run but we have got slightly stuck in the groove, it is time for the next generation to seize power.

The manager, Eugenio Rigo, appears, gliding smooth as a gondolier in his dark suit, shiny shoes, towards us, with that air that only the best and most experienced of hotel managers have that seems to say: I could play impeccable service or I could play impeccable service and let you into some secrets that I don't let all the guests into. Humour and basic human curiosity seem to have been erased from the boutique-chic hotels staff training manual, and the words 'family run and owned' deleted as uncool, old-fashioned. Here, however, they exist unashamedly, and when Eugenio suggests, almost dismissively, as though we might take offence at being dragooned into it, that, since we are so hungry, it is now nine twenty, we are tired, the dining room is one of only two Michelin-starred restaurants in the city, why don't we try it, our normal resistance to such an entreaty evaporates instantly. We want to please him. We have entered into the 'impeccable service with extras' relationship immediately. He must be really good at his job. We book dinner in ten minutes time, just before the restaurant closes, and are ushered up to the first floor to our bedroom.

Like a cake that has been iced twice and then some, we are shown a bathroom mosaiced like a Moroccan mosque and a bedroom where even the walls have been top to toed with shiny, slubby, crushed brown velvet that looks almost, but not quite, like suede, or could it be Venetian leather? There are two glass domes like museum exhibits, spot-lit, on two tables, with what look like curlicued golden sheep's horns inside them. If the golden fleece were flung casually across the gilded bed I wouldn't be surprised. There are ancestral portraits, though more recent than the word ancestor might suggest. I know instantly that Rob will either laugh and love it or feel so oppressed and horrified by its excesses and knobs-on décor that he will get the fastest water taxi out of town or demand to be taken to the Danieli four doors down. He looks around with obvious bemusement. We are here to stay.

The Met restaurant, in its eagerness to promote the talents of its new chef, has unwittingly hired the services of an amateur translator, eager to practise his fledgling English and embellish it in the florid style of the hotel and, presumably, the chef. Thank God its pretensions are funny, as in 'Ingenious his patent for using a coffee mixer to mix different foods – liver, vegetable broth, raspberries. You can't explain. Tasting is believing!' The idea of twinning raspberries with liver and adding vegetable broth is enough for one to want to reach for the sick bag, especially since the implication is that they are liquidised into a sort of gastronomic Complan for the unsuspecting guest. There's a great deal of 'acrobat of taste', 'juggler of flavours', 'sometimes choreographic and baroque' that prepare one for the Big Top rather than the restaurant table, but what appears on the plate is less a symphony or melange than a bloody wonderful, straight-forward fugue.

Bigoli is a Venetian dish. It consists of home made whole-wheat pasta with a simple, feisty but sweetly comforting sauce of anchovies and onions clinging to it. Now this probably has been put through the coffee grinder, though I am beginning to wonder whether the ersatz translator looked up the wrong appliance in the dictionary and really meant the liquidiser, for it is a delicious velveteen-rich bagna caoda of a sauce, in this case probably made with fresh anchovies from the lagoon, but which I will go home and attempt with a jar of the salted equivalent. The pasta is al dente and nutty and absolutely spot on, as is Rob's beef cheek with its sticky dark reduction of gelatinous gravy.

It is late, the auguries are good, I am already impatient for the morning, can hardly wait to open the shutters and look out across the lagoon to San Giorgio.

The next thing I am aware of is a constant burble rising from below — we are on the first floor — that suggests this merchant city is already bustling, breakfasting and open for business. I don't know why it isn't annoying, it would be were I at home, but it's somehow all part of the picture, none of which I've seen yet. And there is a less familiar sound, the roar and whirr of marine engines, the hooting, warning, sonic bass notes of ships talking and advising each other of their presence, their intended direction. It is still shy of eight o'clock, yet the sounds alone are enough to get me to the window to draw back the heavy brocade curtains and push the shutters open out onto the street.

And there it is, spread before me, the dream.

Unpeopled though my dreams of Venice have been, this first vision is of a crowded Hogarthian street transposed into modern dress. A stream, no, a great wave of people is sweeping towards San Marco and the Palazzo Ducale like fleeing refugees, six or seven deep, flowing like a gathering tide along the wide walk, beyond which are the boat stops, the jetties, the moorings at the water's edge.

The strollers all seem to be clad in the national dress of tourism. You can tell the flotillas of Americans immediately, the women with not a teased, coloured, sprayed hair out of place, in loose-arsed slacks, 'leisurewear' and new white trainers; the men, mostly wide of girth, with cameras, baseball caps, talking loudly, in high-waisted shorts or voluminous, belted and pressed jeans, white socks pulled high and trainers. Then there are smaller, slimmer bevies of Japanese looking slightly anxious, quieter, flapping like birds with clicking cameras and open maps and floppy hats; then Germans, English, French, the larger groups shepherded by guides holding flags aloft on tall sticks like ageing cheerleaders so as not to lose anyone from their party of squalling school children. And out beyond, the real street life, which all takes place on the water.

Boats, tugs, cargo ships, gondolas, vaporettos, power boats, steamers and all kinds of marine craft are skimming the water, ducking and weaving across its surface, some backing out at top speed from the little canal that abuts us and turning hard and fast onto the Grand Canal ahead, avoiding the nearest boat by a sliver of spun spray as they head out, like playboy racers, onto the water for work. There are boats tying up in front of us and discharging their cargoes swiftly, and clusters of rocking boat buses waiting for the lines of people to fill them. Ahead, the great dome and the island of San Giorgio, the lagoon merging imperceptibly into the Grand Canal, and breakfast.

Eugenio has decided that our first foray should be to one of the smaller, less frequented gems, the Scuola Dalmata of St George and St Tryphone, whose brotherhood became recognised in 1451, before they built their seat towards the end of the fifteenth century. It is a short stroll from The Metropole and on entering the small building, the idea that there are any other tourists in Venice simply evaporates. There is a penetrating quiet in the place, the few visitors hushed by the intimacy and majesty of the Renaissance-style oratory and its simple splendour. Here is housed the famous 'teleri' cycle painted between 1502 and 1507 by Vittore Carpaccio, telling the stories of saints Giorgio, Tryphone and Jerome in nine breathtakingly beautiful paintings.

The upper hall with its magnificent painted walls and ceiling, a central octagon surrounded by four ovals and four gores featuring Matthew, Mark, Luke and John, displays the works of painters from several different schools, and is quieter still, more suited to contemplation, but I have found the Carpaccios an epiphany, could come back time and time again to breathe in their colour, texture, detail, light and their epic story telling.

The still calm of Carpaccio's first picture for the Scuola, *The Prayer in the Garden of Olives*, is magnetic. Then there is the symbolic victory of good over evil depicted in the belt of the young girl the saint is holding like a bridle in *The Triumph of St George*, whose tranquillity is in direct contrast to the fiery picture of *St George Killing the Dragon*. When I mention to Paul Johnson later how captivated I have been by them, not quite knowing whether he will chastise me with one of his beady-eyed, load-of-tosh, you should know better reactions, and make me doubt my eye and taste instantly, on the contrary, he is thrilled and delighted and professes Carpaccio to be one of the greatest and most under-rated of painters, in his top ten.

It is a morning well spent, without the taxing nature of the huge museum or gallery where one is always somehow diverted into looking at too many pictures too quickly, rather than my preferred fewer viewed as slowly as the eye and the brain demands. Why looking at pictures should be exhausting I have never fully understood. A concentrated gaze is not exactly the equivalent of a six mile run, but I find the latter energises while the former exhausts. The Scuola leaves one replete somehow, replete and dazzled in equal measure, but starving. It is time for lunch.

The Osteria Oliva Nera is tucked away up a back alley near San Giorgio dei Greci, and the new owner seems eager to please his tourist lunchers — all American, bar me. Pretty soon we get down to discussing food, Venetian food, and Dino reveals that, no, his chef is not a local, indeed, is not even an Italian, he is from Japan. That his precision and attention to detail were such, when he came to Italy to learn how to cook Italian food, that he has become as good as, if not better than, any chef who has cooked for him over the years. And he is not just a master of classical Venetian cooking, he has the land of his birth and of its famous tempura to thank for his light handedness with the batter.

So we allow ourselves to be steered by this knowledge and order the fiori di zucca farci su letto di melanzane marinate, a plate of stuffed courgette flowers with fresh ricotta and buffalo mozzarella, locked, we are led to believe, as tightly as Houdini into their battered box and served with marinated aubergines.

The batter is so light it could almost lead you to believe it isn't several thousand calories a mouthful, is virtual batter, a homeopathic potency of deep-fried nothingness. It is primrose pale, so crisp it shatters in the mouth once its hermetic seal is broken and the intensified flavours within are released to flood onto the tongue in a whoosh of perfect contrast: creaminess, springy softness, milkiness with a lactic twinge. The aubergine errs on the side of al dente, never a good idea with an aubergine, but we are both deeply impressed by the fiori di zucca.

We continue with two local dishes, a replay of the bigoli in salsa Veneta that I have eaten the previous night and a dish of Goth-style pasta, its thin, inky black locks dyed with sepia, tagliolini neri fatti in casa con coda di scampi e fungi finferli. The scampi are from the lagoon, the fungi are local, the dish impressively simple, full of clear-cut flavour, honest and seasonal. It is a habit that not all cooks and chefs can agree upon, the fish and fungi combination, the firm rubbery with the soft, squishy, fishy, and it reappears throughout our stay in Venice. The bigoli Rob professes delicious, robust and piquant though not quite in the same league as last night's. We seem to have struck lucky for the second time, and whatever the warnings of high prices, bad food and bad tourist attitude, we leave with a bottle of the owners' favourite olive oil having been well fed, well looked after and educated and at a reasonable price.

Meandering back along the Grand Canal and down past the hotel, we stop off at the Gelateria San Giorgio on the Via Garibaldi and get talking to the owner, another Giorgio, since we are quite unable to pick a colour or flavour from the stupendously good-looking ice creams which he makes in a tiny room at the back of the little shop he sells them from. 'I only have 23 square metres but I make everything here,' he says. 'It takes me one and a half hours a day to travel into Venice from Ario and I work seven days a week.' He suggests we should taste his peach ice cream, he has made it that morning with the last of the peaches. 'Tomorrow you come back for pumpkin ice cream,' he orders. The ice cream is a delicate shade of dusty pink and utterly smooth, creamy and aromatic. 'I use no cream,' Giorgio says. 'Just peaches, water and sugar and it is whisked until it feels like cream.'

It is so strange being a tourist. I can never properly shake off the sensation of being out of my element, of making a temporary home where you will never feel quite at home. We never really think about it now weekend travel and the easyJet era has swept us all off to foreign cities more quickly and more cheaply than the railways take us back down to the country. Yet I am never quite comfortable not being a native, not having a connection, an acquaintance or at least an introduction in a new place.

All my friends who know Venice well speak of friends with crumbling palazzos, of masked balls, for which there are almost as many shops selling the most elaborate confections to hide behind as there are hidden corners or restaurants; of their time studying here, of gradually feeling at home, being invited behind the scenes into real Venetian life. Ours is a different experience, a glimpse from the stage door. Seeing Venice like this, in this timeframe, one has to consciously ignore and not be annoyed by the crowds as thick as they are down Oxford Street; likewise by the gawping and clicking, the bumping and jostling, the fact that even the hidden corners, the back-street restaurants, are full of people just like us also trying to avoid people just like us.

The light begins to leave the city; the domes turning apricot pink in a brief, attention-seeking glimmer, the sea losing its glitter and fading, like the sky, to black.

We have been invited to have drinks with Gloria Beggiato, the vivacious, flame-haired Venetian who has taken over The Metropole from her parents, who have owned the hotel since 1967. 'Venice was sleeping for a long time,' she begins. 'Because it is an island and it didn't care about new trends, it has always relied on its past, always been full. It's only in the last five years I started to give my imprint and run it like it is my house. My parents had collected everything. We cared so much about quality, but we needed to restore the cuisine. It was my father's idea that we should find a new chef who knew how to do that.'

Eating in hotels had fallen from fashion some time ago in Venice, just as it had all over Europe, and Gloria realised that if she were going to make the restaurant work, her first major problem was to find a good chef who didn't see it as second best to be running a hotel kitchen.

In fact Corrado Fasolato found Gloria. 'He came from a

restaurant in Trentino in the mountains, where he cooked mountain food, down here to the sea.' A Venetian by birth, Fasolato had won a Michelin star in Trentino a few years earlier. 'It is the first time I have found someone who cares as much for my place as I do,' Gloria says. 'Corrado started cooking here in January 2005 and that December they gave us a Michelin star. It was a shock, we felt panic, in our hearts we weren't ready.'

It is now nearly a year later and the dining room, run by Fasolato's wife, feels full of confidence from the moment the home made bread arrives, the most telling indicator in any establishment.

They have started to see the return of the local Venetians too, regulars who come to dine here and stop the restaurant from feeling no more than just another tourist destination. The fact that The Metropole is the only hotel with a Michelin star in the city – the second and only other Michelin star belongs to a restaurant called Da Fiore – seems to have secured both their reputation and their acceptance with the local bon vivants that hotel dining is in vogue again. And then there is the old-fashioned comfort factor, the fact that there are seventy members of staff for the seventy guests, some of whom have worked at the hotel for over three decades and who are so knowledgeable and attentive that they help with our itinerary by measuring us up as closely as a bespoke tailor would and suiting us accordingly.

In the tiny bar we sip the most delicious house cocktail, a Tiziano, which consists of prosecco and the thick, dark, pulpy juice of the small, black local grapes called fragola, which have a bouquet of strawberries as their name suggests. Were we to come back in the winter months we could clink glasses of Puccini, sparkling white wine with fresh tangerine juice.

The following morning we join the throng on a crowded

vaporetto and disembark at the Rialto which resembles nothing so much as a crowd scene in an epic Fellini movie. We veer off to the Accademia, crossing the Rialto Bridge which, with the Piazza San Marco, should probably only be visited when the city and its floating population have drifted off into a deep slumber, or some time in darkest November or dankest February which appear to be the only months where Venice is almost returned to its inhabitants.

We visit Peggy Guggenheim's house which is open to the public, to look at her collection of modern art and objets and, just as interesting, to wander round her perfect, small, formal, beautifully laid out town garden filled with modern sculpture, which leads down to its own landing stage on a bend in the Grand Canal. Every stone and slab is laid in geometric patterns, some raised, some lowered, around the trees and shrubs and flowering bushes, stone and gravel, brick and slate, each in turn adding texture and perspective; its design as much about shapes as about planting.

There is a stone pergola with a circular stone table and bench enclosed within it, and stone pillars reaching up to a circular stone ring like a halo above it, on which a tree rests its sinewy, weary old branches and leaves almost like a tired traveller, ensuring shade and shelter, one imagines, for the sumptuous al fresco picnics in the days when it was a Guggenheim home. Today there is a group of students sitting quietly inside the stone circle, copying some of the sculptures that are dotted around the most exclusive back garden in Venice.

The Saturday morning fish market is in complete contrast to the pictures ancient and modern with which we have been acquainting ourselves with a sense of earlier mediaeval and renaissance Venetian life. It makes us feel, for the first time, that we have gone backstage and found a corner of real Venice. It brings all layers and all types of Venetian society to its huge, ice-strewn counters. The fish stalls are vibrant with reefs of coral coloured crustacea and slippery-fresh fish from the lagoon and the Adriatic. It is in a somewhat chaotic and down at heel neigh-bourhood. By midday when we arrive, it is already beginning to shut up shop, and the crowd is mainly old Italians, stylishly dressed for the occasion, even the older couples holding hands, old ladies with their dogs, black-clad grandmothers bargaining for their lives. At the side of the market a butcher's shop has whole fat hens and pheasants hanging in their bronze and beige plumage, a counter of milky-fleshed veal and one selling thick tranches of horsemeat, its pink, slightly soft looking meat not looking nearly as robust as the ruby red beef.

Rob leads us into the Campo Cesare Battisti which feels like suddenly coming out from under a tarpaulin of dark and shade into bright light almost for the first time. The same happens in the vast space of the Piazza San Marco. Elsewhere the light is always brightest on the water, looking back to the city. We are in search of a hit of mid-morning espresso, and find ourselves in this huge, unexpected, near-empty square off the market. Rob dives into the nearest small café, the Muro Santa Elena, where the cicchetti, or small snacks, are stacked up like trays of exotic canapés so that you simply have to order one of each. The porchetta sandwich with aubergine and mustard, and the shrimp with Tabasco have us squabbling like pigeons over the crumbs. Next door is a small vegetable stall of such perfection its produce looks like the painted miniatures you can buy at vast expense for Georgian dolls' houses. There are beans as long and slim as bodkins laid out in elegant rows, babies' fingers of zucchini and bouquets of their trumpet-like flowers ready to stuff; there are porcini like large parasols with their hairbrush handle stems and finferli, the egg-yellow chanterelles, in waxy heaps alongside clusters of chiodini, those little fungi that are attached like Siamese twins, one to another, in groups.

We pass the stand-up market bar, Al Marka, where traders and families are already drinking and snapping up mouthfuls of small snacks out in the piazza, and the old cheese shop Casa del Parmigiano, established in 1936; we duck down the dingiest, meanest and eeriest of alleyways barely two arms'-span across, where old butchering warehouses and foundries are interspersed with more modern artisan craftsmen: paper makers, blacksmiths, framers, furniture restorers. We cross courtyards and squares, trace and retrace our steps, enter the musty, marble chequered-floored churches of San Polo dating back to the ninth century and Santa Maria del Giglio in all the crenellated wedding cake splendour of the seventeenth and see the astonishing Tintorettos and Tiepolos, Veroneses and Vittorios, Schiavones and Rubenses hung in the solemn, gloomy spaces, reminding us of how great religious art can at once fill us with hope and a sense of sadness and impotence.

This evening we will celebrate; meanwhile, we will return to the hotel after we have walked to the station and the final vaporetto stop at the end of the island, the place where many travellers catch their first glimpse of the city. It is run down and rough here, the smart shops have been replaced by cheap, tatty cafés and everything is down at heel. But the picture before one's eyes is still majestic. You can see the sweep of the Grand Canal, the distant domes, the boats, the skyline, sagging wrought-iron balconies on the flaking facades.

My neighbour Nick Anderson, in Somerset, tells me on my return, that he arrived at the station on his first trip to Venice, and saw '...this Canaletto before my eyes and promptly burst into tears'. It is a picture which, surely, could never grow stale or wearisome.

We come back down the Grand Canal reflectively, hugging each other for warmth as the cold gathers on the water. At one stage I see a plaque half-way up a house in front of us and shriek in excitement, it is where Byron lived. Back at The Metropole a bucket of champagne on ice awaits us in our bedroom. Rob is convinced I am responsible, but I am not. That is just the sort of place it is.

I have booked Rob's birthday dinner from England on Susan's advice. She ate there on Christmas Day last year. It was her favourite place over her whole ten-day gastronomic stay, and her taste on matters of gourmandising has been tried, tested and trusted for over a decade now.

Alle Testiere is a tiny restaurant, possibly the smallest in Venice, with room for only twenty people, and a galley kitchen behind the bar through which one can see the kitchen staff pas de deuxing just to avoid anointing one another in boiling oil or branding each other with their hot pans. It has two sittings to cope with the crowds, one at 7pm and the second at 9.30pm. It gets booked weeks in advance. We set off on foot for the early sitting, and end up hopelessly lost despite our map. It seems to happen each time we set foot outside the door. Perhaps the maps are designed specifically to befuddle the unsuspecting tourist and lead him astray. It is squid-inky black down the lost alleyways and a bone-damp chill is rising off the water. I am shivering, my hands tucked into Rob's inside his pockets.

Finally we discover the narrow Calle del Mondo Novo and look inside to the pre-prandial clinkings of the first diners in the intimate small dining room. We hear only American and English voices, but for the owners, Luca and Bruno. Within minutes Luca is asking us if we know Johnny Apple, the illustrious American bon viveur and food writer, who, he says, frequented their restaurant whenever he was in Venice and who has died that day.

We are brought plates of baby gnocchi, gnocchetti with scampi and porcini, and ravioli alla zucca e ricotta in un ragu di tonno bianco, ravioli stuffed with pumpkin and ricotta in a ragu of white tuna, and then main courses of pietro alla griglia, a plainly grilled whole John Dory, and Rob's tagliata di tonno al balsamico which is the star of the night. It is a perfectly fresh and rare cooked chunk of tuna in a pool of dark, mellow balsamic which has been reduced to syrupy sweetness and scented lightly and expertly with rosemary and a few crushed juniper berries. The tuna, being one of those fish that can withstand the pressure of equally strong tasting ingredients, and meaty enough for the astringent herb and the berry one associates more with game than anything else, is both complemented and invigorated by these three ingredients, and it is the dish that I am most eager to get home and attempt to reproduce.

I imagine little knobs of butter must have been dropped and stirred into the sauce to give it its polished black shoe-shine appearance and its plush, velvet richness; that the rosemary must have been infused cautiously into it and then withdrawn; but at this stage who knows, the guesswork is all part of the fun, or will be when I return to puzzle it out in my kitchen. I just wish I'd had the sense to order it for myself. It's always a mistake to think that you've got to order different things in a restaurant, although it has become received wisdom that one should.

The lights flicker and dim alarmingly as we finish our fish. We look at our watches. It is still only ten past nine, but Rob feels uneasy: 'It's a bit rude to lower the lights to make us eat up more quickly,' he says, surveying the growing queue of people standing outside the restaurant awaiting the second sitting.

At that moment Luca switches on a tinny old recording of 'Happy Birthday' sung in Italian, and arrives at our table with a slice of torta di gianduia on which is balanced a sparking silver candle, and a bowl of gelato di fragola e basilico. I had asked for a birthday cake when I had rung from England to book the table, but little did I expect a small restaurant in Venice where we were unknown to the owners to actually remember. The other diners have all put down their forks to sing. Immediately the celebration seems real and we tuck into the chef's mother's recipe for this dense and brittle cake, full of roasted hazelnuts that crunch under their own weight in chocolate, and a delicious strawberry ice cream infused with a lick of fresh basil, the making of which Luca, in his element now, is determined to go over step by step with me.

Help. My feet are killing me in my new Manolos, a sort of Courreges revisited pair whose heels are backed with black crocodile as shiny as liquorice that looks good enough to eat. And how I wish I hadn't drunk so much.

Checking my notebook when I get home, I can't begin to decipher the process, which appears to involve warming the sugar and strawberries, cooling them to 40 degrees before adding the basil, then using a Pacojet when the ingredients have fallen to 20 degrees to keep the 'nose' of the leaves and finally adding cream.

Forget getting lost in Venice, I am now lost in Heston Blumenthal country, and as far as I'm concerned, molecular gastronomy is for the boys who want to stretch themselves, gastronomically speaking, over the test tube, in their kitchen equivalent to ski goggles, and play with Bunsen burners, dry ice and 24-hour water baths. Molecular gastronomy is a term that really means extreme cuisine, so should only be served in the restaurant dining room of a genius like Heston, not in the home kitchen.

Luca adds, finally, that the ice cream had only been made two hours previously, at 7 pm, to retain its intense flavour, and that he bought the ingredients for the chef's mother's torta himself and gave them to her, otherwise she wouldn't use the best quality. It is always reassuring to hear of a similarly ingredients obsessive cook, the mutual recognition dilutes the madness somehow, or at least makes one feel one isn't alone in it.

Luca brings me a list of the dishes we have eaten before we leave, but insists that the torta remains a house secret which the chef's mother will carry, I guess, to her watery Venetian grave.

'I don't know how you did it,' Rob says, as we get even more lost down a tangled pappardelle of alleyways before eventually arriving back at the hotel. 'Each meal has been better than the last.'

We are far too full to sink into the splendour of the baroque bed quite yet. The full moon is up, it has been as romantic an evening as the New York cynic could possibly countenance and we are beginning to succumb to the strange magic of this extraordinary city. I stand and stare out of the half shuttered window across the silver light that diminishes to a point way out in the lagoon.

Perhaps after a night like this Rob will sleep, will at least not awaken in the early hours and walk the empty streets and dank, echoing alleys for several hours as he did the previous night, trying to reconcile himself to the idea of the year ahead. Perhaps.

There is a famous photograph of my father, seated next to Stephen Spender and Wystan Auden, taken outside a café in Venice by Stephen's wife Natasha in 1948 at the international

PEN conference. Despite the 'poets of the thirties' label, this was the first time the three had all met up together and the historic picture has recorded it for posterity.

It was three years before my parents came back to Venice briefly in 1951 on their first trip abroad together, honeymooning with the Spenders in an albergo by Lake Garda. Because of post-war restrictions, they were only allowed to leave England with £25 each, and, according to my mother, lived on £1 a day which included the fish and the wine they had for dinner. So did you go to Harry's Bar? I asked her.

It turns out that another friend staying with the Spenders, who had a car, drove my parents to Venice from Lake Garda and brought them to Harry's Bar for a glass of the legendary Bellini. My mother was not impressed, it meant they couldn't afford dinner that night, and she would far have preferred my father to have spent the money '…on something more romantic. I wanted to go on a gondola with Cecil,' she told me. 'But we simply couldn't afford it.'

I, on the other hand, had begged Rob to take me to Harry's Bar; for me it held a kind of mystique that, despite its obvious American tourist-trap connotations, was infinitely preferable to the gondoliers and their raffish, spray-on charm.

We took the short walk there from The Metropole past the Piazza San Marco for lunch. Since Rob was wearing his mandatory American tourist shorts, we were banned from the downstairs bar which is where Harry's debutants should know to ask for a table, and were shown instead to the room upstairs.

I had imagined something larger; something wood panelled, with whirring fans and outside tables and a stand up bar where artists and writers had once gathered to drink grappa or prosecca and smoke and talk and linger into the night. I had thought the walls would be papered with pictures painted and given in lieu of cheques after drunken debauches and extravagant lunches. Instead, both rooms, upstairs and downstairs, were surprisingly small and intimate and comfortable and subdued and everyone was sitting at their respective tables, angled so that you could comfortably and obviously survey everybody else in the room and the moving tableaux of boats slinking past us outside the window on the canal.

So what is the secret of Harry's Bar? How has it kept its allure, its cachet, its glamour in the same way as perhaps only The Ivy, the Caprice, The Ritz and Annabel's in London have, for several decades and several generations?

Arrigo Cipriani says in his book about his world famous bar: 'I think the real secret is that there is no secret. Anyone who visits Harry's Bar always finds three things: quality, a smile and simplicity.' We know that is not all, we know that it is not enough, but it is a brilliantly disingenuous thing to say. Fill in the gaps and you would add another three things: exceptional courtesy, no snobbery and impressively, sneer-in-the-face-of-money expensiveness. Our lunch would have bought my parents a couple of months of Bacchanalian living in the early 1950s. 'It's the £100 risotto,' Rob told everyone after the event. So was it worth it?

I would say yes, although I didn't pay for it. Right down to the starched primrose linen – every little detail is there for a reason: 'Green doesn't reflect well on a lady's complexion, pink doesn't on a man's', Cipriani also declares in his book.

The service is neither over-servile nor over-familiar. We are on the lookout for the tiniest of faults, judging this place with no mercy, giving it no room for error, almost willing the legend to debunk itself and snare itself in its own unassailable reputation.

Flaky rolls arrive with cold, sweet butter. Rob orders the

Risotto Cipriani which sounds vile. It is a curried chicken and mushroom risotto. A mongrel of a cultural collision, surely. I order a risotto of shrimp and zucchini. We sip our fresh peach Bellinis from glasses the shape of miniature kegs which have probably been designed specifically for the purpose, although the reason for the unusual ergonomics is not obvious.

The Bellini is celestial and makes me feel light-headed instantly. The risotto is brought to the table on a trat-style trolley — remember them from Mario and Franco's in the 1960s? — from which both dishes are served by two waiters working in unison, as though they are playing the spoons in a musical theatre production.

I have always thought I make a pretty special risotto, and that over the years, with endless mastering of the subtleties, perfecting of the best ingredients and methodology, inventing or re-working of every different subspecies of the dish I could dream up around the four seasons, that I would be unfazed at having to serve one up to a serious Italian chef or even to one of my two most esteemed and illustrious Italian food writers, Anna Del Conte and Marcella Hazan.

This — these — risottos are better, even, than I could make or even imagine how to make. I just can't work out why either, though Rob is goading me to. Could it be the water, I can't think of anything else? Unless there is a special paddy field in the Po region where, like a great first growth, the Ciprianis harvest the best carnaroli rice exclusively and bring sackfuls of it back to Harry's Bar.

Rob's mongrel of uncertain pedigree is stupendously the best. Probably the best risotto I have ever eaten. The texture falls the right side of starchy crunch; there is attendant butteriness and soupiness but not too much of either; the finest Parmesan, grated finer than dandruff; a whiff of spice, a depth of flavour, and that's it. My risotto has a doll's-sized dice of zucchini, tiny pink apostrophes of sweet-salt shrimps from the lagoon, and not much more. It is almost as good as Rob's.

The waiters reappear and dish up second helpings, a thing that I last remember and lament the passing of from George Perry-Smith's Riverside in Helford; it is a civilised custom that is one step from extinct. If I never go to Harry's Bar again, I will savour the memory for ever. The staff have made us feel that our happiness is the one thing that matters to them. They are the most professional and cordial staff in the world. Arrigo Cipriani, we are told, is dining with a table of friends next door. I like the idea not just that 'le patron mange ici', but that he probably has done every day for fifty years or more.

Great dining experiences are very often not about serious gastronomy, and if they are, I find, they tend to be somewhat overwhelming; they can too often feel formulaic and removed from any sense of one being in the hands of a generous and welcoming host who has retained that all-important thing, the personal touch. Had Signor Cipriani not been dining in his own restaurant, his mark, his touch would still have been as pro-nounced and obvious. Often, top restaurants are too busy being sacred to make one feel comfortable and at ease, and the sense of expectation acts like a barrier rather than a spur to the enjoy-ment. They are intimidating even to those of us who really do know about food. They are all about the chef. Here, the simplicity that Cipriani speaks about is the defining characteristic and the guest is considered more important than the chef, just the way it should be.

You may decide that a Bellini and a plate of risotto is not worth getting into debt over, and I wouldn't blame you. You may think that the fact that when we slipped out of the door at 2.45pm we found a queue of Americans still waiting to get in, is enough for you to decide it's all too much hype and deserves to be given an indecently wide berth. I felt neither of those things, partly, admittedly, because I had the added curiosity of wanting to know what it was like now compared to when my parents went a half-century ago, of being curious about whether it could, in the face of modern tourism, have retained any or all of its former qualities, and because Susan had said she and Garech had been twice at Christmas they had enjoyed it so much and that they had been able to entirely discount the criticisms. The thing is, it *is* still like a small club, but one doesn't feel excluded or merely tolerated entering it on a day pass, so to speak, as one of that intolerable species 'the tourist'. You do take on temporary membership at an obscenely hiked-up price, there is no point in complaining about it, and you either accept, as Rob and I did, or reject the fact that Venice would be all the poorer, as we are, after paying, without it.

That evening we sit outside in the garden at the Corte Sconta, or 'hidden corner,' near the Arsenale in the Calle del Pestrin for a dinner of typical fresh fish from the local waters, cooked and served Venetian style. A carpaccio of paper-thin tuna and sea bass with a smidgeon of olive oil and raw celeriac is followed by canestrini, scallops so tiny they are smaller than our little 'queens' from Brixham, which I imagine have been roasted in the oven, in the shell, with butter, a little tomato and basil.

There are spider crabs with olive oil and lemon juice; a dish of squid, octopus, shrimp and crayfish; there is a stiff, salt paste of bacalau served with a small slop of the grainy white Venetian polenta, followed by the famous agro-dolce dish of sarde in saor, fresh sardines with softened sweet onions, raisins and pine nuts. There are Mantis prawns, then some pasta with swordfish and aubergine, soft-shell crabs that you crunch every pincer and morsel of and crisply fried artichoke hearts.

There is nothing particularly complicated about the saucing, nothing particularly exotic or unusual about the ingredients or the dishes. This is about showing off the freshest and sweetest and smallest of fish, leaving them un-interfered with, served up tasting of themselves and the sea. There appear to be more locals at the Corte Sconta than at any of the restaurants we have visited so far, but the husband and wife owners who are also taking orders and waiting table don't discriminate in their enthusiasm to share news of today's catch with the tourists or the locals. The individual dishes are small but substantial and the cohesion of the whole dinner, its progress from course to course, from raw to cooked, from fried and stewed to deep fried, is well timed and well judged. There are a couple of dishes that we are less enamoured of, a crab pate whose flavour and texture is more pasty than pâté and the sea bass carpaccio which didn't entirely stand its ground next to the more muscular-tasting tuna. However, this is another memorable and cosy, intimate dinner in a true family-run restaurant, that continues to tell us a story about what the Venetians eat, how they cook it and how local tradition has survived and flourished despite the polyglot stampede of tourists eating at every watering hole in the city.

If I were to give a party in Venice, this is where I would give it. The garden at the back of the restaurant where we have sat down to dine could easily accommodate 150 people, so my fantasy is for a line of trestle tables to be laid out for Rob's serious birthday next year, with bowls and plates laden with every tiny fish from the lagoon; of this hidden corner of Venice being the secret garden we invite everyone to meet up in to celebrate, and that we continue the party over a long, weekend orgy of spectacular feasting.

We are lying on the baroque bed tossing up which island we should go to from the various recommendations for our last day, a Sunday. Should it be Murano, Torcello or Burano? I have all the information on the various restaurants, churches, occupations of the islanders, from Venetian glass to lace making, from vegetable growing to wild fowling and fishing, but we're still not quite sure how to make up our minds.

It turns out there's not much point in us even trying to decide. We go downstairs and prise Eugenio out of his lair at the back of reception to ask his advice, and he tells us that he has already lined up somewhere special for us and that he will book us a water-taxi for the following day. 'I have booked you into the Gatto Nero for lunch,' he informs us definitively. 'It's on the island of Burano where the Venetian lace is made. It is a very special place, I know you will love it, and the restaurant is exceptional.'

It takes about 40 minutes to speed from The Metropole by water taxi to Burano. As you approach the island, the first thing you see is rows of brightly painted houses that look as though a child has run riot with a new paint box. Each owner has picked a colour louder, brighter, brasher, clashier than its neighbours'. Kia Ora orange, puce, lime green, raspberry, electric lemon, mustard, cobalt blue; vermilion, deep purple, lilac, the palette is wide ranging, eclectic and wonderfully garish. Later, at lunch, when we ask just how this visual kaleidoscope came about, we are told that the individual colours are picked by the fishermen so that when they are away from home at sea they will be able to pick out their own house as they return towards the shore with their catch.

Burano is low and flat and incestuously small. The only big building is the enormous church which dominates the whole island. The houses are built along small canals with narrow walkways and bridges and the water level looks as though it has risen so dramatically recently that there are sandbags hugging the doors and steps and stacked up on the flimsy decking that has been erected over the original paths. Small fishing boats litter the little channels. There are only a handful of streets, all bathing in the autumnal light warmly and smugly. We venture into the small tourist area which seems to consist of one whole street of lace shops and restaurants, and comes alive in brief, crowded spasms as each boat disgorges its short-stay cargo of passengers.

One shop stands removed from the rest, Merletti dalla Olga. It consists of three floors of lace work, the most ornamented and filigreed that the human eye could see to sew and the fingers to work. What a connection, it strikes me, between the nets the fishermen must work to stitch and patch and mend on an island that has surely lived for centuries by its fishing, and the skills of the women with their lace-making. Think of the many hours and days the women must have passed in their husband's absence, through long nights of storms and worry, awaiting returns, anticipating departures, their hands flicking and poking the linen, knotting cotton, stabbing needles into silk, earning the little extra, I imagine, that will keep the children in shoes and books and food while their husbands are away at sea.

The most intricately worked lace looks as though it has been sent to elf out-workers, or that it should long since have been taken over and manufactured by the whirr of an industrial Chinese or Taiwanese sewing machine, but, perhaps, for the last handful of the island's remaining lace-making grandmothers. But no, there are groups of women of all ages demonstrating their skills in front of the customers, sewing so fleet fingeredly you can almost see the leaves and stems and petals and bows take shape like time-lapse photography.

The moment Rob intimates that he might be there to spend, we are targeted by a well-dressed lady who exudes ownership, and assumes we will be impressed by her telling us that Elton John and David Furnish visit every year and buy everything they can lay their hands on. We are almost deterred. We leave with a set of simply embroidered place mats and napkins that look as though they have been stained in weak tea, a colour that stops lace looking doily-ish, old lady-ish or as though it has been worked for that most hideous of inventions the antimacassar.

We walk down the narrow waterways and find the Gatto Nero. It is just before one o'clock. Our waiter, one of those darkly vulpine-featured Italians, short, skinny, nervy, shakes us by the hand inside the restaurant as though we have come to dine as friends at his home, offers us a table inside or out, and as we step outside, offers us a Bellini, insisting, like everyone that week, that it is positively the last of the season's and adding, 'It is made with local organic peaches.' His English is an extraordinary mix of Scottish glottal with Italian intonation. The chef comes out in his whites, grey-haired, a man of substance and practised confidence, shakes hands and introduces himself as the owner, Ruggero, and tells us his son, our waiter, is called Massimiliano.

'I hope you're hungry,' he says.

'Sempre,' I reply. Always.

'Are there any fish you don't like?' Massimiliano asks. I tell him that Rob is not a great lover of anything inky and tentacled, otherwise all-comers please. The menu is out of bounds: 'The wine is from Istria. I don't know your taste, but it is salt and will go with the dishes.' The whole experience is already becoming as consensual as sex, once the partakers have agreed to it and jointly relinquished control. It is something the Venetians are very good at, without obviously bullying one into going along with it. Looking back, it has been like this since Eugenio managed to tempt us when we had only just arrived.

'Where are you from?' I can't resist asking Massimiliano.

It turns out that his wife came to Burano on holiday from Edinburgh one year, they fell in love, and he followed her back there for long enough to have picked up fluent Scottish before they returned to Italy.

A plate appears with a thick smattering of the local snow-white polenta, with tiny, sweet shrimps embedded in it and a little olive oil and garlic. Massimiliano delivers the dish with a summary of the ingredients and their manner of cooking like a priest from the pulpit. We swallow the sermon whole. He brings the next dish.

'Now this is the spider crab in its shell with just a little Tuscan olive oil and lemon juice. I buy direct from the best fishermen. I don't offer a price, they will only deal with you if they like you. I clean the fish myself. That way I know if I see worms in them that they weren't stolen by the fishermen from the fish farms.'

An older English couple have taken the table next to us, he the perfect Englishman abroad one associates with Venice, folds of crumpled oatmeal linen, lean, dun suede loafers, slightly abbreviated gestures, subsiding into a chair in a caricature of overweight exhaustion, with a look of eager bonhomie which, at the same time, is careful not to invite our approach. She, more imperious, better preserved, her voice that little bit louder, tells us several things: she wants us to hear what she is saying, she is checking us out and she wants us to recognise her position in the social firmament, but as yet, she is not prepared to address us directly. Their first bottle of wine arrives and is dispatched swiftly. They are not a couple about whom Kingsley would have offered his most damning insult: 'shy on the booze'.

A dish of tiny razor clams, still in the shell, with scallops cooked with a little tomato arrives. The razor clam, like the octopus, can, if ill treated, resemble nothing so much as a band of rubbery muscle. In the right hands it is a different animal, a yieldingly soft and delicate wand of flesh. These are the tiniest, most baby razor clams I have ever tasted, as sweet and tender as the scallops, their long hinged shells opening awkwardly like the spines of a new book to reveal the pencil of fish cooked, as the Italians would say, 'morbido', creamy soft.

'Last night when I finished my job sometime after midnight, I was too wired up to sleep,' Massimiliano says, with the kind of intensity that verges on the not entirely sane. Now he can see we mean business he is illustrating the dishes with greater colour and gusto.

'So I went out fishing with a friend in his boat at one o'clock and came back just before dawn with today's fish.'

He has returned to our table with some baccalau on toast and his father, Ruggero, has stolen out of the kitchen to explain that it is 'particulare', a recipe that is particular to him.

'The cod is dried, not salt,' Massimiliano tells us. 'They were kept in a bucket of sea water for three days after I'd killed them. I changed the water every day, then they were boiled and skinned when they were still hot, and the olive oil and milk were whisked in.'

176

The English couple watch as our next course arrives. A squirl of squid ink-dyed pasta, langoustines and cherry tomatoes. The sweet teamed with the sour in the same way as they do in Sicily and Puglia. It is, Ruggero says, the 'matrimonia perfetto', the perfect marriage, pasta and fish.

'Sometimes I have a little row with my father if the tomatoes are too sharp,' Massimiliano says. 'I like to buy them on the island from my friend Marino because there are no chemicals. I don't know what my father's doing now...' he trails off.

We are about to find out. Ruggero reappears with a huge plate of tiny, deep-fried fish in batter. 'Lucia, my mother, fries the fish,' Massimiliano tells us.

The English couple, lubricated by more wine and impressed by the stalwart way we have tackled dish after dish and sent back each plate empty, introduce themselves. This is one of the best places they know. They come back often, have an apartment in Venice, a house in Calabria, the last unspoilt region of Italy, they say, largely because people are frightened of the locals, think they are all Mafia, bandits, though they are, in fact, wonderful, generous, welcoming people. Where have we eaten since we arrived? (Judgement Day is finally upon us.) I mention Alle Testiere and she says, 'We know Luca and Bruno well, we have been going there for years. Yes, it's one of the best restaurants in Venice.'

We are forced to tackle a brace of sickly, boozy, creamy puddings which arrive unbidden. They are cool and rich and entirely unnecessary. The English couple ask, 'Have you ever tried sgroppina?' Dammit. I've never heard of it and I couldn't willingly put anything else in my mouth at least until Monday morning. They insist on ordering us two. 'It is lemon ice cream whizzed up with vodka and prosecco and served cold in a glass.'

And it is drunk chilled and thick and pale and tart through a straw like the most alcoholic shake you have tasted. And, indeed, it is delicious, as has the whole lunch been. But look at the time. It is 5.30 pm, the dusk has gathered and we have to skim the choppy waters back to the city one last time before we fly home. Massimiliano calls for a water taxi and insists on walking us briskly to it and waving us off. Everything has been 'particulare', the familial hospitality, the food throughout this four-and-a-half-hour lunch, the colour and character of the tiny island of Burano.

Back in Venice we say goodbye to Eugenio and speed back to Marco Polo across the black lagoon.

It is midnight when we get home to Somerset, and Venice is already beginning to feel like a dream, though less the fantasy it was before. Now it is a place I have begun to map and flesh out and somewhere I know I want to return to.

It is two months before I sit down to write about it. The writing is as intimidating to contemplate as the trip was, not least because there is that sense of what can I possibly say that hasn't been said before? There are painters who avoid painting Venice for the same reason. My friend Caroline Parker in New York is one. She lives around the corner from Rob's flat on Prince Street and I call her to talk about it.

'I found Venice quite unnerving too,' she says. 'Every day we found ourselves in the same restaurant, we couldn't resist it, we were drawn back to it. It was the quality of the colour, the mossy dark green, the dark lights and the reds. We sat downstairs and were looking out onto the water, which was on an equal footing with the land, and the gondoliers who were bending at waist level to us out on the canal. The water was stinky and earthy.'

'Yes', I say. 'And muddy and inky like the food, and the whole time you sense this sort of closed in sadness and you are always in shadow.'

'We felt we'd finally gone back-stage and got away from the touristy Venice that is a caricature of itself when we went to the fish market. We came out of the darkness into the market and the wide, sunny square behind it, it was the only bright light,' Caroline says, echoing Rob's and my feelings about that very same square adjacent to the fish market. The only other place I'd felt it was emerging into the colossal white space and light of the Piazza San Marco.

'Write a mood piece about Venice,' Rob had said. 'How food is about forestalling death; eating you're alive, it's like sex.'

We are all fending off death like Venice. The water will eventually take over. There is sadness at its heart, but there is also sublime beauty; preserved, ancient, ageing, ageless, defiant, and it overrides the sense of sadness and loss and triumphs over it. The spirit that hovers over Venice and its dark shadows and corners is suffused with light and life and the death and darkness are somehow held at bay in their midst.

Looking out onto the water from the land or looking back to this glorious city from the water one feels the triumph and vigour and power of the human spirit, a reminder of what it possesses that makes it seem both mortal and immortal, fragile yet strong, beautiful and alive precisely because of its transience. Venice. It is the picture in the dark.

Bigoli

SERVES FOUR

My come-home version of the
lovely Venetian bigoli, though
I couldn't find the fatter, whole-
wheat pasta that they make
specially for it, so used skinnier
strands of spelt pasta. I think the
idea is to make the dish branny
and nutty so am not worried
about the switch. It's so luxuriant
and laid back and intense a dish
that it seems to conjure up the
Venetian spirit and feist to the
letter.

450G/1LB PACKET spelt or whole-
wheat spaghetti cooked the
dangerous side of al dente as it
will be heated through in the pan
with the sauce afterwards
2 VERY LARGE organic onions,
peeled and very thinly sliced into
rings
Venetian or fruity extra virgin olive
oil
½ JAR of anchovies in olive oil
KNOB of unsalted butter
black pepper
flat-leaf parsley, chopped

Sweat the onions down slowly,
slowly, in a few tablespoons of
extra virgin olive oil for 10
minutes, then continue to cook
extra slowly under a lid. I do
this in the baking oven of the
Aga, stirring every 10 minutes,
for about 40 minutes; do the
same on top of the stove.
Remove the anchovies from the
jar and mash them with a fork
down into the onion, cooking
them in for 5 minutes. Season
with black pepper but no salt,
the anchovies are salt enough.
Throw in a knob of unsalted
butter the size of a walnut. Blitz
in the Magimix until smooth.
Co-ordinate the pasta cooking
time so that you drain the al
dente pasta just after you've
blitzed the sauce. Put the not
quite fully drained pasta into
the large, heavy-bottomed
frying pan you've cooked the
onions in and return the sauce
to the pan, turning it over a
very gentle heat to coat and
cook the pasta through a little
more for a couple of minutes.
Throw over a fistful of chopped
parsley and bring to the table
in the pan to serve in warmed
bowls.

Tonno Balsamico

SERVES TWO

Inspired by Alle Testiere, I made my own version of their stupendous dish when I got back to New York, serving it with fennel steamed and then braised in white wine, water and olive oil until tender, with the addition of a couple of crushed anchovy fillets at the end.

2 THICK tuna steaks
sea salt and black pepper
1 TBSP good, extra virgin olive oil
6 bruised juniper berries
2 SPRIGS rosemary
8 TBSP aged, good but not wildly
  expensive balsamic vinegar
4 TBSP Barolo or good, red Italian
  wine
45G/1½OZ or so best unsalted
  butter

Salt and pepper the tuna straight from the fridge on both sides and leave out for an hour at room temperature.

Heat the olive oil in a pan and add the juniper berries and chopped rosemary. Cook very gently together for a few minutes before turning up the heat and adding the balsamic vinegar. Reduce it by a third, stirring from time to time before adding the Barolo or red wine and reducing it further. Taste to make sure the alcohol has lost its raw edge and the balsamic has similarly mellowed.

Remove, cover and leave for 30 minutes for the flavours to develop.

Griddle the tuna on both sides until medium rare, then leave to rest while you finish the sauce. Strain the sauce through a sieve and reheat it over a gentle heat, adding a scrunch of pepper and the butter, a little at a time, in small knobs, whisking it in as you go. Eventually the sauce will look like dark, shiny velvet. Pour it over the tuna steaks and serve.

Curried Crab Risotto

SERVES FOUR

It's surprising how the introduction of Indian spices enhances this inimitable Italian dish and accentuates its crabiness, perhaps more so than even Parmesan would in a more conventional rendering, but it just works beautifully.

450G/1LB fresh crab meat, white and brown
1 SMALL organic onion, peeled and finely chopped
3–4 TBSP extra virgin olive oil
1 TSP each fennel seeds, cumin seeds and coriander seeds
⅓–½ TSP cayenne, to taste
1 TSP garam masala
sea salt and black pepper
340G/12 OZ carnaroli rice
150ML/5 FL OZ dry white wine
2 MEDIUM courgettes chopped into dice or 8 whole baby ones with their flowers
UP TO 850ML/1½ PINTS fish stock made with the crab shell, prawn shells and anything like a salmon head you can get hold of
unsalted butter
A LITTLE cream
1 TBSP fresh dill

Pick the crab to extract the meat, or get your fishmonger to dress you a freshly boiled crab with no additives like rusk.

Sauté the onion in some warmed olive oil over a gentle heat for a few minutes. Meanwhile, in a small pan heated over a brisk heat, temper the fennel, cumin and coriander seeds, erring on the generous heaped side with the cumin, for a minute and then crush them all together in a mortar with the cayenne, garam masala, a little sea salt and a few black peppercorns. Throw most of this mixture over the cooking onion and stir it around for a couple of minutes before adding the rice and stirring well to coat it on all sides.

Add the wine and let it bubble for a couple of minutes, then start adding the heated fish stock a ladle or two at a time, stirring all the while.

After 10 minutes, heat a little more oil in a separate small pan and throw in the courgette dice, turning to coat in olive oil over a medium heat. You don't want the courgettes to brown or start to exude juice, you want them to cook to al dente and retain crunch and colour. When they have reached this stage, remove from the heat.

Keep the risotto stirring at the same time and after about 20 minutes, throw in the crab meat and stir it in briefly. Taste and add the rest of the spice mix if you need to, as well as more salt and pepper.

Add a good lump of butter, a ladle more hot stock and a few tablespoons of cream, remove from the heat immediately and cover with a lid for 5 minutes for the flavours to marry.

Remove the lid, add the warm courgettes, give a final stir and bring to the table.

Pralinéed Hazelnut Cake with a Chocolate Ganache

In no small part inspired by the Piedmonte hazel groves and my addiction to the black stuff.

Preheat oven to 180°C/350°F/
  GAS 4

225G/8OZ unsalted butter
225G/8OZ unrefined vanilla sugar
  + 2 TBSPS
4 organic eggs, separated
225G/8OZ organic plain flour
1 ½ TSP baking powder
PINCH of sea salt
180G/6OZ whole hazelnuts, the skins removed as for the hazelnut ice cream recipe on page 40, and ground to a paste similarly, plus a few extra whole, toasted and skinned nuts to decorate

Cream the butter and sugar together thoroughly in the Kitchen Aid until light and fluffy. Add the yolks one by one and beat them in. Fold in the praline.
Beat the whites to soft peak. Add the final 2 tbsp sugar and beat to firm peak.
Fold ⅓ of the sifted flour into the creamed mixture then stir in ⅓ of the whites. Fold in the next third of each and then the last third.
Grease and line a 9-in (22cm) Springform tin. Scrape the mixture into the tin and bake for 40 minutes or until a skewer comes out clean.
Cool in the tin on a rack.

For the ganache:
120ML/4 FL OZ organic double cream
225G/8OZ Valrhona or other good bitter chocolate

Heat the cream to scald point, then drop the squares of chocolate into the hot cream off the heat and stir until melted. Cover the cooled cake with the ganache and decorate around the outside of the top with whole toasted hazelnuts.
Serve with creme fraiche.

7

Two for the Tour

Back at Fawlty Towers, the Alitalians have finally delivered Rob's luggage but mine is still scudding around in transit who knows where… I am hallucinating over the possibility of having several pairs of Manolos half-inched by an Alitalian baggage-handler's moll… I put on a pair of Rob's fetching y-fronts and clean my teeth with his toothbrush. It's time to go in search of a good dinner…

The life of a travelling food writer isn't all a bed of fresh foie gras or glossy oiled carciofi. Sometimes we have to eat up our greens, bitter greens.

Rob and I have been invited to Puglia, a region neither of us knows anything about, other than that it is in the heel of the boot, is one of the poorest and least well known, and one we are keenest to explore. We are never more excited than when we are winding our way off-piste down a wilfully lost Italian hillside or up a misty, fruity valley, eating Italian food and drinking in the landscape. Unfortunately, life can't always be so sweet.

People always ask us, Italian or French, if you had the choice and had to pick your ultimate cuisine, which would it be? Despite the received wisdom and supposed gastronomic superiority of the French and their haute cuisine, give me bas cuisine any day, Italian 'peasant' food – though even the word peasant has become a phoney, foodie aphorism – from any one of the regions of this fertile, exuberant, traditional nation that has never had its roots shaken let alone allowed them to be pulled like teeth and industrialised, transmogrified, convenienced. The very fact that the regions of Italy have remained resolutely, insolently, distinct-ive and recidivist despite globalisation, urbanisation, is, for me, the deciding factor.

The Italians still cook. They still make their own pasta even if they only have time to cut and hang it out to dry on Sundays. They still spend the major part of their earnings on their chief pleasure in life: eating. Thus, by association, we are honorary Italians. Any excuse to explore a region we only know from the cookery book shelves and far distant restaurants of its émigrés and we are captive; but in this case, we don't even have those to go on.

One thing is certain about Puglia. Its cooking hasn't travelled.

I want to know why. Is it so poor that it can't afford the postage even though it is known as the breadbasket of Italy? That it hasn't been able to merchandise itself in the peasant-hungry cities, or that its own émigrés haven't been able to convince their new-found nations that they are the new Tuscany? I have never heard tell of a Puglian restaurant in any region of Italy I have ever visited, let alone in England or America, to which thousands of Puglian émigrés have fled over the last hundred years, and would doubt its authenticity if I found one. I am wholly ignorant of the cuisine, the people, the place, the cheeses, the oils, the wines, and the way the Pugliese use them.

Wait a minute. The word Pugliese. The region's eponymous loaf, if not in as common parlance as the words 'baguette', or 'croissant', has at least skimmed the radar, though beyond the words 'peasant' and 'crust' and 'bread basket', I don't know what its defining characteristics are supposed to be.

In the meanwhile I have bought a bottle of olive oil off a supermarket shelf, the only one that says it is Puglian, but after dousing it liberally, would not begin to change my views on the best olive oils of Europe and their provenance. However, as we know, the supermarkets are driven by cost rather than taste. Taste comes a pretty poor second.

Rob is on the overnight plane from New York to Rome and I am meeting him there after a heinously pre-dawn start from Heathrow. Perhaps I should have begun to feel uneasy at the American organization who had invited us to Puglia putting me on a flight so early as to warrant getting up at 3 am and the Heathrow Express not having even hit the tracks at that ungodly hour. Instead I have shifted airlines, booked a taxi and risen before the dawn chorus has fallen off its perch. The British Airways breakfast being one of those damp, indigestible dough-balls filled with mechanically recovered pink slurry, which I had left steaming in its packet, meant my stomach was gavotting and rumbling as I ran from the main terminal to the domestic one in Rome, heading straight into the arms of the sleepless, unshaven, deliciously grouchy American awaiting me at the gate. We boarded our Alitalia flight. Lunch? Forget it. We were handed a packet of the ubiquitous terralis, the Italians' national snack, and that was that.

At Bari airport there was bad news. The baggage handlers in Rome had decided not to load any of our luggage. Had we known there was some kind of industrial action we would have attempted to carry it on board, but naturally the Alitalia check-in attendants hadn't wanted us to outsmart their mutinous baggage handlers and ensure our comfort, good humour, make-up and knicker elastic. We were forced to join a school-dinner length queue to fill in forms that might, presumably, match our luggage to us at some unspecified time. The Alitalians said they wouldn't be able to get it all on the later flight. Forty minutes later we escaped and, unwilling to wait hours longer for the last of the luggage-free from our group to make it onto the tour bus, caught a taxi to our hotel. By the time we arrived it was late afternoon, we had been travelling all day and all night respectively, hadn't a toothbrush between us, were starving and not a little disputatious.

The Nicotel in downtown Bisceglie is a concrete block well away from the town's action, off what appears to be its industrial hinterland. It looks out across more concrete blocks, through smaller, sugar cube sized ones down below our balcony, which straggle along the unprepossessing promenade to the Adriatic.

The room is travelling salesman, carpet-square-and-fablon with mustard coloured drapes and the usual drainage problems one associates with the above. So we have a week of this? Rob and I are on the verge of bailing out instantly until we realise we have no bags and no getaway car. We check the itinerary. We are already meant to be on the coach heading for the first lecture. With nothing to unpack, we take our places on the bus, two for the tour, and head off for some illumination on the subject of Puglian olive oil. Its being mid-November, the olive harvest should be approaching its zenith, so we are looking forward to sinking a few wellsful of Puglia's best.

One and a half hours into the droning, simultaneous translation going on in our headphones and passing alternate-lined limericks to each other to keep the brain cells firing and from dying off with unrelieved tedium, we can stand it no longer. We rise. We head for the room at the back where we are supposedly going to be given 'substantial snacks' with drinks later. The schedule has also, alarmingly, told us that there is no dinner provided for our inaugural night. We find a cruising helper and signal that we are going to need full resuscitation and de-fibrillation if we can't ingest anything substantial orally pronto, prestissimo. Nil by mouth is over.

A few minutes later a kindly waiter releases a few plates of fried food. Deep-fried food. Here we are in Puglia and our first degustazione is some tiredly, oh so deeply fried battered vegetables and unidentifiable fishy things, the tepid oil seeping into our fingers as we snaffle them up. On another dish there are circles of indifferent mozzarella tooth-picked to a tomato and a circlet of mighty white bread, the sort of thing you might expect at parents' evening at a minor – or even major – English public school. At least the Prosecco is better than rocket fuel. A few more people leave the audience and fall like fledglings out of the nest onto the proffered worms.

Eventually we are disgorged back into the mighty charabanc with the 100 or so other delegates, and delivered back to our hotel. We take a taxi into the seaside town of Bisceglie that has shut up shop in the way any English equivalent would have done at least a month earlier, as the crowds and warmth have faded and winter approaches. We have not been equipped with the names and addresses of the best local watering holes. Most of the cafés and restaurants are closed. Eventually we find a small, welcoming, family-run place where Nancy Harmon Jenkins, the distinguished American food writer, whose book *The Essential Mediterranean* has kept me good company in Rob's New York flat (and whose daughter Sarah Jenkins is the chef of whom I have spoken so highly earlier in the book, late of 50 Carmine Street and Bread), discusses the menu in fluent Italian. This is our first real taste of Puglia. Our fellow diners are a friendly food writer called Patti Unterman from the *San Francisco Chronicle* and a delightful Florentine food buyer called Anna Mignani.

We fall upon bowls of tiny onions, bitter greens with chilli oil to drip onto them, salt cod, dried broad bean purée and slices of pizza from the wood-fired oven.

The telephone rings and it is my friend and editor Anne Fulenwider from *Vanity Fair* in New York asking if I can do an emergency job over the weekend – it is Friday night in Italy – and write a short piece about the playwright Peter Morgan. He has written the spectacularly brilliant script for the films *The Queen* and *The Last King of Scotland*, has a current triumph on the London stage, *Frost/Nixon*, his first stage play, which is transferring to Broadway in the spring, and the film rights have just been snapped up by director Ron Howard. And Morgan's

recent television film *Longford* about Frank Longford's relationship with Moors murderer Myra Hindley has to be odds-on
favourite for a BAFTA for Jim Broadbent and Morgan. This is
his moment. How can I say no? Even though we have already
discovered there is no wireless or internet connection at Fawlty
Towers, and I have to send the piece through willy-nilly on
Monday morning, I accept. Anne says she'll get together a slim
volume of press cuttings and FedEx it to Puglia, and in the
meanwhile she'll fax me the script of *Frost/Nixon* in the absence
of the internet.

We arrive back at the hotel to find the Alitalians have failed
us. What hope a FedEx, I think, and call New York to ask for
everything to be duplicated and sent by fax.

We over-sleep.

When we go downstairs in the morning the bus for the
conference centre has long since departed. We are due on the
panel for this morning's session at 11am. The hotel informs us
that there are only five taxis in the town and they are all taken.
By five to eleven we have negotiated with another group from
the party to commandeer theirs. We race to the location, arriving
twenty minutes late, but relieved to find people are still standing
around drinking coffee after the first session. The American tour
organiser, sylvan, clipped bearded and uniformed in a trust-me
tweed jacket, a little too new and well tailored to look as profes-
sorial as he would wish, and his two female cohorts, who seem
to be shepherding the troops rather than looking after the more
prestigious guests, have barely exchanged glances with us, let
alone offered help and commiseration over our stray luggage,
nor have they briefed us on the nature of the session. We will
just have to busk it, which feels awkward and unprofessional.
The session is wildly over-long and meandering and its leader,

a discursive Italian, appears to veer madly off-message in between introducing us, the guest speakers. Even the Japanese look bored. And still no sighting of that elusive substance we have come to drool and dribble over, Puglian olive oil. No tasting, no dinner, no introduction to it from a local grower. Given that the rest of the day is to be spent in further lectures, and the morrow on a coach leaving at an unreasonably early hour for a five-hour spin to an ex oil-mill that closed some time in the last century, before a buffet lunch in a golf club, Rob and I and several of the other better informed and less patient journalists and food writers are beginning to fray at the cuffs.

It is revving up to Thanksgiving and Christmas, Rob's busiest time of year, and he can ill afford an unproductive week, particularly since he is doing a pre-Christmas Puglia promotion in the shop and needs the best artisanally produced goods to stock it with. And I can ill afford the time off from the book if I don't find a chapter here.

We decide to go AWOL. We take a taxi back to the airport at Bari and hire a freedom vehicle, a car. Suddenly we are in demand. Several journalists begin schmoozing us for a seat in the freedom vehicle, but we have decided, for reasons of politesse, that we won't play away tomorrow, but will make our own way, at our own pace, to the dreaded golf club lunch, in convoy with Nancy Harmon Jenkins, and begin to decipher the landscape, the architecture, the region. We may even get to drive through an olive grove.

Back at Fawlty Towers, the Alitalians have finally delivered Rob's luggage, but mine is still scudding around in transit who knows where. Notwithstanding the knicker shortage, I am hallucinating over the possibility of having several pairs of Manolos half-inched by an Alitalian baggage handler's moll. I put on a pair of Rob's fetching y-fronts, his size 9 socks, and clean my teeth with his toothbrush. It's time to go in search of a good dinner.

We head to the coast with Anna the Florentine, following Nancy, Patti and another American food writer called Susan, to a locally esteemed fish restaurant, Ristorante da Tuccino at Polignano a Mare. It is huge and packed to the gills with Italians. You don't so much read the menu as head for the wet fish counter by the entrance to size up the species, the tonnage and the combination of raw and cooked that suits you.

Now I know I have already alluded to portion control with reference to the average, super-size me American food junkie, or should I say junk foodie, in my new-girl-in-New York chapter 'You Say Tomato', but this is different. This is something else; leaves me dazzled by its excess. This is conspicuous consumption that could only be American, it has no shame. I trail in the wake of the triad of American female food writers to the counter and cannot believe my eyes. Or, should I say, can't believe their eyes. They, I mean their eyes, are so much bigger than their stomachs it looks like we'll need hoists and pantechnicons just to get the doggy bags back to Fawlty Towers. They have witnessed the naked display of slippery, slimy, scaly pass before their eyes and they have picked everything. Not just everything, but whole shoals and schools of blubbery, oily, fleshy fat fish; flat ones, winged ones, long skinny finny ones, big, bloated roe-filled ones; live ones and dead ones, crustacea and bi-valves, tentacled, barnacled, clammy, cold shiny ones; crunchy-tailed shelly ones and wet, white fishy ones. They want raw, they want more raw, they want, they want...

'Wait a minute,' I say nervously. 'Rob doesn't eat raw fish and he doesn't eat octopuses, squid, cuttlefish, any ugly, rubbery big boys from the deep.'

I order him a pile of mantis prawns cooked in salt over the coals to start with. I leave it at that, as we don't order our main courses until we have finished our antipasti and our primi and Rob has said specifically that what he really feels like is a comforting plate of seafood spaghetti, filled with a modest selection of vongole and gamberi and garlic, as do I.

So far we have about a hundredweight of fish being gutted and primped for our table.

Back in the main restaurant, a character who looks suspiciously like Borat arrives at the table. He is our waiter for the night. He hops awkwardly like a stork from foot to foot, is as loquacious as they come, fingering his moustache and addressing us in soliloquy with a list of the 'secondi', with the obvious pleasure of an am-dram pro.

'You look just like Marcello Mastroianni,' Rob exclaims, when we have had time to digest the script.

'Actually everyone else tells me I am Clark Gable,' Borat says in all seriousness, striking a languid pose. It is only then that I realise that the moustache has, indeed, been sculpted and topiaried on the Gable principle, and that his eyebrows have something of the cultivated, yearning lothario about them.

At that moment the first trawler of raw fish arrives and the triad fall upon it in ecstasy. We three at the other end of the table feel that we are watching from the wings as they tear head from tail, break shells and bones and suck sloppy brainy things from heads and fingers and other strange, fishy orifices. This is an almost anthropological experience, watching the vim and succour, the swoon and slurp, the swig and crack of two of the food mavens, breaking off only to write down the names of the poor raw swimmers they're sucking up.

Nothing has arrived for Rob so far and he is looking on with rumbling dismay. I am doing my best to unfurl fleets of shrimp shells, wrapped like cigar papers around their tender, raw frames, but even I am having difficulties with the idea of the nubbled tentacles, splayed soft and sloppy yet as chewy as uncooked tripe on a huge platter.

Rob whispers in my shell-like, 'What did you order me, I can't eat any of this?'

'Try a prawn,' one of the mavens orders Rob. He looks unhappy and on the verge of uttering that time-worn Ozzy warning signal: 'Don't come the raw prawn with me.'

Earlier on, Rob had said to the assembled group of us, with casual, but obvious to me irony, that he wouldn't mind stopping off for a hot dog. I know what he means. He gets like this on food trips, in hotels and foreign countries where one is constantly grazing off hotel, restaurant and room-service menus, eating strange food and just wanting the comfort of something basic and unpretentious. A little good street food. Something without knobs on. Runny scrambled eggs on whole-wheat toast. A saus-age. In his case, lox and bagels, in mine, a bacon sandwich. In the rarefied world of the food trip this is tantamount to spitting in the soup, and even his fellow Americans seem to have taken Rob at face value. If I had done likewise, I reflect, I wouldn't be here now.

'You'd obviously prefer a hot dog,' one of the Americans says, her mouth briefly emptied of fish flesh.

I try to detect her sense of irony, but there is none. A chill as cold as a fish's eye comes over me. She is insulting Rob. She is taking him to be a food philistine, someone brought up on Dunkin' Doughnuts, Jell-O and Twinkies who has an unculti-vated palate, ergo an uncultivated mind. He may be the greatest cheese guru in New York City, nay, America, but his unassailable good taste in the cheese department has not rendered his all-American palate above suspicion. Am I imagining it? I will never know, and luckily Rob's delicious charred prawns arrive and put paid to his immediate hunger at that point. I almost wish he had ordered prawns Marie Rose — what the Yanks would call 'Russian dressing'. Now *that* takes some nerve and a shovelful of retro irony.

The would-be matinée idol arrives back to sweep the shells and spines away. He brings the maître d' with him who offers, in view of the still extant sea creatures piled as high as the discarded bones, to cook the remaining pile up for us. This is not a place where a local would over-order. This is his way of politely telling us it is bad form. That we have to eat up our dinner like good children, or we may not be allowed to be excused from the table. Ten minutes later the fish is returned to the table fried, and we attempt to do it justice all over again. By the time our seafood spaghetti makes an appearance we can barely masticate.

When we finally get back to Fawlty Towers where, I have omitted to say, the staff entirely make up for the ambience and the location, my suitcase has arrived after its two day walkabout, entirely thanks to one of the hotel staff driving to Bari airport where it has finally flown in solo, and I now have a faxed copy of *Frost/Nixon* to aid the digestion with. I read the script well into the night at a single sitting and begin thinking of how to write the piece and what to ask Morgan when I interview him in Vienna by telephone on Sunday.

In the morning I put on the errant Manolos like two old, long-lost friends who have turned up unexpectedly, and we set off on The Long March behind Nancy 'Hannibal' Jenkins again. We drive through the flat, silver-leafed landscape of mile upon mile of olive trees, some of the smaller, twistier roads spread with canvas as though for a village picnic, the green sheets catching the black and green olives and their leaves which the pickers are pulling from the boughs. This is 'trulli' country. Trulli are the vernacular buildings of the Merge, traditional, stone-built dwellings capped with corbel-vaulted roofs built with overlapping circles of flat stones or tiles called chiancarelle, which make them look as though a strange sect has imposed its architectural vision on a whole region, both the ancient and the modern buildings constructed in the same way, like circular beehives for medieval monks.

When we stop for petrol at one of those Puglian equivalents to a Little Chef, a real chef is coming out of the kitchen with a baking tray full of still warm, dark chocolate squares penetrated like nougat with roasted nocciole. Inconceivable off the hard-shoulder of the M4, but standard even in the poorer regions of Italy. We eat the welcome titbits in wonder with our lethal shots of espresso and career on through the stony, grey, autumnal olive groves.

The only thing that can be said about the golf club at Acaya, other than that there were no golfers, is that it was a heck of a way to go to eat cime di rapa, bitter broccoli tops, cicoriette greste di campagna con le olive nere, wild young chicory with black olives, and ciceria e tria, the local home made pasta served with chickpeas, some of which have been fried – an unsuccessful but authentic local touch, since they have lost their crunch sitting leaking oil into their cooking water at the bottom of the dish.

The best taste by far is the ricotta salata, but given that this is the same food as is eaten all over the region, and that the oil mill – which we in the freedom vehicles had managed to avoid – is no longer operational, and we still haven't been taken to a working one or had a tutored olive oil tasting, I am beginning to wonder if I couldn't have learned everything I have so far learned from this trip by cooking up my own bitter greens from my own back yard with the aid of Nancy's book, my olive oil guides, a dose of the bitter green stuff bought from my favourite oil merchant, Charles Carey, and cheeses from Rob's shop.

The unusually sharp and intensely flavoured aged ricotta is a local speciality, also known as ricotta forte, and one which I found compulsive once I had discovered it. The pasta with bitter greens which the locals often coat in their floury fava bean purée, 'ncapriata fave, is also a staple.

If only Nancy had been allowed to talk to us about Puglian cuisine first, and the whole trip had commenced with us being given copies of her book, *Flavours of Puglia*, instead of its being handed to us at the end of the lunch after the classic and unusual finale of verdure, raw vegetables, we would all have been happier and better informed from the get-go.

'La cucina pugliese nasce come cucina povera,' says a renowned local cook and friend of Nancy's, Paola Pettini, who used to run a cooking school in Bari. 'The cuisine of Puglia was born as the cuisine of poverty.' So much better and more accurate a way of putting it than 'peasant' food; 'cucina povera' it will be from now on. Here the pasta is eggless, the bread made from hard, durum wheat flour that grows in abundance in the region, where it is also used stale, turned into breadcrumbs and sautéed in olive oil then substituted for Parmesan or Pecorino on top of pasta, or thrown over steamed or braised vegetables. The diet is based on vegetables, and includes many wild ones that grow around the olive trees, or in the stony fields and abandoned terraces, like cicorielle, wild chicory, and lampascione, the particularly bitter bulb of the wild tassel hyacinth that we ate on several occasions. It is about as bitter as the aloes you have painted on your nails as a nail-biting deterrent as a child, and is almost, but not quite, too much to take.

It is a diet which includes very little meat, although horse meat is the local preference. Several of the Americans at our table are looking sneerily repelled by the equine meatballs, as though, 'Well what would you expect in a third world place like this?' which always fills me with perverse pleasure. How many times have these well travelled, well heeled, cultured people ventured into provincial French restaurants and unknowingly chomped delicious bifsteak or steak hâché that is really horsemeat?

The cuisine here is not about restaurant food but about home cooking, 'cucina delle donne', created by women cooking at home, and based on what's in the family larder, which can also include salt cod and mussels, and on feast days, 'animale da cortile', farmyard animals like chickens, rabbits and lamb.

Nancy tells us that the rich in Puglia eat the same food as the poor, grains and beans, making Puglia one of those rare places in the world where that still happens, the only difference being '...the rich eat more of it.' As we know, many peoples' diets change the moment they leave poverty for the middle classes, and change for the worse. The first thing they do once they're no longer on the breadline is eat lashings more meat, particularly red meat, which enforces their newfound position of wealth and privilege. I like the fact that fave beans may be known as 'la carne dei poveri', the meat of the poor, but that they are also manna to the rich.

Here in England it all seems to happen in reverse though, perverse as we are; the moment we jump classes, the greater the peaks of social mountaineering we manage to scale, the more we eschew the diet of meat, meat and more meat and head for cucina povera, the only differences being, I suspect, that the baked beans no longer come from the tin, they are soaked and cooked the cucina povera way while the Mighty White is magicked into organic whole-wheat. Yet until comparatively recently the snow white loaf was seen as a symbol of wealth and status in Britain. It is only since the brown rice and sandals brigade of the late 1960s spread the idea that white bread became a symbol of ignorance, disdain and poverty by the snobs and know-it-alls like ourselves at the top of the food chain.

Nancy believes the local diet has barely changed in Puglia in 500 years, apart from one great exception, the tomato. Here, tomatoes are sweet and acid, dense and fleshy, bursting with juice, and available all year round fresh from the garden, sun-dried and packed in oil, put up in jars either whole, or in a sauce, and strung in brilliant scarlet necklaces that, amazingly, will keep in a cool, dry place from harvest to spring-time the following year.

The region of Puglia produces up to two-thirds of the olive oil made in Italy each year. Even deep-fried food is dunked into a bath of bubbling olive oil, so no danger of clogging the internal tributaries with the horrors of trans-fats here. Our only danger seems to be in spending nigh on a week in oil country and not striking an oil well, or at least discovering where the best oil comes from, and whether or not the new season's is good enough for Rob to import in time for his Puglia promotion in December.

We return via Lecce, one of the great capitals of the Baroque, with its elegant churches and houses built of local pink stone. The sixteenth-century church of Santa Croce, with its mighty balcony resting on thirteen caryatids, representing grotesque human figures and allegorical animal shapes, is one of the more stupendous buildings in a town of many minor glories, whose three majestic gateways lead out from its narrow, gilded and decorated streets.

It is Sunday morning. Another day, another coach trip, but we have decided to spend the morning at the hotel so that I can do my telephone interview, before we drive with Anna Mignani to see the greatest wonder of the region, the Castel del Monte.

I get through to Vienna and have a hilarious conversation with Peter Morgan who, despite seriously self-deprecatory tendencies and an almost completely believable disbelief that any of the awards will come to him, does actually confess that if they do, it will be his 'big fat cigar moment'. I invite him to dine with us in New York in December, when he will be in America doing the junket for the films and in pre-production of *Frost/Nixon* on Broadway. I have tonight to write the piece, so we drive off in the early afternoon.

Set on a lone hill, which reinforces its strange, stark, geometric beauty, is the Castel del Monte. It rises out of the landscape, if you approach it from the town of Andria, like a pale, modernist edifice that might be more in keeping with the architecture of the future than of the past. This has to be part due to its rocket launcher sides and the re-building and cleaning that has left it bone-white and scoured like a pebble instead of dulled and pocked and scarred by the many centuries it has weathered at the top of the hill. It looks more as though it has come down like a tardis from above than as if its foundations have risen slowly from this bare, tortured landscape where there is nowhere to hide from the high, midday sun in summer bar a few umbrella-topped trees clinging to the terraced hillside it is set upon. The wind, as we climb the last few hundred yards up to the great castle door, delivers an icy blast that chills the ears, the nose, the hands, the soul.

The Castel del Monte is one of the most beautiful fortresses and great architectural achievements of the Middle Ages, built by the great emperor of the Hohenstaufens, Frederick the Second, who was known as 'Stupor Mundi', the astonisher of the world. It was built in the first half of the thirteenth century to an unusual octagonal plan, with eight octagonal towers marking the vertices of a polygon. Frederick the Second married Constance of Arigona when he was fifteen and she was twenty-five, and made an indelible mark as an astronomer, mathematician and philosopher, but was also known for his brilliance and shrewdness as a statesman and his fearlessness as a conqueror. Could there ever be a modern equivalent?

The upper storey, faced with marble, is warm and light with convivially sized, trapezoid-shaped rooms, the remains of working open fireplaces where it is almost impossible to believe, given the enormous height of the ceilings, that the fires drew and didn't kipper the occupants, warm red corralite surrounds to the doorways, and, apparently, the unheard of architectural luxury of indoor bathrooms and loos with washing facilities that were probably fed by cisterns. It is thought the complicated sewage system took everything away from the castle walls, down deep, one presumes, into the surrounding cornfields. In one of the eight towers an artificial eyrie was constructed for the breeding of young falcons.

Even emptied of life and furniture, inside there is a strange sense of comfort and modernism and none of the chill and un-homeliness of a long uninhabited castle. By the time we leave, it is 4.30 pm and already darkening.

A few hundred yards down the side of the hill is a small restaurant, the Taverna Sforza, where we shelter from the penetrating cold.

'What's left?' Anna asks the owner, who informs us that we are too late to eat, that the chef has gone off duty. We beg and plead and say we will eat whatever the kitchen has left, we will heat it up ourselves, we don't need a menu, just bring hot food.

The restaurant is third generation and Giovanni's pride is at stake. Thank God for the persuasive talents of Florentine Anna, who very soon, short of threatening to besiege the kitchen her-self, has secured us a carafe of wine and a plate of freshly cooked cardoncelli, the local fungi famously eaten all over the region at this time of year, followed by perfect local lamb and cinghiale served with carroti rosso, which turns out not to be a strange strain of mutant carrots, but a dish of beetroot. The chef seems to have mysteriously returned, as everything is freshly cooked and Giovanni sits with us, inspecting every dish as it arrives.

We appeal to Giovanni for help, telling him we have been held captive and that our kidnappers have failed to deliver. That we know nothing of the region and its food, its oil, its cheese, and that we are interested in visiting the small dairies that produce the local formaggio. It turns out he is an active supporter of a local co-operative of producers and eager for the praises of their wares to be sung further afield. He will ring the best producer of mozzarella in the region and get us a tasting and a tour of the dairy the following morning. Andria, after all, is the centre of burrata production and burrata, that divine bauble of buffalo mozzarella enclosing a flood of cream that bursts dam-like onto the tongue in a rich, lactic lake, is one of the reasons Puglia is on our gastro-map.

Back at the Nicotel I write my column for *Vanity Fair* and cajole the hotel staff into letting me send it on their computer, almost more tricky than the writing, as they have had nearly a hundred other journalists cajoling them similarly who they have so far turned down.

In the morning we drive to Andria to Michele Matera, at 234 Via Ferucci. Nino Matera and his wife Teresa greet us warmly and show us the table they have prepared for us in the shop. We are treated like visiting royalty who must be introduced to the pride and joy of the region's best produce, lest we leave without having discovered it. Giovanni arrives. He has taken the morning off from the restaurant to look after us and translate.

Nino has only just returned from the dairy in another part of town where he has been making cheese all night, from midnight right through to 9 am. He is second generation, his father was boss before him, now he and his brother Antonio work every night as Nino has done for 25 years, returning to help in the shop in the morning and finally hitting the horizontal at 1 pm. He is only 38.

Look at the hands of any mozzarella maker and you will recognise them as the hands of a cheese maker, used to plunging his mitts into hot water whose temperature would leave us teary eyed and scarlet fisted. Nino's fingers, blistered and swollen, look like smoked salmon sausages, the hardened layers of skin having formed an orange crust almost like one of the great washed-rind cheeses from Ireland's Beara Peninsula.

Each night, Nino tells us, they make 700lbs of fresh, unpasteurised buffalo mozzarella by hand. In 2003 they won the Premio Italia che Lavora award for their cheese in Bari. This is more like it. The shop is constantly replenished with queues of housewives talking noisily and vehemently to each other, the

owners, us, in that way the Italians and no other race seem to
have mastered quite so well, where all outsiders presume they
are quarrelling but they are, in fact, just passing the time of day
as they wait their turn for the fresh cheeses. It is like this every
day, they tell us, the shop is famous throughout the region.
There is a beautiful salume counter, and the best artisan terrali
we have come across on the trip, which we decide to import to
Murray's, with enough fennel seed pitted into their crisp-baked,
golden rings to complement the cheese. There are Teresa's home
made tortas stuffed with fontina and ham, and bulging strings of
ivory scarmorza affumicata smoked with palia, pine wood, or con
vino rosso, the scarmorza aged with red wine.

Our table is laid with plates of both; with stracciatella that
buyers travel 200 km for, Nino tells us. There is crema di
formaggi, made with the same milk as the mozzarella, and
a quivering, damp, fresh cheese pocked with flecks of brilliant
green wild arugula. We have bowls of the scarmorza, the
mozzarella, the burrata and bocconcini made with white wine.
We taste everything. We have never tasted mozzarella like it.
It is not just the freshness, it is the fact that mozzarella that has
been subject to the pasteurisation process loses fat and protein
at 90 degrees fahrenheit and is machine made, all of which
must affect the flavour. Here it is made by hand at 66 degrees
fahrenheit, Nino tells us and the flavour and texture are
indescribable. It is like skeins of silken, milky, mossy-soft velvet,
pliable, creamy-rich, acidic yet merciful. It is as though we have
never eaten mozzarella before. We eat everything put before us.
Teresa and Nino and Giovanni are enjoying watching as much
as we are enjoying eating. I could breakfast here every morning
and never want for change. After a tour of the dairy Rob and I
depart, inspired by the milk of Puglian kindness and generosity

and suddenly impassioned by Puglia.

Nancy, sensibly, has left. Three days was long enough for her and she has sped to her house in Tuscany. Rob and I are now like a breakaway faction, and although our reasons are more about survival than subversion, we have to continue up this boulevard if we are going to leave with the contraband we need for Rob's business and my book. Anyway, the American tour organisers appear to have zero interest in whether anyone in the group is actually enjoying themselves or realising their objectives, which is wholly unlike any other press or PR trip I have ever ventured upon. We swap notes and findings with the few kindred spirits who have been tethered to the tour bus in the hands of their tormentors, and with the other individuals who have followed our lead, instigated their own mini rebellions, rented their own cars and also headed off in other directions.

It is our last morning and we are on a mission with the three musketeers. Rob has been in touch with a Puglian organisation called AINT that helps local producers sell internationally, and they have offered to take us to meet some of them. When Sabina, Roberto and Cinzia turn up in their tiny car and we all five pile back into it we know we are in for a good day. First stop Corato, where we have finally, finally struck oil. And what a borehole. Giuseppe del Console looks like Father Christmas, jocular, jowly, grizzly bearded and as rotund as one of his barrels. He is supervising the pressing when we enter the mill and the noise is ear-splitting. Giuseppe buys in olives from 600 local farms and they are all pressed within 24 hours of being picked. He uses coratina olives which the area around Corato specialises in.

'I have a unique machine which presses the olives very gently, keeps them cold when they are pressed so that they keep their aroma. The soft pressing is used to harmonise the flavour. Other producers use faster machines but speed is not good. I create a very intense fruit aroma of artichoke and bitter almonds and olive leaves.'

'So your oil is best because, would you fill in the blanks?' Rob begins.

'It is not the best in the world,' Giuseppe retorts. 'But you will only use a little bit of our oil, it is very intense on the throat; it is different because it has a high level of polyphenols, the highest, and is very high in anti-oxidants, so the result is its bitterness. So you don't use too much and you don't get fat.'

'So will you ask Giuseppe why he looks like he does?' I ask Roberto.

Giuseppe roars with laughter, 'It's because I like pasta!'

Rob has a sudden revelation: 'I've been here before, it must have been 10 years ago, I met Giuseppe, I have been thinking about his oil for 10 years, I didn't know how to find him.' The three musketeers are as thrilled as Rob is, and Giuseppe looks as though he has just been deified.

I ask Giuseppe why Puglian olive oil is such a well-kept secret if it is so good.

'The US didn't buy it until now because you only eat rubbish. You didn't even buy extra virgin olive oil until about 10 years ago. Most olive oil is too sweet because it is chemically treated. Ours, the coratina, keeps its flavour and aroma level for a year whereas most oils lose theirs by April after the November harvest. I like bitter oil and bitter greens, it's healthy.'

We try glugs of oil on its own and are sent into choking fits, it is oil straight from the press and it has the characteristic Pugliese pugilism, or fighting spirit, that hits the throat like it's being rubbed with chilli covered sandpaper. Once we dribble a few drips of the viscous green oil onto food, a few sliced tomatoes, the effect is completely different. The note of artichoke hits the palate at the end, but first there is a pleasing, grassy, raspy but bearable hit of almonds and damp olive leaves, just as Giuseppe has said there would be.

'You need only one drop on your fish,' Giuseppe continues. 'A little with vegetables or meat to taste the aroma and smell the artichoke, two drops is 'periculoso', dangerous. My wife thinks extra virgin oil is my lover because I am so passionate about it, see, the bitterness is gone when you eat it with a carrot, it's a pleasure, like when you eat a candy.'

By the time we leave Giuseppe, Rob has determined to buy 90 litres of the green, grassy stuff for the Puglian promotion, and everyone is happy. In fact the oil simply pours out of the Murray's door within four days of arriving, and Rob's merchandising it at the front of the store. He could have ordered double the amount and the same thing would have happened, so relations with Puglia will continue to develop over the coming seasons.

We visit a terrali company before heading off to the hills to Montegrosso, near Andria, back in the Murga region, where, Sabina and Roberto and Cinzia all agree, is situated the best chef, the best restaurant in the whole region.

Pietro Zito looks like a well-seasoned, substantially built, head-shaven bouncer and he has a small, unassuming restaurant called Antichi Sapori, – Old Taste – in the middle of the village. Inside is rustic without being obtrusively or self-consciously so, with a string of the famous tomatoes, pomodori della cocchia, hung drying, just as Nancy has told us they do in Puglia, from the wall behind our table, where they are beginning to wrinkle into senescence without losing too much of their youthful, fleshy-cheeked brightness. I am invited into the kitchen to meet the chefs and see what they are cooking for us. First, some fresh ricotta with a miniature dice of candied celery, a brilliant way to add dolce to agro and a fortuitous pairing. A few thick slices of home made salame with fennel are brought to the table, and two more cheese plates to form a triumphant selection of anti-pasti, a cacciocavallo with candied apple, the apple a 'mela cotogna' which is a local variety, and a delicious Pecorino from nearby, which Pietro serves with candied red onion. So Pietro keeps running his agro-dolce theme through the cheeses and their partners, be they vegetable or fruit, accompanied by chunks of focaccia di grano arso, a toasted wheat focaccia.

We revisit the bitter depths of the lampascione, the wild tassel hyacinth, which Pietro has fried in petals and serves with balsamic vinegar, whose mellow stickiness teases away the sense that we may be being poisoned by this strange bulb that has no equivalent in our cuisine. The simple refinement Pietro has executed shows his imaginative understanding of the limitations of the one thing and their being breached by the two. Next is sponsale, apparently a leek-like vegetable, served in olive oil with parsley and chilli, before a carciofi gratinati, a whole artichoke gratinéed and a crostini of olives cooked in charcoal.

So far this is a feast to make any vegetarian go weak at the knees, which would convert even the most carnassially addicted of humans, and the great thing is, not only do we not feel the need of meat, but some of the vegetables actually feel meaty. A bowl of ciccoria in brodo d'agnello is the nearest thing to meat to tempt the palate after the salame, the bitter chicory vamped up by the sweet, lamby broth, which is followed by the ubiquit-ous cime di rape, a little dish of fagioli with new harvest olive oil, and a taste of scarmoza di capra which Pietro has aged for two months.

The famous local pasta, orrechiette, the Italian word for an ear, is 'tostato', toasted, in this bit of Puglia, to the colour of mud, and has a lovely nutty flavour. Apparently when the rich landowners harvested the grain, they left behind the chaff for the poor people who picked it up when it had been burned by the sun, and turned it into pasta. Extraordinary that the poorest of poor foods should achieve the cachet of the most sought after and desirable and, like once cheap oysters, probably go on to attain exclusivity. When we bring this unknown pasta back to Murray's, it flies off the shelves as fast as the staff can put the bags out in the store.

Our pasta arrives in a hillock with a second mound of finely chopped sweet olives and a third of pure di fave which are left for us to stir together on the plate. Never has a dish, indeed, all these dishes, of such simple, nourishing goodness, left me feeling quite how true they remain to their origins; to an honest, unpretentious cuisine that is still soil-bound and all about gathering, foraging, scavenging and picking wild weeds and grain and fruit and vegetables and working with their flavours and textures to re-create that place on the plate.

And somehow the cuisine translates directly into being about what the body needs most when the place happens to produce it. It speaks reams, or rather sheaves, about cropping and storing and abundance at the same time as it tells tales of husks and stalks and ears of corn; poverty, paucity, hardship, a little going a long way. This is as delicious a lunch as I have ever eaten anywhere in the world, and Pietro has pulled it off without a single air or grace or needless embellishment, and with no kow-towing to excess or waste or richness, in a small, family restaurant where probably nothing has travelled, other than the lunchers, for more than a dozen miles.

Our three musketeers are quietly proud to have shown us a

taste of their region which has left us hungry and curious for more, and we, in turn, have invited them to dine with us in New York at the beginning of December when they come over for the Puglian promotion. We are determined to take them to the Blue Ribbon on Bedford Street for the best American food in town, where they can experience our beloved Southern fried chicken with honey, mash and bitter collard greens. Come to think of it, it is a pretty credible echo of the agro-dolce that the Italians understand better than anyone.

Roberto, Sabina and Cinzia take us on a short trip to an organic farm after lunch, and we finish with a tour of a lovely old chocolate factory, Mucci, in Andria, established in 1894 and now being run by the fourth generation of the Mucci family. The present owner's great grandfather invented the tenerelle, choc-olate coated almonds, which we watch being made in almost the same way as they originally were. Rob manages to find a few hidden corners that I know I can't possibly match, and tries just about every type, colour and creed of chocolate that Mucci produce before ordering a selection for the shop.

Back at Fawlty Towers, my long delayed FedEx has arrived well after the job has been corrected and put to bed, and Rob receives a letter from our American tour boss advising us that our prolonged absence from the charabanc is a deal breaker, and, as a result, he is refusing to pay our hotel bill.

Rob and I deliberate carefully before replying. There are no free lunches. We are old enough and wicked enough to know that. The cliché is without exception true in my experience, but trips such as these are paid for by the local people, not the tour organisers; often by small producers and regional government funds which we are very mindful of. We, in our turn, have a grail we set out in search of, and would always hope to return with, but if we are not properly led we diverge, we seek a different path, as Robert Frost illustrated so presciently in his well known poem *The Road Not Taken*.

We cannot afford to come home empty-handed. Nor have we.

It is unlikely that anyone else on the tour established anything like the business links that Rob did. Already thousands of dollars have gone home to Puglia, and Murray's has begun to put the best Puglian ingredients, the soul and soil of this harsh, poor, captivating country on the gastro-map as, I hope, have I writing this.

We write a short letter of firm politesse with a sting: our point-blank refusal to accept these revised terms. And we stress that no conditions were applied to the original understanding and that we have fulfilled our side of the bargain to the letter. We have no intention of paying the bill.

We ring the three musketeers who agree to the final part of our plan, the getaway. In the morning, like criminals mid-heist, we walk out of the hotel. Naturally we have honoured our extras bill. We stand outside the drive and wait for deliverance. Cinzia screeches to a halt. We jump into the car and race to the airport ahead of the tour bus. Alitalia are on a different strike on the way home and there is no food on either leg of the journey. That's state-run airlines for you, but we have a bagful of wonderful fresh cheeses from Nino, his fennel-pocked terrali and at least a month's supply of Mucci chocolates in our bags.

Next time it's two for the tour.

Summer Vegetable Quick Lasagne

SERVES FOUR

Often I just can't be bothered to make lasagne because of all the different processes involved and the coming together and cooking of it all at the end, but here is one that just cooks itself, the vegetables steamed and roasted and no bechamel sauce to worry about. So it is light, full of flavour, and you really can make it when you get back from work in the evening and eat it the same night.

The other amazing discovery: the second night I ate it cold from the fridge as one would a good ratatouille for dinner, since my daughter Miranda hadn't shown up the previous night, and it was just as delicious in an entirely different way. A proper leftover dinner.

If you're a vegetarian, simply eschew the anchovies, whack up the herbs with extra thyme and savory and rosemary, and scatter some buffalo mozarella over the leek layer and some grated Parmesan over the top if you feel like it. It is lovely without cheese if you're making it fishy with anchovy.

2 LARGE organic red onions
6 CLOVES garlic
fruity extra virgin olive oil
2 SPRIGS rosemary
6 SPRIGS thyme
sea salt and black pepper
24 organic cherry tomatoes or 12 or so ordinary sized organic tomatoes
6 leeks, the whites only, peeled and left whole after washing
8 BABY FINGERS of courgette with the flowers on if possible
6 anchovy fillets
3 HEAPED TBSP creme fraiche
A BOX of lasagne that is high quality but doesn't neeed pre-cooking

Peel and slice the red onions quite thinly, peel the garlic, strip the rosemary and thyme off their branches and chop them small and cook everything together in the warmed olive oil, about 3–4 tablespoons, over a gentle heat for 10 minutes, stirring and adding a tiny bit of salt after a couple of minutes. I now put a lid on them and put the pan in the baking oven of the Aga for 40 minutes, stirring twice. You can do the same on top of the stove on a gentle heat.
Meanwhile, roast the halved large or whole cherry tomatoes in a roasting tin in a hot oven with

a little oil and thyme until beginning to burst and all juicy, and steam the leeks whole until tender when pierced with a skewer.

Keep the leek water in the base of the steamer and slice the leeks in half lengthwise.

When the onions and courgettes are softened, remove the pan from the heat, put the anchovy fillets in the pan and crush with a fork then dollop over the creme fraiche, stirring it in with the anchovies, and season with black pepper, not more salt, the anchovies are salt enough.

Put a thin layer of the onion mixture over the base of your roasting tin and then add a layer of high-quality lasagne sheets that don't need pre-cooking.

Now add a layer of tomatoes, using them all up, and their juices, and spread a layer of all the halved leeks over the top, seasoning them with black pepper. Add another layer of lasagne sheets and then add half the onion and courgette mixture. Add a final layer of lasagne sheets and the rest of the onion mixture, making sure the creamy juice covers the pasta sheets so they don't dry out.

Carefully pour the inch of leek water into the dish at the side, so that everything is well lubricated. A splash of olive oil on top won't go amiss, but don't overdo it.

Bake for 25 minutes or until bubbling and the pasta feels cooked right through to the bottom layer when pierced with a skewer.

Leave for 10 minutes before serving, or serve warm or at room temperature with a green salad.

8

Everything but the Squeak

There is a flurry, a breeze, and the great Bocuse enters with a small entourage that includes his wife. He is heroic of scale in his toque, she smaller and bird-like and immaculately suited in Chanel. His warm brown eyes light up the room. This is a drab Sunday night but M. Bocuse enters, despite his 79 years, like someone storming the Bastille…

If I had had any idea as to what to expect over our five days in Lyon and Roanne, I would have gone into training. As it was, the only clue, other than my scant, flimsy knowledge of saucisson chaud à la Lyonnaise, pommes de terre sautées à la Lyonnaise, and the epically muzzley, muscly, snouty, head-to-tail-to-trottery delights of la salade Lyonnaise, came from my friend Michel Roux Jr of Le Gavroche, in London's Brook St.

'Michel, we can't get a table at Troisgros for Monday night,' I began, knowing that he would probably have a direct line to the emperor of every three-star emporium in France. He and his family, his father Albert, uncle Michel, cousin Alain, are all scions of the emigrant French branch of the Michelin Mafia and have, over a quarter of a century, helped transform the dismal, post-war restaurant eating habits of the great British gourmand from brown Windsor soup and boeuf en gelée to their own modern take on the French classics, and they've managed to garner more stars to their name here in England over the years than the Americans can flaunt on their star-spangled banners.

Michel promised to sort it out, and we got onto the equally serious business of plotting Saturday and Sunday night.

'You must go to Christian Têtedoie, I did National Service with him, it's a one-star and he's a fantastic chef. It's a lovely restaurant down on the quay.'

Where else but Lyon, I mused, would a chef rejoice in the name Têtedoie, 'Goosehead,' and not have changed it by deed poll? I have since discovered that it is a name local to Lyon.

'What should we eat?' I continue.

Michel is in his element knowing that neither Rob nor I have been blooded by the local cuisine, which lays claim to being at the epicentre, the heart, the pulse, the liver, the lungs, even, of great French cuisine.

'You have to eat the quenelles de brochet and the tête de veau avec homard,' Michel instructs. The latter combination alone is enough to drain the blood from my cheeks, conjuring up, as it does, the tender young head with its beefy cheeks, cooked pools of eyes, lolling, pink poached tongue and soft, mushy brain scooped out and braised in a pond of black butter. Perhaps the crown is removed monkey brain style so the king of the crustaceans can be packed, like forcemeat, into the hollow effigy where the brain once was, providing a curious, fishy resonance to the brawny, brainy flesh. Not that I am squeamish about heads en générale or en gelée. I was brought up on calves' brains, which my grandmother's cook, Rhoda Fisher, deemed should be poached for growing children and no nonsense allowed. It is more the surf meets turf combination that my brain is having difficulty with, my personal sense of mismatch and excess, and the fact that 's and t' just doesn't seem very French. But who am I to know?

'And Sunday?'

'Have you been to Bocuse? You can't go to Lyon and not go to Bocuse,' Michel insists.

The almost too shocking to relate gaps in our culinary education are about to be closed. I set about booking Têtedoie and Bocuse with the edict to call Michel if I can't get in, and to offer salutations from 'la famille Roux'.

Rob and I meet in Paris at the airport. We haven't seen each other for over two months and the meeting is more charged than our normal — if they can be called that — airport reunions. We board the Lyon flight and arrive in the damp, slate-clouded mist that Lyon is also renowned for and decide to explore the city whose culinary reputation is as legendary for its charcuterie as it is for its perhaps less applauded talent for cooking fish.

We cross the fast-flowing ribbon of Rhône bordered by high, handsome, palely painted, almost boastful Victorian houses and walk through the old city until we reach a parallel river, the Saône, a slower, slimmer curl. On many of the small street corners we spot the famous Lyonnais 'bouchon' signs.

That evening, our taxi driver jests that there are three rivers in Lyon, the Rhône, the Saône and the Beaujolais, and tells us that 'bouchon' means the corking of the bottle from the hundred-litre casks from which these fiercely traditional Lyonnais restaurants serve their customers. He also tells us that only a handful remain that serve really traditional bouchon food, like Le Garet in the rue Garet where we are headed.

It is thrilling to discover on my return that Elizabeth David, in her *French Provincial Cooking* written 45 years ago, notes: 'I also remember an especially excellent dish of skate with black butter on the menu of one of those rough and noisy but efficiently run little bistros which are typically Lyonnais… One of the great virtues of this little place in the rue Garet was that everything was served sizzling hot. The raie au beurre noir came to our table with the butter and the fish fairly bubbling in its own little dish; and I saw that the patron, having cooked his own steak, brought it to his table in a covered serving dish, ceremoniously decanted it on to his hot plate, and took the empty dish away to the kitchen before sitting down to his interrupted meal.'

This had to be Le Garet and its character had not changed. Right down to the patron, who, though he must have been the son or grandson of Mrs David's original character, worked the crowded tables of local diners then repaired to his own small table to enjoy his evening meal before our eyes.

Rob and I were with a small party, as part of our mission was to attend the prestigious Caseus Awards in the city of Lyon, which I can only describe as the cheesemonger Olympics. Hervé Mons, Rob's affineur from Roanne, was organizing and hosting this extraordinary contest, in which mongers from a dozen countries around the world, including, bizarrely, Japan, not noted for their skill in the dairy department nor yet their love of cheese, were competing in a five-part contest, for the title that would confirm their place in the cheese firmament.

One of our party ordered the raie and it was exactly as Mrs David described. The noise from the table of men next to us, curious as to our choice of dishes; the swift, spirited welcome from le patron bearing bouchons of St Joseph; the obvious approval of the table to our left as each dish arrived and con-formed to some unspoken standard of traditional excellence; the paper table cloths and huge squares of linen napkin, the clatter as the best bread and pats of sweet, white butter were brought with a great bowl of rillette d'oie; the rosette de Lyon, cured pork sausage served with butter and pickles; the saucisson chaud avec pommes vapeur; the salade cochonailles, cured pig from all corners and crannies of porcine anatomy and including everything but the squeak, jewelled with squares of pork fat and accompanied by lentils coated in a piquant, intense mustard dressing; these were all the stuff of a cuisine of confidence and guts and basic, honest, stick with the good stuff integrity.

We sauntered on to huge pelts of calves' liver which was darker and less timid in flavour than we are used to, with that other staunch classic, pommes de terre sautée à la Lyonnaise, small cubes of waxy potatoes sautéed with onions in pork fat, which helps to bring the dish together without overwhelming it.

We were fascinated by two local dishes, the tablier de sapeur, or fireman's apron, of tripe coated in egg and breadcrumbs, fried to definitive crispness and served with tartare sauce, and the cervelle des Canuts. Canuts were the silk weavers who worked in the Croix-Rousse district of Lyon before and during the Industrial Revolution. These dishes, as strong a statement as you could hope to find in a truly regional restaurant, did, however, beg a couple of questions: how do the locals eat like this without a whiff of a green vegetable? And just how were we going to cope with the riches of the Michelin-starred tables to follow?

With that final thought, we fell out of the redoubtable Le Garet, sated and weary, into bed, praying that the digestive juices would realise they were being given a more than usually challenging work-out and would feel stimulated by the task ahead.

Saturday night in Lyon and it is still damp and drear as we cross the swirling Rhône and the swollen Saône and head down the quai Pierre Seize to Têtedoie. No wonder everyone drowns their damp, chilly sorrows in bubbling hot pig fat and drenches, or at least quenches, their thirst with the good old Bordeaux from up-river.

The chic, carpeted comfort, abstract canvases, well-spaced tables are in complete contrast to the rough-edged noise and clatter and homely hospitality for all comers – terrines left on the table in that all too rare spirit of generosity so that you can help yourself to whatever quantity or combination you want of last night's bouchon.

After a day watching giant wheels of Parmesan cut against the clock into precisely gauged chunks, cheese counters installed and displays set up as rapidly as camp kitchens, countermen plying their trade in a dozen tongues to the judges looking for counter service, expertise, the meilleur ouvrier knowledge that a maître fromagier should automatically bring to his customers, the two of us are in need of a little comfort, and the romance of some two-star treatment.

The Irish, led by my old friends the Sheridan brothers, Seamus and Kevin, who keep the two best cheeses shops in the land, in Galway and Dublin, have come in bottom at their first attempt, so I am sure the whole thing is a fix and that the French are bound to win. But they don't. In fact they don't even make the top three. I guess the rules and the judging will remain a mystery to me.

We ask about that most testing of traditional dishes, la quennelle de brochet comme à Lyon au coulis d'ecrevisses, with its pounding of the pike, its panade of cream and egg white, the moulding and poaching and puffing up of the delicate paste, the river of pink sauce fashioned with crayfish; how can we possibly choose between that and le homard et tête de veau confite that Michel has told me is Christian's signature dish?

I am as gently but forcibly led to the tête by the maître d' as good reason could not begin to dispute. Rob is allowed to order le parmentier de boeuf et paleron confit 7 heures. In the mean-while, we are brought little demi-tasses of mealy, creamy, roan coloured chestnut soup, its sweetness tempered by a crisp, salt slice of bacon perched like a Rhône bridge from lip to lip, and with a shipwreck of buried treasure in the form of a soft poached quail's egg buried in its murky depths.

The dish of homage to the king crustacean, its brilliant cara-pace crowning, regally, the head of the calf, is like a dish from a lost empire. There is cheek by jowl and who knows what other protuberance and extremity that current English fashion would eschew and turn its collective nose up at. The meat is part rillette-like shards, part spoon-soft flesh with a crisp, dark crunch of crackling. The lobster sits sweetly in its midst just doing its own sweet, pink, delicious thing, its lobster quadrille.

We wonder, yet again, at the French ability to worship the

flesh, the full fatted flesh, without apology or recourse to greenery. Tomorrow we will have to fast before we feast chez Bocuse, with maybe just a bowlful of pruneaux for breakfast.

'Comme il est difficile d'être simple,' reads Van Gogh's philosophy at the foot of the towering menu that arrives in our laps at Paul Bocuse's temple to gastronomy.

The House of Bocuse is like a Versace palace, painted in carnival colours of crimson and green, with frescoes adorning the courtyard walls, the inside opulence a full-on combination of kitsch and country. You know the sort of French bourgeois taste where heavily shone pink copper pans hang above 'les meubles rustiques'. The kitchen is like a glass goldfish bowl which you have to float past as you are ushered past impossibly smiley and good looking young chefs, before you glide upstairs to one of the dining rooms. The waiters have the looks and coiffeur and brilliantined black hair of silent movie stars, one pair who could be twins, waiting table in the low murmur that seems to emanate wherever cuisine is deemed a religious experience, and infusing the very pores of the room.

There is a flurry, a breeze, and the great Bocuse enters with a small entourage that includes his wife. He is heroic of scale in his toque, she smaller and bird-like and immaculately suited in Chanel. His warm brown eyes light up the room. This is a drab Sunday night but M. Bocuse enters, despite his 79 years, like someone storming the Bastille, striding like a lion between the tables and shaking hands with all the diners.

The fact that Bocuse arrives with the aperitifs, like a host at his party, is a further sign of the unquestioned status he has in the French culinary world, although he is advanced in years and something of an anachronism now. He doesn't need to wait for the praise and afterglow from his worshipful diners. Our brief conversation is like being granted a Papal audience, and indeed, this is how Bocuse is known by his confrères. I stumble through the salutations from la famille Roux and he bows elegantly in reply. Just as suddenly he is gone.

Bocuse's menu pays not the faintest lip-service to modernity. It is confident and unshaken by movements of fashion and fusion and faddery. The volaille de bresse en vessie Mère Fillioux demi deuil, that I notice being carved at the table behind us, is a dish that was invented by one of the great figures of French cuisine in the early twentieth century, La Mère Fillioux, when a generation of women restaurateurs became the celebrity chefs of their day in Lyon. Eighty-five years years ago, she too used to come out of the kitchen to carve each truffled chicken at the table.

We order the loup en croute feuilleté. The fish-shaped pastry coffin is etched with the detail of each scale and fin, and when it is cut into, its shiny, mahogany crust lets out a steamy sigh before the great fish is filleted in front of us with mesmerising skill and precision. The mousseline spiked with pistaches is laid alongside the fillets, the pastry shroud replaced respectfully, each leaf as light and crisp as autumn leaves in contrast to the firm, yet delicately fleshed fish and its slippery silk mousseline.

Bocuse still stands, in his eightieth year, like a Colossus, for a level of technique that defies fashion and is a yardstick for the more contemporaneous style of the younger generation like Têtedoie. I can't imagine ordering his loup en croute anywhere else in the world, and if I did, am sure that it would be a disappointment. Despite the dinosaur, fin de siècle feel of the place, the dish, and its rigorous, refined perfection was as original to me as had I been in El Bulli eating the nouvelle vague, laboratory-led cuisine of Ferran Adria. A master is, after all, always a master.

It is beginning to snow. We are heading towards Roanne where Hervé's affinage is situated, so that he and Rob can do some business before the final grande bouffe at La Maison Troisgros in the town. In this unremarkable French provincial backwater, la famille Troisgros have secured a place in French culinary history over three generations.

Our table at the restaurant has been secured, in the end, by Hervé.

When Jean-Baptiste and Marie Troisgros started in business in the 1930s, it was at the Café des Negotiants in Chalon sur Saône, where Marie cooked the great bourgeois French classics, tête de veau, soupe a l'oignon, coq au vin. They moved to Roanne, buying the hotel opposite the railway station and renaming it the Hôtel Moderne. By the 1950s it had a name as one of the best table d'hôtes in France.

The present La Maison Troisgros is on the corner of the same street as the old Hôtel Moderne, where, Hervé tells us, Jean-Baptiste became the first person in France to serve wine by the glass to his customers.

'He wanted the locals to be able to have a good glass of wine even if they were poor, stop off on their way home after work if they felt like it without feeling intimidated by the restaurant,' Hervé tells us. What a revelation that Jean-Baptiste's concept came about like this, here where we are sitting, and spread worldwide. It was also Jean-Baptiste who brought his sons out from the kitchen to meet their customers, another well-copied custom in the profession.

The day of reckoning happened on 15 March 1958. Pierre Troisgros' response to opening the new edition of the Michelin guide and finding that he and his brother Jean had been awarded a third star, has become part of the legend: 'C'est une catastrophe!'

Imagine the fear at joining the likes of Bocuse and the chic temples to gastronomy in Paris, when your restaurant is still a small, family-run business in Roanne.

Michel Troisgros, Pierre's son, is third generation. After the death of his uncle Jean, Michel returned to Roanne from serving his apprenticeship with some of the greats: Girardet, Taillevent, Guerard; at Chez Panisse and The Connaught, and joined his father until Pierre's retirement in 1993.

It is evident from the menu how much Troisgros the younger has been influenced by his travels in Japan and Asia, taking the nouvelle grande cuisine and the dishes that his grandmother was famous for by the scruff of the neck and reworking them with the sharp, bitter, acidulated, vinegary, citrussy notes that have become his signature. One of the dishes that has influenced him is the Troisgros brothers' famous escalope de saumon à l'oseille.

Michel's touch is light; pretty and witty and gay, with bonnes bouches such as his tomate cerise en carapace caramel au sesame, which arrives looking like a lolly on a stick and is an explosive, sweet-sour burst of heaven. The carapace is a crackle-coated sugary shell with a hint of sesame and ginger until the soft pulp of sharp tomato it is nursing within releases its acidity onto the palate.

My velours de fenouil aux langues d'oursins combines a plush velvet fennel cream, little tongues of sea urchin and a satin smooth fennel custard with tiny, intense shavings of raw fennel.

Rob's cèpes a la saltimbocca is whole, baby cèpes made sharp and salt with strips of prosciutto, fried sage and capers.

We have ordered the canette de Challans laquée, aigre-doux de mangue, pommes soufflées. The duck is carved under our noses, rare breast served with a paper cone filled with cloud-puffs of pommes soufflées that are soaringly brilliant and delicious. The legs are ushered in separately, unannounced, with a second helping of pommes soufflées, just when you are putting down your fork, wiping your mouth, like an impromptu second act that you feel impelled to stay for, full though you are. When Michel comes to the table to talk to us we have fought shy of pudding, but he promises me the cherry tomato recipe.

In the morning breakfast arrives. It is the tipping point. It is not only impossible to do it justice, it is only possible to do it an injustice. We know our well practised limitations and only rarely do we exceed them. And we are still full from last night's feast. I am reminded of the fat Russian couple we once watched sitting on the terrace eating breakfast on a trip to Jamaica, for whom the problem appeared not to exist. We may construe our gourmand-ising here as acceptable because the food is of a higher order, and it is all part of the job, but are we not deluding ourselves?

Looking back, I wonder, has the fat Russian wife conspired and joined her fatter husband on his quest for oblivion, believing her complicity is the only option, like the wife of a drunk appearing to condone his drunkenness by ignoring it? Does the one feed the other?

The Russian husband had ordered a plate of eggs Benedict, the hollandaise sauce slicked over the twin yolks and toasts in a sticky, buttercup bright ointment of emulsification that, one imagined, may have percolated through to his arteries a few hours later. He couldn't quite sit upright to attack them, rupturing the eggs from an awkward distance, his belly jutting from his chest into the table as it did, his well-upholstered wife fielding a plate piled with eggs and bacon and toast opposite him in a more minor act of accord and approval. The impossibly thin, lanky-limbed black waiter with high-set, taut cheek bones, delivered a further plate of 'eggs Benedict' which stood, like a lady in waiting, expectantly in the wings.

Having eaten the lot, he struggles from his chair, his fat fingered fist reaching for the fat cigar he has laid next to his series of now empty, yolk-stained plates. Is the next oral desire always within eye-shot? Is gluttony equally about visual gratification?

He tamps the thick stub of desire, lights it and wreathes the terrace in that peculiarly acrid yet seductive smoke, enveloping us all in his act of dissolution and excess.

Does our smug horror say as much about us as we toy with our papayas and banana bread? Are we complicit in this world where, to eat a three-star dinner at a temple to gastronomy reinforces our taste even in its one-off excess, yet to watch another plug food into themselves like a doomed man strapped to the electrodes is, like torture, only a step away in our new, obese world?

'Our sense of superiority is a reflection of our own fears,' Rob had said as we finished our fruit on the Caribbean terrace, and he left the last mouthfuls of oatmeal at the bottom of the bowl.

'Actually I feel more afraid than superior,' Rob continued, 'though we're just as contemptuous of people who don't ever give in to it but probably long to. I fear the gluttonous fat man inside me, but look at him, he has no guilt and he'll just eat until he keels over, and in a sense I feel a certain respect for the impunity with which he approaches it as I kind of do for anyone who gives full rein to his passions.'

There had been these small, restrained, yet impeccably well-balanced dishes delivered to our room at Troisgros for breakfast: a bowl of thick, home made yoghurt with a compote of apricots in tart syrup; a tasse of cold, loosely shirred eggs with a little liquid crest of green pistou running off it – how confident do you have to be to serve cold, creamy-rich folds of eggs in place of hot scrambled ones – a plate of pâtisserie, some seamed with kibbled nuts, sweet and pliant as you uncurled their brief coils, and small brioches with yeasty button tops. The best brewed coffee, the best squeezed orange juice, the only thing lacking, our joint appetites.

The breakfast returned to the kitchen almost untouched and we vowed to come back to Troisgros one day, have a light supper, stay the night and then really do it justice.

'The difference between us and them,' Rob says later, when I have had trouble deciding if there is one, 'is that the French eat for pleasure and everyone else eats for pain. That's the *real* French paradox. We beat ourselves up.'

'You mean it's not that they can eat all those Lyonnais potatoes cooked in lard without any deleterious effect, it's that they actually believe it's good for them?' I ask.

'They think it's good for them and we think it's bad for us. But you know what? If that obese Russian outlives us by thirty years the theory will be proved, but we won't be around, we'll have died first.'

Now that is unthinkable.

Asparagus, Broccoli Rabe and Goat's Cheese Salad

SERVES FOUR

Here is another inspired antidote to the riches of Lyon which is perfect for late Spring, when you are feeling green-starved and in need of iron and astringence in equal measure.

24–30 asparagus stems
extra virgin olive oil
AROUND 240G/½ LB broccoli rabe
*   or purple sprouting broccoli*
2 fennel bulbs stripped of their
*   tough outer leaves and sliced*
*   paper thin on a mandolin or by*
*   hand and squeeze a little lemon*
*   juice over the slices to prevent*
*   them from browning, turning*
*   them on the plate to coat*
JUICE OF UP TO 2 organic lemons
sea salt and black pepper
120–180G/4–6 OZ Le Chevrot or
*   goat's log like Ragstone or Golden*
*   Cross*
1 DSRTSP chopped savory

Break off the woody bottoms of the asparagus and then brush a griddle or the base of a heavy-bottomed frying pan with olive oil. When it is hot put in the asparagus spears and cook for a few minutes before turning with a pair of tongs. Continue to cook until each spear is cooked through to just tender when the base is pierced with a skewer, removing the spears one by one to a plate as they are ready.

Meanwhile steam the broccoli until al dente.

Slice the goat's cheese or crumble it, your call.

Throw the vegetables, cooked and raw, into a large serving bowl and dress while warm with olive oil and lemon juice.

Season with Maldon salt and a good scrunch of pepper. Throw the goat's cheese over the salad and sprinkle the savory over the top.

Serve at a bare warmth.

Thai Beef Salad

This is a sort of perverse antidote to the richness, the surf 'n' turf 'n' cream 'n' butter of Lyon. It will zing all tired taste buds awake instantly.

4 × 180G/6OZ or so rump steaks, but let your appetites dictate the size

Season the steaks with sea salt when you take them out of the fridge, an hour before you cook them. Brush the griddle with olive oil before you heat it. Griddle the steaks so that they are charred but rare, even if you don't like rare meat, as they will then 'cook' in the sauce overnight in the fridge. Slice thickly when still hot.

For the sauce:
3 CLOVES garlic, peeled and crushed to a paste with a little sea salt
4 TBSP hoisin sauce
1 TBSP hot chili sauce or paste or to taste
4 TBSP mirin
1 TBSP toasted sesame oil
2 CM/1 IN grated root ginger
1 SMALL finely minced onion
2 TBSP sesame seeds
1 TBSP fresh lime juice

Mix this sauce up in a bowl stirring all the ingredients together, then drop the warm slices of steak into it, decant the whole lot into a ziploc bag and put it in the fridge overnight. Bring back to room temperature to serve the following day with salad greens under the sliced meat that you have dressed with the following dressing:

3 TBSP fresh lime juice
2 TBSP soy sauce
2 TBSP runny honey
1 TBSP rice vinegar
1½ tsp mirin
1½ TSP grated ginger root
½ TSP toasted sesame oil
4 TBSP extra virgin olive oil
2 TBSP washed and dried coriander leaves tossed into the salad leaves

9

The Twelve Pins Club

'You lot set off with your marathon stride leaving Nick and me behind …' Rob warns, '… him *shvitzing*, me wondering if I'm about to have a heart attack. I have a torn meniscus, Nick has a twisted kneecap and wears completely unsuitable shoes. We are both praying the weather will call the whole thing off so we can get down to the main event which is eating and drinking.'

The duck breast is speared to the skewer on one of those hooks children draw to play hangman. It is dripping blood, as are the neck, heart and liver, onto the pile of pommes Dauphinoise below. There is a braised endive and a tomate farcie to the side.

This is duck country, where rillettes, confit de canard, foie gras, haricots Tarbais and garbure Gasconne, the famous local cabbage soup, rule the roost.

The Twelve Pins Club are sitting in La Petite Auberge in the square of the small village of Marciac, each attacking their brochette on its metal hook with the sense of entitlement that Brits tend to bring to the table when they feel justified at their excess. We have climbed high in the Pyrénées for upwards of five hours, now we will reward ourselves.

This is our first trip to Michael and Ruth's new house in Gascony. Up until now, The Twelve Pins Club has met each summer over the August Bank Holiday weekend at my house in County Mayo on the west coast of Ireland, for our annual attempt at climbing one or more peaks of the eponymous range of mountains that straddle the middle distant view the far side of Killary Bay in Connemara.

When my publisher, Michael Dover, had told us the previous summer that he and Ruth had bought a wrecky old château in duck country and that he was inviting us all to come and climb in the nearby Pyrénées the following April, we started making plans.

Michael is Irish and has the gentle, straw blond good looks, manner and manners that win in every situation. There is a ferrous edge to him, though; he may sit at a desk all day, but stand him up with a map and compass and he will yomp Olympian distances at Appachean speed, route marching his troops with effortless skill and insouciance. His directions to the ruinous house and army style map reading and tactical manoeuvring that have seen all of us reach high into the snow-line near the crest of the last of the Pyrénées before you hit Spain, and enjoy the strange, ear piercing screeches and game playing of the first black and white striped marmottes we have ever clapped eyes on, have impressed all the Twelve Pins Club members bar one.

'You think it's fun, we think it's torture,' Rob had said, making sure to discriminate between the madness of the British competitive spirit and the sanity of the Americans who see gyms and treadmills as far superior to Wellington boots and the great outdoors.

I was just pleased to know Rob had agreed to come. When I came up with the Twelve Pins idea originally and before it became an annual event, I was post marriage and pre-Rob and sometimes felt like I had a great alternative career as a seaside landlady, getting people together, feeding them sumptuously, introducing them to each other and to the beauties and wildness of the west but, as the only half without another half, never quite having the experience they were all having.

Since I had met Rob all that had changed, but I had something else I hadn't bargained for, his 'kvetching' (his terminology, not mine).

'Why do you come and then complain about it?' I ask, signally failing to grasp the point of 'kvetching' or imagining that it might actually make him feel better.

'If I'm going to suffer, you're going to suffer too,' he says by way of explanation.

'It's verbal therapy. This is all bullshit and you're all out of your minds, it's a New York thing, not a Jewish thing.'

'You mean you'd never admit you're enjoying it?' I say,

beginning to think I understand.

'Never!'

What's more, Rob believes he is entirely justified in doing what no Brit would ever do: question the sanity of what we are about to do and whether we are fit for it.

'What's the point?' Rob began as we started the upwards assault. 'I'm forced on this ridiculous trek by a bunch of over-enthusiastic Brits who think they're demi-gods trying to capture the glory days of the Empire, but it all comes down to a pretence. Why do none of you admit that it's really just an excuse to over-eat? As it is, nobody understands my whingeing.'

Not quite true. Ruth, Michael's wife and a highly respected consultant radiologist, had listened persuasively when Rob had asked her, almost as he breasted the first slope, to listen to his racing pulse since he believed he was about to have a cardiac arrest.

There is no one I know who has the gift of calm like Ruth does. She listens, offers a quizzical look, a disbelieving smile and her deceptively quiet yet firm tones are un-negotiable.

'Your pulse is absolutely normal for someone of your age who has just exerted themselves a little.'

Cared for and decisively dismissed in one, it's an art form perfected by the British medical profession.

Rob took a bite of the splendid sandwiches Susan and I had made — black Russian rye bread made with a trace of coffee, caraway seed and dark chocolate and filled with lashings of wild smoked salmon and cream cheese — and continued to doubt the sanity of our mission: 'I wouldn't even consider going on one of these treks if there weren't a doctor on them,' he remonstrated.

Underplaying his fitness and his competitive spirit doesn't fool us. We know he will get to the top even if he isn't first to plant the flag, spurred on by the home-grown therapy of complaint which is enough to make the rest of us feel all the better about ourselves and our efforts. I think he does it on purpose.

The trip has been hardest on Nick and Susan. Nick Welsh was my son Harry's tutor at Eton, and he and his wife Sal have become great family friends. Nick's idea of exercise is wobbling down Eton High Street on his sit up and beg bike with a pile of books under his arm and in his bicycle basket, and he is not under-endowed in the weight department. What he brings to the table is a world-class appetite, a lifetime of exceptional story-telling, and a wisdom and bonhomie that endear him to just about everyone he meets. But he is not fit.

'You lot set off with your marathon stride leaving Nick and me behind…' Rob warns, '…him *shvitzing* (perspiring) me wondering if I'm about to have a heart attack. I have a torn meniscus, Nick has a twisted kneecap and wears completely unsuitable shoes. We are both praying the weather will call the whole thing off so we can get down to the main event which is eating and drinking.'

In fact Rob is a veteran of the gym and a founder member of the personal trainer brigade, taut calved, muscular, and a one-time captain of his 'school swim team', and he actually '…enjoys lagging behind with Nick. Nobody carries on a conversation better than an Eton school master and I can count on the fact he's in a worse position than me.'

Susan Haynes, my Australian editor, was a gung-ho queen of the outback in her past life, and jogged solidly and uneventfully for 20 minutes a day over 20 years. She shamed me into coming out from behind my desk and putting on my running shoes, though up to that point I had thought the activity quite ridiculous and only carried out by deluded morons who believed it would cosmetically enhance their sagging bottoms. While my innate competitiveness resulted in three London Marathons — what is the point of running nowhere for no good reason — Susan's virtuous existence was finally rewarded with a gammy hip which has begun to give her considerable gyp, not that she will discuss it and which she is clearly trying to ignore until the surgeon's knife is inevitable and firmly planted in her well-honed and exercised buttocks.

'Susan's hip is just the beginning,' Rob says ominously, imply-ing future casualties and catastrophes amongst the Twelve Pins brotherhood that can only be guessed at.

We also discovered on our very first climb, the assault of a brace of Pins, that Susan is an even more unlikely candidate for a wining, dining and climbing club than Rob or Nick. She suffers from terminal vertigo. Naturally she hadn't told anyone that either. Indeed, if it hadn't been for John K, my mussel fisherman friend, talking her up and quietly keeping her focused on the ledge above rather than the abyss below, we would probably have had to blindfold her and stretcher her off mid panic attack. It just goes to show that the stiff upper lip that Rob has branded all Brits with also made its way Down Under and became as firmly embedded in the Ozzie psyche as it did in ours.

The emigrant eastern European Jewish American psyche, well that's another matter, and I'm not sure I'm in a position to generalise, though I know it has something to do with being prepared to pay for an intermediary once you can afford to if you have the will but not the willpower. Rob has a string of them all helping to keep him fit, trainers and Pilates teachers, masseurs and physical therapists, who we look down our noses at, whilst secretly suspecting that he will have the last laugh.

I put some of it down to the pursuit of youth that seems to

have strayed off course from its Hollywood home and hit the East Coast with the unplanned vengeance of a hurricane. In LA it's practically illegal to be over 35 and if you're not surgically enhanced and physically frightening, you're invisible.

However, Rob admits to 'seething anger' at the fact that he knows he's lost it and will compare himself endlessly to our physically fit teenagers who leap up mountains without a pause for breath. Harry, only the year before, had made the top of Mweelrea, whose granite peak rises shale strewn from its bare saddle behind my Mayo house, is sheer for most of its 360 degrees and subject to sudden and impenetrable cloud cover, in under an hour and then raced back down it and across the bog home. I think my record is three and a half hours up and back to his one and a half hours.

'English kids are just not like American kids,' Rob declared. 'Regardless of their boarding schools and universities and the terrible school food they've all been brought up on, they're all candidates for the élite forces. In the US all their thoughts would be given to avoiding this sort of weekend at all costs. It's easy to see why our empire might be in decline, but harder to see why you lost yours at all, given the standards you've maintained for generations. And it's more difficult to keep up with the kids each year.'

He's right there, but I'd never let him know it.

This last bon mot pierces the soul with the kind of honesty that most of we members are much keener to avoid or at least ignore. We hare after the teenagers, like shadows in their slipstream, convincing ourselves that our brief stops to admire the view – the kids don't even glance backwards over their shoulders – are really just that, to admire the view. They are certainly not to catch our breaths and get our second and third and even fourth wind.

So the leisurely duck dinner has been the high point for some of us greedy guzzlers, higher even than the snow lined peaks and crevasses we've just traversed in the Pyrénées, returning via a tortuously narrow ledge of path that Michael had somehow forgotten to allude to during his briefing of the troops, which was roofed by great rapiers of dripping icicles. The weekend has been a triumph, the house is wonderful, we can all see its potential.

I had also seen that Rob had been shocked to arrive in the dark and find the house still a building site. Indeed, he caught the foreman pissing in the yard the following morning.

'It sure ain't the Hamptons,' he had said, adding: 'You could kill yourself on the staircase.'

There are no banisters and several holes where stairs should be. The kitchen hasn't been built yet and though there is a cooker, it hasn't been connected. At one stage Ruth started telling us about a friend's recipe for 'a delicious Martini omelette made with mayonnaise', which went no way to convincing Rob of her culinary credentials. The bedrooms have beds but no curtains, furniture or doors, so the privacy element is somewhat compromised. The bathrooms have loos and showers which have been plumbed in but not fixed to the walls.

'I'm thinking, let me know when it's finished and I'll be back,' Rob comments.

I am thrilled. It means my usual role as kitchen commandant is supererogatory and I can relax, we can barbecue in the field and eat out at the local restaurants. The Dover priorities have been to build the swimming pool first, so we can swim and lie in the sun and stick our glasses under the multiple bottle-necks of champagne, white wine and beer that Michael is constantly producing.

In bed on that last night, after the duck dinner, the begrudger summed things up in a wholly uncharacteristic way. It was almost as though he had had a revelation. 'I guess it's really all about the people.'

Brilliant. It means he'll come back next year. That he might stop complaining about the damp and rain and lack of Irish sun for long enough to walk the headland and the strands, swim naked in the waterfall, climb a mountain or two and enjoy the great spirit of middle-aged adventure that we Twelve Pinners are intent on carrying on for as long as our pins will carry us.

The following year we re-grouped in early summer in Gascony. Now there is a flight to Toulouse from Bristol, Rob and I can get to Duck Town with greater ease and speed. Michael and Ruth's son Linden has arrived with some university friends, otherwise the cast remains as before.

The house has become a home over the course of the year, though the workmen are still ensconced. The kitchen is up and running and we can close the bedroom door on our fellow club members and our shutters on the light. The early June sun has warmed the pool and we can sit out for breakfast and drinks in the evening, looking out over the gentle, mature treed pasture land and the woods beyond.

On the day of the climb, Rob has spotted further signs of weakness in the élite forces almost before we leave base camp. Susan's hip is considerably worse and she is limping and Nick is looking heavier and less fit even than last year. He is dabbing at his damp face with a handkerchief almost before the off. Sal will keep pace with him alongside Rob and Susan.

Michael and I strike out with the Edinburgh boys, determined we can match their pace and stamina.

'Michael's delusion is that he's the same at 57 as he was at 37 and will continue to be at 97,' Rob said, after the event.

'He will refuse to believe anything's changed at all, and if he's slower it'll be because the path was muddy. Ruth is the only person with no delusions, she's the only sensible one who knows her limits.'

I always wonder whether anyone knows their limits until they test them, and maybe that's half the battle, wanting to test them in the first place, though I do concede that Michael's and my competitive spirit does share certain similarities. It knows no limits.

Eventually the lads — Linden is actually about to enlist in the army so is in peak condition — stop at a panoramic and shockingly high edge where we wait for the others to catch up with us. The ascent has been such that my legs have that involuntary tremble that I only ever experience when Jean Christian, my ski guide, has sadistically forced me down a piste noire at breakneck speed and I think I have lost control.

The boys start swinging from a branch on the tree above us, effortlessly doing push-ups that casually but obviously draw attention to their virility and youth. Rob decides to have a go. I suppose I should have stopped him, but there is nothing worse for the vanity of the middle-aged male ego than being bossily told 'don't do it' by the female who you are really showing it off to. I wanted Rob to be up there with the boys, the envy of the other oldsters, pumping iron up a Pyrénéan tree.

Linden and his cohorts lifted Rob up so that he could grasp the branch. He raised himself up like a gymnast. And then he fell out of the tree and onto his back, in the sort of slow motion that we have come to expect, where you just stare in disbelief unable to move or help.

'It all came crashing down for me when I tried to do that pull-up on the tree in the Pyrénées and fell on my arse,' he said some time later.

'It was the official moment when I knew I was getting older.'

'And you blamed me for not trying to stop you,' I said.

'Absolutely. If you gave a shit about me you'd never have let them hoist me up.'

'You wouldn't have listened to me anyway.'

'I noticed you failed to extend any sympathy. Thank God Ruth was there.'

Thank God indeed.

That night we headed back to Marciac to La Petite Auberge, Rob sore, Susan sorer — she had had to abandon the climb and wait for us by a stream with the picnic.

Have you noticed how impossible it is to recapture the perfect experience, although one always forgets and tries?

Rob and I had fantasised for a year about going back to La Petite Auberge. The restaurant was filled with a coach party when we arrived, and our lovely outside table of last year looking out onto the market square was already taken. The coach party would certainly not be volunteering any new members for the Twelve Pins Club, they were a party of French pensioners heading back to Normandy who filled two long trestle tables in the back room where we were seated, at the third.

The service was painfully slow. The garbure Gasconne had been simmering for so long that the cabbage resembled boiled bedclothes. La brochette Gasconne, the hangman's duck arrived, the speciality of the house, but this year the thick, bloody tranche of breast that should have been sopping the potatoes was over-cooked and the fat had begun to congeal and drip instead. The vegetables were over-cooked and weary.

Quite soon, and several bottles later, our sense of

disappointment degenerated into speculation. If we had to have sex with one of the septuagenarian coach party, which one would it be?

There was one white haired old ram flirting brazenly with two elderly ladies; he had clearly not lost the charm or the inclination. Ruth and I said we'd both pick him. Rob picked a jolly but tooth-less lady for, as he put it, 'obvious reasons'. Nick looked shocked and refused to participate. Sal and Michael looked at us as though we were mad. That just made Ruth and I laugh all the more uncontrollably. Susan played the cards of life as close to her chest as ever and didn't reveal who her beau would be. Ruth and I caught our stud's eye and he appeared none too surprised that we were looking at him, clearly ladies had been admiring him for many a year. And then he did something shocking. He got up from the table and headed over towards us, introduced himself to Ruth and me and informed us that there was another two hours before the bus departed for Normandy, if Rob and Michael had no objection. What lovely young ladies we were. We declined. We shook hands and he went back to his table.

Another memorable night at La Petite Auberge.

Last summer we met up for the August Bank Holiday weekend again at my house in Mayo. The boat over to Inis Turk bucked the Atlantic breakers like a bath tub in a storm. Nick not only looked scared to death, he was green as jade almost before we left the harbour at Roonagh. We were somewhat diminished in numbers, with Susan crying off because she was finally awaiting a new hip, and my old Irish friends Merci and John K, bereft at the recent loss of her brother John, unable to come. The seven remaining Twelve Pinners were headed off to this remote island of only seventy something inhabitants, six miles off the Mayo coast, since once again the mountains were obscured by low cloud.

As the waves slooshed over the deck, some of us sheltered inside the small ferry's cabin while the rest of us hung off the doorway inhaling the ozone. Nick was leaning right over the deck railings in hideous communion with the remains of his lunch, alternately coming up for air, spray, and to close and squinch his eyes heavenwards to pray for it all to end. Sal, as ever, was at his side.

Once on the island we headed in convoy in the floorless car-wrecks that had arrived to take us up the hill to Paddy and Ann O'Toole's b and b. Nick didn't make the short journey up the island's single-track road without incident either.

Far from eschewing dinner, after a brief nap, Nick pronounced himself restored and ready to join us at the table. He did full justice to the three-course dinner, but it didn't seem to do the trick. He retired back to bed while the rest of us walked down to the local community centre to hear the Irish singer Sean Keane, who comes in to the island once a year from Galway, and to dance sets until well into the early hours.

In the morning, with the males of the party fuelled by Ann's full fry, complete with a checkerboard of black and white pudding, we set off to walk the island.

'Have you noticed how the degree of difficulty in each successive year is in inverse proportion to the relish with which we attack our pre- and post-hike meals and the quantity we put on our plate?' Rob asks. 'The less exercise, the greater the pleasure of the table. In fact we are all only taking exercise so we can eat more, except Ruth,' he adds, 'who wouldn't know decent food anyway.'

Martini and mayonnaise omelettes notwithstanding, Ruth is ruthlessly ascetic and consistent in her habits, exercises seriously, is fit, trim and stunning, and appears immune or resistant to the pangs of hunger the rest of us satisfy at lunch-time.

We battle the great sea breeze coming straight at us like a quarter-back off the Atlantic and head for the farthest peak on the island where the gulls wheel in the cliffs below us, circling and steadying themselves on the great, spooling currents, and beyond, like the end of the world, is just water all the way to America.

It may not be a mountain, but this remote, elemental place nourishes the soul; seems part of a more ancient civilization, yet away from civilization in a way that so few places in the world still are. Seems more remote to me than our climbs in the Pyrénées. We walk an entire circuit of the island before stopping at the little harbour café, where we consume a great platter of home made soda bread sandwiches.

Ruth and Michael branch off to look at the graveyard. Nick, Sal and Rob follow Charissa and me down to the island beach. The water is always colder this far from the mainland and the currents tug with a hideous stealth, sweeping one away from the beach and out into the open sea. Charissa and I plunge straight in, she unmoved by the cold and as at home in the water as Rob. He comes in cursing us, cursing the cold, swimming straight out ahead with powerful, carving strokes.

'I can't stand how after a three-hour hike we have to walk down a cliff and plunge into *ice* cold water in the middle of the Atlantic. It's suitable for whales, spiny lobsters and mackerel,' he says, shivering yet thrilled that we, the hardy three, have knocked spots off the others, the wimps.

Funny that he should be one of the three to do it, though; that he is always game, whatever the challenge, and always comes back to tell the tale, in comic form, having experienced it first-hand.

His willingness has something to do, Rob believes, with the fact that the Americans have lost all their rituals, while we, the Brits, still have them. And that we need modern rituals to anchor ourselves to when the old ones die.

On the ferry home the swell is with us, the giant rollers outpacing us as they sweep relentlessly to the mainland. Michael and Nick stand close on the faintly listing deck in apparently unbreakable, mutual concentration. Michael doesn't say a word, just nods occasionally. Nick appears to be giving an impromptu, non-stop lecture. Once on shore, it emerges that Michael's plan to scotch Nick's sea sickness had been to get him to keep his eye on a fixed point whilst concentrating on telling a story. Nick had described the plot, scene by scene, act by act, of *Twelfth Night* which he is preparing to teach as a set text at Eton the following term, and made it to the shore.

We celebrate our latest escapades with a sirloin of beef I have cooked on the bone with the undercut, the fillet, accompanied by all the tracklements and trimmings and followed by a blackberry, blueberry and raspberry cobbler, the fruit bleeding stickily into the sweet, scone top and tattooing its edges purple. After dinner, Rob and Sal play their guitars and we all sing as the turf fire smoulders and Michael's case of Rioja is steadily drained.

'The truth is,' Rob muses in bed that night, replete with good food, good wine and good company and all the better for being safely back on terra firma, 'each expedition is considered a success if a) everyone survived, b) there are no permanent injuries, c) the dinner is up to snuff, d) there is a sufficient quantity of good wine, e) the music is good. It's not a failure even if one of the party has vomited over a boat deck several times, eaten dinner, vomited again, had a sleepless night, eaten the full fry and walked Inis Turk before the event dinner.'

He's absolutely right. And has also made us all aware that, no matter quite how we airbrush or magnify our infirmities, the indomitable spirit and determination of The Twelve Pins Club looks like it will see us up a few more peaks, through a few more dazzlingly good dinners, over the hill and into our declining years and remain, as Rob said in Gascony, 'all about the people'.

Garbure Gasconne

SERVES SIX

From the word 'garbe' meaning a sheaf or bunch, in this case of vegetables – potato, cabbage, thyme, garlic, parsley, marjoram, beans – this hefty, peasant soup normally has chunks of bread dunked in it, browned in the oven first, or sliced and cooked in the stockpot in a little duck fat.

In Gascony we have it before the duck dinner, pigs that we are, a great cauldron of it brought to and left at the table. The danger is in letting the cabbage simmer for too long and almost bio-degrade. If you can't get the haricots Tarbais that are a speciality of Gascony, use ordinary dried haricot beans.

225G/8OZ dried Tarbais or haricots beans, soaked overnight and drained

1.5 LITRES/3 PINTS water or duck stock

3 MEDIUM potatoes, peeled and thickly sliced

A FEW SPRIGS each of thyme, parsley and marjoram

6 CLOVES garlic, peeled

½ A SMALL HEAD of cabbage, the leaves cut away from the thick ribs and core, and roughly cut, not shredded

A FEW SLICES of bread baked in the oven or bread spread with a little duck fat

ANY left over meaty shreds of duck to include liver, heart and neck if you want to make the soup a little meaty

sea salt and black pepper

Cover the beans with cold water in a large, heavy-bottomed earthenware or enamel pot, to come just above the level of the beans, bring to the boil, and cook for 40 minutes or until the beans are resistant and need another 30 minutes or so. Add another pint or so of stock or water and bring to the boil before throwing in the slices of potato, herbs, garlic and cabbage, turning down to a simmer and putting a lid on the pot.

After 25 minutes, season, throw in the cooked duck bits and the bread and leave to simmer with the lid on for another 5 minutes.

Serve straight from the pot.

Roast Duck with a Wheatberry, Sour Cherry and Sage Salad

SERVES SIX

Aside from the gorgeous snowy duck fat to cook your roast potatoes in for months to come, I always try to find side dishes to accompany roast duck that act like blotting paper and sharpeners to the grease. Back from the bouchons of Lyon to the Sullivan Street kitchen in New York, where Rob's friend Greg and I cooked this dazzling duck dinner one night.

Preheat oven to 210°C/425°F/ GAS 8

2 organic, free-range ducks
2 onions
1 orange
sea salt and black pepper

For the salad:
225G/8OZ wheatberries
110G/4OZ dried sour cherries
A BUNCH of spring onions
6–8 sage leaves
A SMALL BUNCH of parsley
55G/2OZ flaked almonds
ZEST of the orange used to stuff the duck
extra virgin olive oil

JUICE OF 1–2 organic lemons
sea salt and black pepper

Peel and slice 1 onion and put it on the bottom of the roasting tin. Peel and quarter the other onion.

Zest the orange and keep the zest on a plate for the salad. Quarter the orange and stuff it alternately with the onion into the two birds' cavities. Place the birds breast up on top of the onions and season before putting them into the very hot oven.

After 30 minutes drain off the fat and gently prick the breast and plump part of the legs with a sharp skewer. Turn the heat down to 200°C/400°F/GAS 6 and continue to cook.

Drain off the fat after a further 30 minutes, if you don't, it will blacken and smoke out your kitchen. Put all the fat into a bowl to cool for the fridge later.

The ducks will take 1–1¼ hours to cook, the juices should run pinkish not red when the fat part of the leg is pierced with a skewer. Remove from the oven and rest for 20 minutes.

Boil the wheatberries until cooked. They have quite a firm texture even when cooked. While they are cooking, roughly chop the sour cherries and roll up the sage leaves and slice them into slim ribbons. Chop the parsley and the spring onions. Toast the flaked almonds briefly until their edges are tinged mid-brown. This will take three or four minutes, they turn very quickly. Drain the wheatberries and toss in all the ingredients when still hot. Pour on a few tablespoons of good olive oil and squeeze over the juice of a lemon. Season. Toss and taste and adjust the seasoning, adding more olive oil and lemon juice if needed.

Now add the meat juices from the carving board where the birds have been resting.

Carve the breasts and legs and place them on top of the salad which you have heaped onto a large serving dish. Sprinkle over the orange zest and serve.

Yoghurt, Almond and Lemon Cake with Pralinéed Nuts on top

A post-duck sharpener, with lots of zesty citrus intensity. Sticky, gooey crunch on sharp apricot jam; underneath a dense, zesty, moist sponge. Just make a compote of apricots or berries to sit alongside it, and you have a perfect pudding cake.

Preheat oven to 175°C/350°F/ GAS 4

1 SMALL CARTON of sheep's yoghurt
110G/4OZ blanched Marcona almonds, toasted until pale gold in the oven
225G/8OZ plain flour
1 ½ TSP baking powder
pinch of sea salt
110G/4OZ unsalted butter
140G/5OZ unrefined sugar
4 organic eggs, separated
3 TBSP grated lemon zest from organic lemons
2 TBSP unrefined caster sugar

For the topping:
½ POT best apricot jam
100G/3 1/2OZ unrefined caster sugar
85G/3OZ blanched Marcona almonds

Strain the yogurt for 30–40 minutes in a muslin-lined sieve. Grease and line a 23cm/9in Springform tin.

When you've toasted the almonds, blitz them to a crumb in the Magimix, keeping them a tiny bit on the coarse side for texture, if you over-do it they'll turn oily. Sift the flour, baking powder and salt together into a bowl. Add the ground nuts and stir together.

Cream the butter and sugar together in the Kitchen Aid until light and creamy. Add the strained yoghurt and beat until smooth.

Add the egg yolks one at a time. Fold in the lemon zest. Add the flour and fold together.

Beat the egg whites to stiff peak before adding a tablespoon of caster sugar, beating again, adding the second spoonful of sugar and beating to satiny peaks. Fold briefly and gently into the cake and scrape the mixture into the prepared cake tin.

Bake for about 50–60 minutes or until a skewer comes out clean. Remove to a rack to cool in the tin.

Meanwhile, pralinee the nuts by putting them in a non-stick pan with the sugar and heating them together until the sugar melts then turns the colour of bubbling mahogany.

Remove from the heat before it burns and pour onto a greased baking tray to cool in a molten cluster. Then break it up into chunky shards and a bit of crumb with any hard-core implement like a rolling pin.

When the cake has cooled to just warm, melt the apricot jam in a small pan and pour it over the top of the cake, smoothing it across with a rubber spatula. Decorate with the pralinéed nuts and serve with creme fraiche.

10

Braving Broadway

It seems extraordinary that the small, shy boy she had met all those years ago is utterly unintimidated about talking stagecraft with the screen legend who is, after all, just one of his mother's friends to him. And she, in her turn, is as eager to discuss the problems of going on stage and how she has faced them ...

It is a big week on Broadway. Julia Roberts is opening in *Three Days of Rain* at the Jacobs Theater and Harry is singing a solo at the Lincoln Center's Alice Tully Hall in the finals of the international collegiate a capella championships.

I am rooting for both of them.

A month earlier, on the afternoon of Julia's first preview, Rob and I had taken a taxi uptown to the theatre where she had told us to ask for Gay at the stage door. Gay is as solid as a steel girder, tank-shouldered, black and guards Julia with a scrupulous and watchful charm that could disarm at twenty paces, unusual in his profession. I have come armed with a copy of *Tamasin's Kitchen Bible.* Julia loves to cook.

We followed Gay backstage, tiptoeing through the wings and down into the dark auditorium. Julia had told me to be there at 3.30 pm, when she thought they would take a break after their first run-through. The play was to start previewing that night, but on the telephone she hadn't betrayed the slightest sign of what she must have been feeling, knowing that the butchers of Broadway had been sharpening their nibs like arrows and probably dunking them in curare too in anticipation.

This time she has taken on the biggest challenge of all. It's not that she can sneak her first stage performance in off-off Broadway and learn her craft away from the headlines. No, *Three Days of Rain* will pour column inches and be the most hyped Broadway opening of the year with the biggest advance box-office and ticket price: because Julia is daring to set foot on stage.

Rob is nervous about meeting her, I can feel it as we watch her at work, wondering, perhaps, as he watches, how she can appear to go about her business in such an apparently casual way, with an old friend sitting in the auditorium waiting to catch up on a year's gossip and only four hours to first curtain-up.

Upstairs in her dressing room, we hug excitedly for so long that I almost forget the most important introduction. Julia instantly gives Rob a huge hug and a kiss and I am reminded of years back, Harry a small boy, her coming to stay in Somerset, arriving and bounding up to him to ask him for a kiss.

'Actually there's only three people allowed to kiss me,' he says gravely, with the almost lisp he had back then. 'Mama, Gladys my nanny and my godmother Mart.'

Julia, not used to being turned down so blatantly by the opposite sex, laughs her inimitable laugh, the most infectious laugh I know.

'But I suppose you can, just one kiss, on my cheek,' Harry continues, barely missing a beat as he proffers it.

'Gee Harry, I feel like I've just won the Olympics,' she says, quick as a flash, when the deed has been done.

So Julia and Rob have finally met, but I still have to meet Danny and the babies. We fix a date for when I return to New York, the day after Rob and I have tickets for *Three Days of Rain*.

A month later, and the atmosphere in the auditorium is unlike any I have ever experienced. One lady gasps with shock when Julia comes on and audibly stage whispers, 'Oh my God, it's really her.' She looks like a case for smelling salts and bodice-ripping. In the interval they stand in the stalls, men as well as women, hugging their mobiles to their ears to tell their friends where they are, tell husbands and wives what she is *really* like in the flesh.

At the end of the performance Julia comes on and flashes her mega-watt beam at a man far to our right in the stalls who we had already clocked as the one most likely to be her father-in-law, mouthing 'Happy birthday' to him. We find Gay, who whisks us through a secret door, into the wings and upstairs to Julia's dressing room.

'I was so nervous with you in the audience,' she tells me excitedly, the adrenalin from the performance still high octane, and: 'I heard your laugh.'

It isn't what you expect to hear, and yet when she says it, you know she means it. It's no easier for Julia to perform knowing her friends are in the audience than it is for any other actor.

'It all went wrong the first time Danny came and I'd so wanted him to be proud of me, but the whole thing fell apart, we all lost it.'

To say that Julia's greatest strength is in her essential honesty and vulnerability is only a part of it. The warmth that burns through the screen is no less true in real life, and somehow, though God knows how, she has retained a sense of what is normal; lives as normally as her circumstances will allow, keeping the old friends whose lives she blends into seamlessly, at least finding a little of the normalcy there that she isn't always granted.

Tonight she is going on to a birthday dinner with her father-in-law and Danny, tomorrow we are all going to meet for tea at her apartment before the evening performance.

Naturally I bake a cake and Rob brings cheese. It is one of my dark chocolate cakes made damp with almonds rather than flour and spiked with a hit of espresso. I carry it to the apartment in the tin so that it doesn't collapse on the journey.

When we arrive, the babies are sitting in adjoining high-chairs in the kitchen eating a chicken casserole which Julia has sitting simmering on the stove. They are picking out little jewels of carrot and courgette and chicken, very precisely, one by one, from their tray tops to eat in their fingers. Hazel has the palest skin and huge saucers of watchful, china blue eyes fringed with long lashes, her little face framed by wispy blonde hair. She is just like a Victorian doll. Finn has copper locks, green eyes and the more fleshy, boyish, humorous face of a real little bruiser.

Rob and I meet Danny who takes the cake saying, 'I've heard so much about you, wow, this looks amazing, I love chocolate. Julia says you're a fantastic cook.'

Meanwhile, Hazel decides that enough is enough. Having seen her mother unwrap some of the cheese we have brought, she throws out her arms and shouts, 'Chee.'

I cut her a little finger of Hoch Ybrig, a delicious cow's milk Gruyère bathed in white wine and named after a Swiss mountain. A pretty sophisticated cheese. The finger disappears rapidly and Hazel throws a hand out dramatically crying, 'Chee, chee,' again.

I give her several more fingers before the babies get down, with Julia saying firmly, 'Do your chores,' at which the little tots go off obediently to put things in the bin before they start running hectically round the room with their toy strollers. Danny cuts the cake and we tuck in, though Julia is already withdrawing, beginning to focus and make ready for tonight's performance and leaves hers for later.

We watch the babies' bath-time, Finn corkscrewing crazily around like a slippery dolphin, his copper head going under and emerging with a surprised, joker's grin each time he comes back up for air. Then Julia heads back to the theatre and we say our goodbyes.

The next night Harry and the Out of the Blue boys fly in. He is only 10 days away from finals, so, as usual, is cutting things finer than cheese wire.

We invite the boys over for a New York brunch late on

Saturday morning, knowing they won't be able to face eating any later in the day, any closer to tonight's ordeal. They steam through bowls of home made granola and on through another three courses. I fry dozens of rashers of Niman Ranch bacon until they're snapping crisp, and break the eggs into shuddering water to poach. I've made bundles of griddled asparagus glossed in olive oil and aged balsamic. I toast repeated short orders of raisin and walnut bread. We've bought legions of 'snails', coiled, sticky pastries smattered with currants and apricots from the Granddaisy Bakery on Sullivan Street and we pump coffee and fresh orange juice into the boys before giving them a final shot of vitamins, a huge fresh fruit salad of pineapple, mangoes and bananas. They eat like predators, with the watchful, nervous energy that spells preparing for the kill.

'God, I wish it was tomorrow,' one says. 'I'd have done it far more justice once it was all over.'

They head off to spend the afternoon rehearsing and brushing up their choreography in Central Park.

That evening I am beginning to feel sick with nerves too. The trajectory from zero to Harry's Lincoln Center debut seems like a dream. I cook Catalan Chicken, rattes baked with ramps and thyme in olive oil and Green Market pousse with a spritz of lemon and a knob of butter. Chopping and peeling, watching and stirring, the calming rhythms of the kitchen soothe for as long as I perform them. Andy Reiss, a painter friend of Rob's and his girl- friend Cindy come over and join us for supper. I can barely eat.

The Lincoln Center is full. An audience of nearly 1,500. There are twelve groups in the finals, all American bar our Oxford boys, and each has twelve minutes to sing three songs.

When Harry comes on to sing his Coldplay solo, *Fix You*, I am almost breaking Rob and Andy's fingers on either side of me.

The high notes dance on the air, chip at the heart, hold the breath, still the auditorium.

'Best solo goes to…' then best choreography, fifth place, fourth place: the announcements send the hope soaring and falling again… they didn't expect to get anywhere… it's a fix… the judges are mostly American… we're the outsiders… 'And in third place…' …they are the unknown group, they won't give the Brits anything first time out… 'And the runners up, all the way from Oxford England (don't you love that, Oxford where else?) Out of the Blue.' We stand and scream. Shred our vocal chords. The boys are in shock. The group they had mentally placed first have indeed come first. Outside, an unknown woman comes up to me and says that Harry had moved her to tears. Me too. They all had. And their rendition of *Sex Bomb* had moved us to tears of laughter.

The next morning Julia and Danny arrive at the apartment around 11 am. They have strolled downtown with the babies in their backpacks.

'My God, Harry you look just like your Uncle Daniel,' Julia gasps, seizing the 6 foot 4 inch boy and hugging him. 'D'you remember Ireland that New Year? Sitting on all our clothes on the beach to stop them blowing away?'

It had been a belter of a wind, tearing at the strand, sending a desert storm of sand in waist high gusts whipping across the legs. We'd decided to have a crazy New Year's Day bathe in the Atlantic, and all stripped off leaving Harry to sit on a tumulus of clothes to stop them blowing away. We put a turban of towel around his head and there he sat, Buddha-like, not allowed to move a muscle until we returned from the sea.

Hazel takes one look at us and asks for 'chee' and we re-christen the newly famous Hoch Ybrig 'Hazelcheese'. When I look it up in Rob's *Murray's Cheese Handbook* later, I find, with astonishment, that it is described as having: 'layers of hazelnut and butterscotch on the finish'.

Rob starts playing the new Dixie Chicks album. It turns out to be a Moder favourite.

'Do your moves Hazel, do your moves Finn,' Julia says and the little people dance across the floor to the music. Harry and Julia start talking about what they do to preserve their voices on stage.

It seems extraordinary that the small, shy boy she had met all those years ago is utterly unintimidated about talking stagecraft with the screen legend who is, after all, just one of his mother's friends to him. And she, in her turn, is as eager to discuss the problems of going on stage and how she has faced them.

'Bet you never thought you'd be sharing your Broadway debut with little Harry Shearer,' I say to Julia.

'I wish I could have come last night Harry, I would have done if I hadn't had a performance,' she says.

When they leave, Rob heads out to buy wine for the celebratory lunch, and comes back empty-handed but for Bud Trillin in his bicycle clips. All the off-licences are closed. Calvin Trillin, known to his friends as 'Bud', is a brilliant humorist and writer on the *New Yorker*, who has long been a customer of Rob's and lives nearby in the Village. I invite him to stay for an English Sunday lunch and explain that Harry's friends are about to show up after their a cappella triumph.

'I love a cappella,' Bud says. 'I'd have come to the concert if I'd known about it. Let me go home and get some wine. I won't be long.'

At the present count I am now feeding eighteen.

I explain to the boys when they arrive that Bud was widowed not so long ago, on September 11 2001 to be precise, and has recently published a brilliant piece entitled 'For Alice' in the *New Yorker* about his late wife, which seems to have struck a chord as both tribute and love story and that, Bud tells me, people have started talking about as a recipe for marriage. The perfect marriage. Cynical New Yorkers aside, he seems utterly perplexed by its effect: 'I really didn't realise that was how people would read it when I wrote it.'

He has managed to write about Alice through a series of cameos and events, and include the way they brought up their children, perceived family, coped with illness, fear of death, tragedy, entirely un-self-pityingly and it is one of the funniest and most moving pieces I have ever read.

When Alice died, Bud '…got a lot of letters like the one from a young woman in New York who wrote that she sometimes looked at her boyfriend and thought, "But will he love me like Calvin loves Alice?"'

The boys seem to take all this in, then get together and decide upon a surprise.

When Bud returns, all thirteen go and stand against the huge, open French windows before bursting into song. The scent of rosemary and roasting garlic floods the room as I watch smiling and baste the two huge legs of lamb. Bud listens entranced as they serenade him, the sun is shining its uncertain spring warmth and tentatively setting the room alight, the music carried out onto the street below, where people are beginning to incline their heads upwards to see where it is coming from.

And then the boys are gone. They have laid waste to the lunch and left almost as soon as they have arrived, heading for the afternoon flight back to the reality of the exam room. Everything about this week seems a series of defined, highlighted moments of anticipation, nerves, waiting; meeting, feeding, departing. In the sudden shock of quiet after they depart the excitement has ended.

The following Sunday Rob and I head back up to Julia and Danny's for brunch. I have offered to bring everything but Julia is adamant that she will get the champagne — we have always cracked a bottle together whenever, wherever we meet up — the bagels and the fruit. She will shop for it in the morning, she insists. We arrive with eggs and bacon, wild smoked salmon and cream cheese and in the end can't even be bothered to cook. Julia toasts the bagels, Rob and I fill them, Danny pours the champagne. There is a huge plate of sliced fruit and we stand round the kitchen table with the twins scurrying around between our legs. We make plans for Charissa to see *Three Days of Rain* when she flies out for her school business week, the last week of its run. When I see the play again with Charissa, the most determined girl in the universe has taken it to another level.

She was never going to prove her detractors wrong, or not so that they would admit it, but she has done what she set out to do when she took it on.

Julia, like Harry, has just decided to commit to an imperative act of courage, of doing the thing she was most fearful of. Harry had taken years to stand up and sing, and now he had gone out there at 20 and sung in a New York concert hall.

'It is not the mountain we conquer, but ourselves,' Edmund Hillary once said. And both had reached the summit that same spring weekend in New York.

11

Christmas in Somerset

No longer bothered by the subterfuge
needed to copy the letters before
they go up the chimney, or of finding
an answer to the question of just how
he can drink all the brandy and eat
all the mince pies left out for him in
every house in the land, there is still,
nevertheless, the annual dread of
disappointing.

Father Christmas has been coming to this house for a quarter of a century, and it doesn't look as though he's in any danger of hanging up his sack and calling time.

No longer bothered by the subterfuge needed to copy the letters before they go up the chimney, or of finding an answer to the question of just how he can drink all the brandy and eat all the mince pies left out for him in every house in the land, there is still, nevertheless, the annual dread of disappointing. After all, it is a parent's unerring duty to fulfil the hopes and expectations their children have of Christmas, even if their children are beyond the age of consent and expectation. Witness Harry's most recent Father Christmas list which is funny, thoughtful, un-greedy and as edifying to read as a good book:

'Dear Mater Chris'mush of X-Farm-Land
Here are the few things I forgot to write down as possible desirables:
A few Boxers (of the 'cool' but not 'ball' clenching kind)
Natural soap/shampoo/shower gel 'cos the stuff I normally have is chemical ridden
A couple of cool pairs of socks if you see any – Not boring everyday ones!
A funky tie – preferably with blue and black patterning that would go with my shirt and suit as I lost my old one! Only if you can find one.
MAYBES:
A music CD of any well known small choral group singing classical stuff – dunno what choir!
David Attenborough's *The Life of Mammals* DVD box though this may be too expensive. Haven't checked but best place is normally www.play.com

Bubble bath, pens, pencils, lots of small things I never get round
    to using!'

So I have to pull off an annual coup where inter-familial bickering
and end of year exhaustion are dissipated or at least minimised
by excessive quantities of delicious food and alcohol, a well-
mixed cocktail of waifs and strays to dilute things still further,
and not too much togetherness for not too long. Even the best
guests tend to over-ripen like cheese after a few days.

Repent ye those who 'Bah Humbug' the whole shebang and
either take off alone to eat lobster on a coral reef or complain
bitterly about how much Christmas costs and how much they
are dreading it. Remember, if you are Scrooge-like, that the thing
that supposedly causes you the greatest stress, and takes up the
most time and money, but which you do none the less, because,
presumably, you still have the honourable stamp of tradition
engraved somewhere upon your resentful torso, you also do
because you would actually be bereft if you no longer had to
do it.

In my case it is the Christmas stockings and the nine days
of feasting and partying that I seem incapable of whittling away
into anything shorter and less onerous. I am unquestionably
a candidate for early sainthood or at least devout and abject
martyrdom when it comes to Christmas and I admit to being
inspired by the shocking, hair-shirt sense of pleasure that goes
with being a giver and that makes giving so much more pleasurable than receiving. You are, after all, choosing exactly what you
want to give and cooking and eating the things you and your
dependents love best. How selfless is that?

Pleasure, appreciation, hedonism, too much of a good thing;

Christmas is the time when it is all guilt-free simply because everyone else is doing it too.

If I were to count the hours of stocking present buying and wrapping I have spent, I wouldn't be surprised to find that a whole year of my life had gone up in a rustle of tissue paper, but I wouldn't have it any other way. And far from cutting back and making do, my stockings seem to have ravelled and grown as have the three children over the years, outside whose bedroom doors the bulging, lumpy leg attire and overspill pillowcases are placed, invariably at 2 am. after a final three-night frenzy of wrapping and sticking and stuffing, and vehement 'You can't come ins', as they beg to borrow and scrounge my wrapping paper, Sellotape and scissors.

Each year I vow to get more organised; to make the Christmas puddings, as I tell readers of my cookbooks they should make them, at least six weeks before Christmas. Likewise with the home made mincemeat which should be turned regularly like an egg timer to flood and plump and macerate the dried fruit at the top of the jar once the liquor has sunk to the bottom – this year mine has two days to do what should take a month. I vow to do more armchair shopping, online ordering, gift-box buying. To start thinking of presents in the July sales. To make lists, plan, invite; freeze, send, prepare.

In reality I get more hopelessly behind each year, busking in the knowledge that what I have pulled off each and every year for so long, I can now pull off in less time and with far less effort.

It isn't quite true. This year I was too late even to send a Christmas card. And this year it all went spectacularly wrong, although it sort of righted itself at the end in time for a riotous and spectacular New Year's party.

As my elder daughter Miranda said after the event, 'You're at

that stage in between children and grandchildren. You've got
a boyfriend but not a husband, and once you're divorced it's a
different kind of Christmas. It's been a long wait for us to realise
that you need a stocking too, and what do we give you in yours?
After all that food shopping you've done for Christmas, you just
get more food. Nuts, chocolate, jars of pâté and tapenade that'll
sit in the cupboard until next Christmas.'

'Actually that's not true,' I say. 'They'll come out on New Year's
Eve or when people come over for a drink and I've gone on strike.'

'And then,' she adds, 'the three of us leave you the day before
Christmas Eve to go and have lunch with Grandma because she
won't come and stay here for Christmas, so you're left on your
own to do it all.'

And, as she fails to point out as I am popping cranberries, frying walnuts, apples, onions and celery for the chestnut stuffing,
squelching Somerset cider brandy butter through my fingers,
a car draws up and out falls Miranda's ex-boyfriend Tom, plus
friend, plus Julietta, a house-guest friend of Miranda's who I am
not expecting until the following day. Come to think of it, I have
only just been told that she is definitely coming which means
I have another stocking to conjure out of the ether at the last
minute.

I had been expecting the turkey to arrive by carrier, not a
carload heading for Cornwall, but the bird, ordered from Clive
Wreathall's Appledore Farm in Kent, may as well have been sent
by carrier pigeon. And tomorrow, Christmas Eve, is a Sunday;
I have no idea if there are any deliveries then.

Now, if you are sitting there thinking why doesn't she just
go down to the supermarket like a normal person and pick up
a Bernard Matthews turkey... well no, if you have read this book
so far you would know I'd sooner serve the trimmings toute

seule than sink to an avian apology for a free-range Kelly Bronze, or drive down to Jason Wise at The Ark Chicken Company in Devon, personally pluck him from the farm and get him to wring the neck of any last stray goose or turkey in the county as long as it came from a nice class of address.

'Clive. I hate to ring you, you must be up to your wattle in feathers, but it hasn't arrived.'

Sharp intake of breath in acknowledgement. I feel almost more sorry for Clive than I do for us, but not quite.

'I'll check with the carriers, it definitely left here this morning.'

Perhaps it's already being stuffed and trussed in another county.

I still have metres of pastry to make for the mince pies, a fresh orange jelly to set to a quiver, cupboards full of unwrapped presents, and tomorrow's Christmas Eve dinner to think about. And then there is the Christmas tree. I have bought the last remaining tree from outside the village shop and it is so tall it will have to be trailered over here and craned into the house unless I can saw off a couple of metres of it. Then there is the horror of keeping it upright which I singularly failed to do with last year's tree which I had planted in a bucket of earth. The earth dried out and cracked and the tree listed gently to port until it fell gracefully over and had to be tied to the radiator. It is the girls' job to decorate it, which I am rather hoping they will find time for before Twelfth Night when the whole lot has to come down.

Christmas Eve.

We have decided to have some friends round for drinks before Midnight Mass, which should keep us awake for long enough to walk to the village church for 11.30 pm, meanwhile it is late afternoon and whitevanman is knocking at the door.

'So where exactly did it spend the night?' I ask, more than marginally worried that my lovely bird could now be the harbinger of something disastrous it picked up at a DHL Christmas party. The driver looks sheepish and says it was out in the van overnight and it was pretty cold. I bring the blighted bird in to assess and stuff. It is a beauty and doesn't appear to have the faintest whiff of anything untoward about it. I call Clive who sounds even more stressed out than he did yesterday.

'This must be your worst day of the year,' I say, somewhat unimaginatively.

'I'm flying out to the Caribbean,' he jokes.

Then Julietta, who took ill when she came for Christmas last year, takes to her bed again. She says she has been up all night and has got severe food poisoning. It *can't* be from my food, surely; it seems too much of a coincidence, as that is exactly what happened on Christmas Eve last year, so she never did get to eat her first English Christmas dinner.

I get down to making something of a tribute dish for the rest of us, a crab risotto in imitation of Harry's Bar's, adding my own roast and ground curry spices, a pile of langoustines and the light and dark meat picked from a succulent Brixham crab.

By dinner time things have got worse. Julieta, Miranda tells me, is near delirious and thinking she may have appendicitis. We should call a doctor. Is this the greatest test of the National Health system I wonder, Christmas Eve in deepest Somerset and a South American guest with possible peritonitis? Should we just fifth-gear it to hospital?

We go through a ridiculous rigmarole with the out of hours service who ask a series of questions that appear to have no relation to the patient's complaint, urgency or the necessary facts and are told we will be called back when they have decided which doctor and what to do. Julietta is so distressed that she is hyperventilating.

Eventually a car draws up and out steps a ghoulishly pale, elderly figure in a pale, elderly gabardine mac. He heads upstairs and we carry on drinking with the friends who have just arrived.

After a thorough examination, the exhausted doctor tells us that it is definitely not a burst appendix, it is acute food poisoning, and hurries to his boot where he seems to have a complete dispensary of lethal drugs. We thank him profusely, excusing ourselves by saying it is the first time we have called the doctor out since Charissa was a baby nearly eighteen years ago and feeling that the Third World health service which we are becoming increasingly known for still has pockets of excellence if you really put it to the test.

I have started to get a migraine. The carols and gluwein at the church don't help. I drag the stockings to the bedroom doors and fail to sleep a wink. At 9 am I pad downstairs to release the bird from the cold clutches of the fridge an hour before it is due in the Aga.

It is only when the stockings have been ransacked and the children are alternately nibbling on life-like casts of black chocolate ears Rob and I have found in the Redding Market in Philadelphia and swigging tequila from their miniatures that I grind to an end-of-the-line halt.

'I just can't put the turkey in...' I say, wholly uncharacteristically, '...and do the whole thing.' The migraine is a blinder.

'Forget Christmas lunch today,' Harry says immediately.

'Gladys and Nigel aren't coming 'til tomorrow anyway and they really didn't want to miss Christmas lunch with us.'

This is the best Christmas present of all. The pressure is off. Miranda digs up a few fat leeks for a Vichyssoise and makes a hearty, oily tortilla stuffed with a soft bank of sweet onion. Nobody seems to mind. At least there are four dozen mince pies, the lethal brandy butter and a huge stack of films for BAFTA voting to fend off any danger of too much conversation.

Julieta is beginning to get better; I am beginning to feel worse. After another bad night comes the sickness. Charissa tends me like a ministering angel, brings hot-water bottles and drinks then rushes back downstairs and peels for her life, parsnips, potatoes, Brussels sprouts. Miranda takes over the complete Boxing Day Christmas dinner. Thank God for competent children. She makes bread sauce and gravy, wraps sausages in bacon; steams the pudding I've made with prunes and dried apricots, dates, figs and rakes of dried vine fruits; smothers and bastes the bird in butter; crisps roast potatoes and parsnips; steams the sprouts. Everyone sits down around 4 pm, and it strikes me I could just keep the one role next year, play Father Christmas to Miranda's brilliant impersonation of a professional cook.

Julieta still hasn't managed to eat an English Christmas dinner, but I suppose there's always next year.

Three days later Rob arrives from New York, there are friends staying on their way to Devon, more friends staying for the New Year and a dinner for sixteen starring two geese, which stand a better chance of not getting lost or waylaid than the turkey as I only have to collect them from the farm down the road.

I have entrusted the party games to the capable, commanding hands of a neighbouring army colonel, my friend Michael Kingscote, who we are all convinced is the real 007. Troops and teams are his lifeblood. We will range in age from 17 to 75 which I believe is the key to a great party.

The colonel arrives looking like Bond's country cousin, resplendent in 'my grandfather's 1926 Huntsman smoking jacket', muddy boots that he swaps for velvet slippers, and a double brace of pheasants in full plumage dangling off either arm.

'I got onto the net and looked up adult party games,' he says in a suitably suggestive tone and takes a couple of balls of nylon string tantalisingly out of his pockets, leaving me none the wiser. 'You wouldn't believe what I found!'

After the celebrant roast geese, the chocolate St Emilions, orange custards and lemon possets we fall into line at Michael's command and play charades. The adult party games that follow culminate in two teams, one headed by a boy and one by a girl, starting head to head, whose task is to thread the nylon string up one trouser leg and down the other of each male, and up one arm, across the bust and down the other arm of each female. Somehow this is impossible to perform without men unzipping flies, trousers falling down around knees, women undoing buttons, bra straps entangling with hands and twine and everyone ending up practically welded together like glue, since Michael has ensured the length of twine is just too short for comfort.

We stop at midnight to toast the New Year with kisses and champagne. Nobody leaves until 2 am, the final games spun out to see the new year in as much as the old year out.

The old house creaks to itself, the wind wandering through the slate roof, the last wisp of oak smoke rising to scent our room as we climb into bed.

It is strange how different the house feels when it is full, containing and reflecting the happiness and hope we share collectively, children, loved ones and old friends. The turning year will see the three children heading back to school, jobs, auditions in a matter of days.

So where does the journey, the story end?

Well of course it doesn't end here.

Rob deliberates long and hard before reminding me of what, at first, seems an unlikely analogy with one of his favourite stories, E.B. White's classic, *Stuart Little*. No ordinary mouse, Stuart Little was born to a family of humans and lives in New York, but when his best friend, a beautiful bird named Margalo disappears, he is determined to track her down. He sets out on an adventure, but doesn't find his friend. The way, however, is left open like the road, for a further adventure: 'Stuart rose from the ditch, climbed into his car, and started up the road that led toward the north. The sun was just coming up over the hills on his right. As he peered ahead into the great land that stretched before him, the way seemed long. But the sky was bright, and he somehow felt he was headed in the right direction.'

In two days time we fly off to New York.

Seafood Spaghetti

SERVES TWO

Everyone has their own favourite version of this, mine varies seasonally and according to what the fish shop has in that day, but it wouldn't be right without a stack of shells and pink carapaces. Carpetshell clams from Devon are as pretty as they are salty-sweet, and with langoustines, mussels and scallops the dish is done.

225G/8OZ clams
225G/8OZ mussels
4 langoustines or large, raw
prawns
2 LARGE OR 4 SMALLER scallops
with their coral
2–3 TBSP extra virgin olive oil
1 MEDIUM onion peeled and very
finely chopped
2 CLOVES garlic, peeled and finely
chopped
1 BULB fennel, outer tough layer
removed, finely diced
1 STALK celery, strung and finely
chopped
110G/4OZ or so freshly podded peas
large pinch saffron stamen soaked
in a few tablespoons warm water
for 20 minutes
2 TBSP Pernod
½ GLASS or so of dry white wine,
whatever you're drinking
4 organic tomatoes, skinned, seeded
and cut into dice
1 TBSP each chopped flat leaf
parsley and basil
sea salt and black pepper
225G/8OZ spaghetti

Scrub the clams and mussels and remove any weedy looking beards. Clean the scallops and separate the coral from the white, cutting each disc into 2–3 slices.

Warm the olive oil in a large, heavy bottomed pan and stew the onion, garlic, fennel and celery gently until they are softened and translucent.

In the meanwhile, get a large cauldron of water to the boil for the pasta ready to cook to al dente and co-ordinate with the sauce.

Put the peas in a small pan with a little water and a knob of butter and stew gently until tender. Leave in the pan.

Heat a little olive oil in a small frying pan and put in the langoustines. Cook until the underside turns pink before turning over and cooking the other side similarly. Remove from the heat.

Pour the Pernod over the softened onion and allow it to bubble and steam for a minute

before adding the white wine
and saffron. Bring to the boil,
add the clams and mussels and
cook under a lid briefly until
they have opened.
Throw in the scallops with their
coral to cook briefly in the pan,
they will take no more than
a minute, adding the langoustines at the same time. Season
and throw in the tomatoes and
peas. Remove from the heat
immediately and sloosh the
sauce into the almost drained
pasta in the pan, adding a knob
of butter. Turn to mix over the
heat for a minute. Remove from
the heat, throw over the herbs
and serve in hot bowls with an
extra bowl on the table to hurl
the empty shells into.

Tunisian Orange Cake

This is a cake to get excited about at Christmas time as it enters into the whole sticky, scented, citrussy spicy spirit of things and its sharp edge is just what you need. Stephen Markwick, one of my favourite chefs, who trained with our great mentor George Perry-Smith, serves it in his excellent restaurant Culinaria in Bristol sometimes.

Preheat oven to 180°C/375°F/ GAS 5

120G/4OZ stale white breadcrumbs
400G/14OZ unrefined vanilla caster sugar
200G/7OZ Marcona blanched almonds ground in the Magimix
3 TSP baking powder
400ML/14 FL OZ sunflower oil
8 organic eggs
ZEST OF 2 organic oranges and 1 lemon

For the syrup:
JUICE OF 2 organic oranges and 1 lemon
2 cinnamon sticks
4 cloves
140G/5 OZ unrefined vanilla caster sugar

Grease and line and flour a 23cm/9in Springform tin.

Mix the breadcrumbs, sugar, almonds and baking powder together in a large bowl. Whisk the oil and eggs together and add to the dry ingredients. Mix well. Add the zests and mix them in well.

Pour into the tin and bake for 45–60 minutes or until golden and a skewer comes out clean. Put to cool on a rack in the tin.

Heat all the syrup ingredients together gently and then simmer for about 5 minutes. Strain. Pour the syrup over the cake while the cake is still warm. You can skewer holes in the cake to do this if you like.

Serve with creme fraiche laced, if you like, with a little Cointreau and sweet orange oil.

Glossary

Relais San Maurizio
Hotel del Monastero, Località San Maurizio, 39
–12058, Santo Stefano Belbo (CN), Italy
Tel: (+ 39) 0141 841900
Fax: (+ 39) 0141 843833
www.relaissanmaurizio.it

Castello di Verduno
Albergo e Ristorante, Real Castello,
Via Umberto, 19 – 12060, Verduno (CN), Italy
Tel: (+ 39) (0)172 47 01 25
Fax: (+ 39) (0)172 47 02 98
info@castellodiverduno.com
www.castellodiverduno.com

Ristorante Belvedere
Piazza Castello, 5 – 12064, La Morra (CN), Italy
Tel: (+ 39) (0)173 50190
www.belvederelamorra.it

La Cristina
Frazione Valdivilla – 12058, Santo Stefano Belbo
(CN), Italy
Tel: (+ 39) (0)141 847168
E-mail: lacristina@ristorantiitaliani.it

La Campagna Verde
Madonna, Strada Provinciale Balbi, 22
12053, Castiglione Tinella, Piedmont, Italy
Closed Wednesday
Tel/fax: (+39) (0)141 855 108
Email: mirellabiacno2@virgilio.it

§3 *Fishy Fishy Café*
Market Place, Kinsale, County Cork, Ireland.
Tel: (+ 353) (0)21 477 4453
www.fishyfishy.ie

Murray's
254 Bleecker St. (between 6th & 7th Ave.),
New York,
NY 10014
Tel: (212) 243-3289
www.murrayscheese.com
Store Hours: Mon–Sat: 8am–8pm;
Sunday: 10am–7pm

The Pink Tea Cup
42 Grove Street
New York,
NY 10014
Tel: (212) 807-6755
pnkteacup@yahoo.com
www.thepinkteacup.com

Russ and Daughters
179 East Houston Street, New York, NY 10002
Tel: (212) 475 4880
Fax: (212) 475 0345
www.russanddaughters.com

Ottomanelli Brothers
1549 York Avenue (corner of 82nd Street)
Tel: (212) 772 7900
Fax: (212) 772 8436
www.ottomanellibros.com

Home Restaurant
20 Cornelia St., New York, NY 10014
(near 4th St.)
Tel: (212) 243 9579
www.recipesfromhome.com

Mamoun's
119 MacDougal St., New York, NY 10012
(between Bleecker St. and W. 3rd St.)
Tel: (212) 674 8685

Katz's Delicatessen
205 E. Houston St., New York, NY 10002
(at Ludlow St.)
Tel: (212) 254 2246
Fax: (212) 674 3270
www.katzdeli.com

Pearl Oyster Bar
18 Cornelia Street, New York, NY 10014
Tel: (212) 691 8211
www.pearloysterbar.com

Bread
20 Spring St, New York, NY 10012
Tel: (212) 334 1015

New York Strip House
13 E. 12th St., NY 10003
(between University Pl. and Fifth Ave.)
Tel: (212) 328 0000
www.theglaziergroup.com

Blue Ribbon
97 Sullivan St New York, NY 10012-3663
Tel: (212) 274 0404
www.blueribbonrestaurants.com

§5   *Chez Panisse Restaurant and Café*
1517 Shattuck Avenue, Berkeley, CA 94709-1516
Tel: (510) 548 5525
www.chezpanisse.com

Delfina
3621 18th Street, San Francisco, California 94110
Tel (415) 552 4055
www. delfinasf.com

The Huntington Hotel and Nob Hill Spa
1075 California Street, San Francisco, CA 94108
Tel: (415) 474 5400
Fax: (415) 474 6227
www.huntingtonhotel.com

Tartine Bakery
600 18th Street, San Francisco, CA 94110
Tel: 415 487 2600
www.tartinebakery.com

§6   *Hotel Metropole*
Castello, 4149 Riva degli Schiavoni – 30122,
Venezia, Italy
Tel: (+ 39) (0)41 52 05 044
www.metropole.hotelinvenice.com

Gelateria San Giorgio,
1342 Via Garibaldi, Venezia, Italy

Osteria Alle Testiere
Calle del Mondo Novo – 30122, Venezia, Italy
Tel: (+ 39) (0)41 52 27 220

Harry's Bar
San Marco 1323 – 30124, Venezia, Italy
Tel: (+ 39) (0)41 528 5777
Email: harrysbar@cipriani.com

Ristorante Corte Sconta
Calle del Pestrin 3886

Tel: (+ 39) (o)41 522 7024

Osteria Oliva Nera
Castello 3417 Salizada dei Greci,
(near Ponte dei Greci)
Venezia, 30122, Italy
Tel: (+ 39) (o)41 522 7024
Email: Oliva-nera@libero.it
www. www.osteria-olivanera.com

Osteria Gatto Nero da Ruggero,
Fondamenta della Giudecca 88,
Burano, Venezia, 30012, Italy
Tel : (+ 39) (o)41 73 0120

§7 *Castel Taverna Sforza*
Castel del Monte, Andria (BA), Italy
Tel: (+ 39) (o) 88 356 9996

Antichi Sapori
Piazza Isidoro 10, Montegrosso, Andria (BA), Italy
Tel/fax: (+ 39) (o)883 569529
www.internetrestaurant.it/ristoranti/scheda
.php?idristorante=1301

§8 *Restaurant Christian Tetedoie*
54 Quai Pierre Seize, 69005, Lyon, France
Tel: (+ 33) (o)4 78 29 4010

Paul Bocuse, L'Auberge du Pont des Collognes,
40 Quai de la Plage,

69660 Collonges au Mont d'Or, Lyon, France
Tel :(+ 33) (0)4 72 42 90 90
Fax: (+ 33) (0)4 72 27 85 87
www.bocuse.fr

Restaurant Le Garet
7 Rue du Garet, 69001, Lyon, France
Tel: (+ 33) (0)4 78 28 16 94
Fax: (+ 33) (0)4 72 00 06 84
www.achat-lyon.com/viti1178-RESTAURANT-LE-GARET.htm

La Maison Troisgros
Place de la Gare, 42300, Roanne, France
Tel: (+ 33) (0)4 77 71 66 97
Fax: (+33) (0) 4 77 70 39 77
Email: troisgros@relaischateaux.com
www.troisgros.fr

§9 *La Petite Auberge*
Place de L'Hotel de Ville, 32230, Marciac, France
Tel: (+ 33) (0) 5 62 09 31 33
www.marciac.net/fiche_14_11.htm

Index

50 Carmine, New York (Greenwich Village) 91

A Voce, New York 34
Acaya, Puglia 197
Acme Bread Co, San Francisco 125
Adria, Ferran 224
AINT, Puglia 206
Aix-en-Provence 29
Al Marka, Venice 161
Alba 26
Amis, Kingsley 59, 61, 62, 63, 64, 176
Anderson, Nick 161
Andria 203, 204–5, 208, 211
  Castel Taverna Sforza 203, 280
  Michele Matera 204–5
  Mucci 211
Antichi Sapori, Montegrosso 208–11, 280
Apple, Johnny 163
Appledore Farm, Kent 265
Aqua, San Francisco 136
The Ark Chicken Company, Devon 266
Arthur 107–8
Auden, Wystan 165–6

Badger 106–7, 106–12
Balcon, Jill 65
Barolo vineyards 22
Basilicanova, Parma 15
Beara Peninsula 74
Bedales 56–7, 64
Beggiato, Gloria 157

Berkeley
  Chez Panisse Restaurant and Café 117, 130, 132, 133, 134, 278
  Peet's Coffee Shop 132
Bisceglie, Nicotel 188–9, 190, 204, 211
Blahnik, Manolo 45
Blue Ribbon, New York 8, 90, 211, 278
Bocuse, (Paul), L'Auberge du Pont des Collognes, Lyon 217, 222–3, 281
Bogathy, Zoltan 27
Boman, Eric 45
Bonati, Giorgio 15
Bord Bia symposium, Kinsale 74, 75, 76
Borel, François 29–30
Bra
  Caffe Converso 23
  Slow Food Cheese Festival 10, 22
Bread, New York 91, 278
Broadbent, Jim 191
Broadway, New York 252–4, 260
Brown, Michael 85
Burano 172–8
  Merletti dalla Olga 173

Café des Negotiants, Chalon sur Saône 224
Caffe Converso, Bra 23
Cambridge 49–50, 58
Campagna Verde, Madonna 17–21, 276
'Car' (grandmother) 50, 51, 52, 53
Carey, Charles 198

Carmellini, Andrew 34
Carpaccio, Vittore 153-4
Casa del Parmigiano, Venice 161
Caseus Awards, Lyon 218-19
Castel del Monte, Puglia 201-2
Castel Taverna Sforza, Andria 203, 280
Castello di Verduno, Verduno 30-4, 36, 275
Cavele, Carolyn 76
Chalk Farm, Marine Ices 63
Chalon sur Saône, Café des Negotiants 224
Chez Panisse Restaurant and Café, Berkeley 117, 130, 132, 133, 134, 278
Christian, Jean 240
Christmas, Somerset 262-71
Cielo (Murray's) 79
Cipriani, Arrigo 167, 169
Cora (Rob family cook) 83, 84
Corato, Puglia 206
Corrigan, Richard 76, 107
Courchesne, Al 125-6, 127, 130
Cowgirl Creamery, Point Reyes 125
Cranks, London 133-4
La Cristina, Valdivilla 10, 12-13, 14, 275
Culinaria, Bristol 273

Da Fiore, Venice 158
Danny, Julia's husband 253, 254, 255, 257
David, Elizabeth 50, 125, 218, 219
Deborah (cousin) 55
del Console, Giuseppe 206-8
Del Conte, Anna 168
Delfina, San Francisco 119, 278
Dirty Girl Produce 125
Dover, Linden 239, 240
Dover, Michael 232-3, 238, 239-40, 244, 245
Dover, Ruth 232, 234, 238, 240, 241, 242, 244
Downtown Bakery, San Francisco 125
Dublin, cheese shop 221

Elliott, Tony 46
Epicurious Garden
  Socca Oven 135-6
  Soop 134
  Taste 135

Fasolata, Corrado 157-8
Fillioux, La Mère 223
Finn (Julia's son) 254-5, 258
Fisher, Rhoda 53, 70, 217
Fishy Fishy Café, Kinsale 76, 276
Flavours of Puglia (Jenkins) 198
Florence Meat Market, New York 99
Florence (Rob's mother) 83, 105
Forman, Lance 84
Fortnum and Mason, London 51, 56
Frederick II, Emperor 202
Frog Hollow Farm 125, 126
Frost, Robert 212
Fulenwider, Anne 190

Galway, cheese shop 221
Garech 170
Gascony 232-42
Le Gavroche, London 216
Gelateria San Giorgio, Venice 156, 279
Granddaisy Bakery, New York 256
Greenwich, England 58
Greenwich Village, New York 8, 85, 91, 115

Grigson, Jane 50
Guggenheim, Peggy, house, Venice 159

Hamnett, Katherine 46
Harry's Bar, Venice 166–70, 267, 279
Haynes, Susan 147, 162, 170, 234, 235, 236, 239, 241, 242
Hazan, Marcella 168
Hazel (Julia's daughter) 254–5, 258
Heale Farm, Devon 102
Hertfordshire, Hadley Common 59
Hodgson, Randolph 74
Hog Island Oysters, Tomales Bay 125
Home Restaurant, New York 90, 277
Hotel Metropole, Venice 149–51, 157, 157–8, 162, 279
Hôtel Moderne, Roanne 224
Howard, Elizabeth Jane 59, 60, 61, 62, 63, 64, 65, 66, 69
Howard, Ron 190
The Huntingdon Hotel and Nob Hill Spa, San Francisco 131–2, 279

Jacobs Theater, New York 252
Jamaica 226–8
Jenkins, Nancy Harmon 190, 192, 196, 198, 199, 200, 206, 208
Jenkins, Sarah Harmon 91, 99, 190
Jerez, La Mesa Redonda 84
Johnson, Paul 154
Julieta (Miranda's friend) 265, 267–8, 269

K, John 236, 242
K, Merci 242

Katz's Delicatessen, New York 90, 277
Keane, Sean 243
Kingscote, Michael 269, 270
Kinsale
  Bord Bia symposium 74, 75, 76
  Fishy Fishy Café 76, 276
Knickerbocker, New York (Greenwich Village) 115

Langhe 10–21
Lecce 200–1
Lemmons, Hadley Common, Hertfordshire 59
Lewis, Cecil Day 28–9, 35, 43, 49, 52, 57–66, 71, 165–6
Lewis, Daniel Day 51, 62, 64, 115
Lewis, Rebecca Day 115
Lewis, Sean Day 66
Lifethyme, New York 98
Lincoln Center, New York 138, 252
The Little Pie Company, New York 82
Lyon 216–28
  Caseus Awards 218–19
  Paul Bocuse, L'Auberge du Pont des Collonges 217, 222–3, 281
  Restaurant Christian Têtedoie 280
  Restaurant Le Garet 218–20, 281

Madonna, Campagna Verde 17–21, 276
Magnolia Bakery, New York 136
La Maison Troisgros, Roanne 216, 224–6, 228, 281
Mamoun's, New York 8, 90, 277
Mann, Sargy 59
Marciac, La Petite Auberge 232, 241, 281

Marine Ices, Chalk Farm 63
Mark (Rob friend) 84
Markwick, Stephen 273
Martin, from Holland 23
Matera, Antonio 204
Matera, Nino 204–5, 212
Matera, Teresa 204–5
May, Robert 134
Mayo 79, 80, 237, 242–6
Merge 197
Merletti dalla Olga, Burano 173
La Mesa Redonda, Jerez 84
Michele Matera, Andria 204–5
Mignani, Anna 190, 193, 201,
    203
Miller, Arthur 78
Monkey, Jane's brother 59, 63,
    64
Mons, Hervé 29, 30, 31, 35, 219,
    224
Montegrosso, Antichi Sapori
    208–11, 280
Morath, Inge 78
Morgan, Peter 190–1, 196, 201
La Morra 22, 25, 30
    Ristorante Belvedere 25, 26–7,
    275
Mucci, Andria 211, 212
Mura S. Elena, Venice 160
Murray's
    New York 10, 15, 17, 29, 78–80,
        102, 116, 117, 118, 127, 205,
        210, 276
        Puglia promotion 192, 200,
        208, 211, 212
Murray's Cheese Handbook (Rob)
    258

New York 74, 78–97, 252–60
    50 Carmine 91
    A Voce 34

Blue Ribbon 8, 90, 211, 278
Bread 278
Florence Meat Market 99
Granddaisy Bakery 256
Home Restaurant 90, 277
Katz's Delicatessen 90, 277
Knickerbocker 115
Lifethyme 98
Little Pie Company 82
Magnolia Bakery 136
Mamoun's 8, 90, 277
Murray's 10, 17, 78–80, 102, 116,
    117, 118, 127, 205, 210, 276
    Puglia promotion 192, 200,
    208, 211, 212
New York Strip House 92, 278
Ottomanelli Brothers 277
Pearl Oyster Bar 278
The Pink Tea Cup 83, 276
Russ and Daughters 84, 277
Nicotel, Bisceglie 188–9, 190, 204,
    211
Nigel and Gladys (Somerset
    friends) 109, 110, 111
Niman, Bill and Niman Ranch
    116–24, 127, 129–30
Niman, Nicolette 119

Odermatt, Thomas 127–8
Osteria Alle Testiere, Venice 162–5,
    177, 279
Osteria Gatto Nero da Ruggero,
    Venice 172, 174–8, 280
Osteria Oliva Nera, Venice 154–6,
    280
O'Toole, Ann 243
O'Toole, Paddy 243
Ottomanelli Brothers, New York
    85, 99, 277
Out of the Blue 114–16, 129, 130,
    137–8, 255, 257

Parker, Caroline 178–9
Parma 15, 27, 28
Paul and Marigold (friends) 104
Pearl Oyster Bar, New York 278
Peet's Coffee Shop, Berkeley 132
Perry–Smith, George 169, 273
La Petite Auberge, Marciac 232, 241, 281
Pettini, Paola 198
Philadelphia, Redding Market 268
The Pink Tea Cup, New York 83, 276
Polignano a Mare, Ristorante da Tuccino 193
Pollard, Mr and Mrs 54, 55
Premio Italia che Lavora 205
PRN conference, Venice, 1948 166
Puglia 8, 186–212
    see also named towns and villages

RECIPES
    Apple Sponge and Hazelnut Ice Cream 40–1
    Apricot Tart 142–3
    Asparagus, Broccoli Rabe and Goat's Cheese Salad 229
    Bigoli 180
    Black-Eyed Pea Salad 140
    Carbonnade of Beef 68
    Curried Crab Risotto 182–3
    Garbure Gasconne 247
    Lemon Chiffon Pie 70
    New York Spicy Spare Ribs 98
    Peperoni alla Siciliano 36
    Perfect Scrambled Eggs 67
    Pralinéed Hazelnut Cake with a Chocolate Ganache 184
    Profiteroles 71–2

    Quiche Lorraine with a Crisp Bacon Top 141
    Ratatouille 100
    Risotto Balsamico 37–8
    Roast Duck with a Wheatberry, Sour Cherry and Sage Salad 248–9
    Seafood Spaghetti 272–3
    Short Rib of Beef and Borlotti Bean Casserole 69
    Spiced Leg of Lamb with Tahini Sauce and Ratatouille 99–100
    Summer Vegetable Quick Lasagne 213–14
    Thai Beef Salad 230
    Tonno Balsamico 181
    Tunisian Orange Cake 273–4
    Vitello Piccante 102
    Vitello Tonnato Without the Tonnato 38–9
    White Truffle Pasta 39
    Yoghurt, Almond and Lemon Cake with Pralinéed Nuts on top 249–50
Redding Market, Philadelphia 268
Reiss, Andy 256
Relais San Maurizio, Santo Stefano Belbo 11, 14–16, 275
Restaurant Christian Têtedoie, Lyon 280
Restaurant Le Garet, Lyon 218–20, 281
Rigo, Eugenio 150, 153, 172, 175
Ristorante Belvedere, La Morra, Italy 25, 26–7, 275
Ristorante Corte Sconta, Venice 170–1, 280
Ristorante da Tuccino, Polignano a Mare 193
Riverside, Helford 169
Roanne 29, 216, 224
    Hotel Moderne 224

La Maison Troisgros 216, 224–6, 228, 281
Rob
  birthdays 26–7, 146–8
  cheese buying 15, 22–3, 208
  Christmas 269, 271
  early meetings 7, 11, 74–97
  Murray's Cheese Handbook 258
  telephone conversations 104–6, 109
  Twelve Pins Club 233–46
  see also Murray's
Roberts, Julia 252–3, 257, 260
Roberts, Michael 45
Roli Roti Gourmet Rotisserie, San Francisco 127–8
Roux family 216, 217, 223
Roux, Michel 216–17, 221
Russ and Daughters, New York 84, 277

Salone del Gusto, Torino 24
San Francisco 114, 116–17, 118, 128, 130–1, 138
  Acme Bread Co 125
  Aqua 136
  Delfina 119, 278
  Downtown Bakery 125
  The Huntingdon Hotel and Nob Hill Spa 131–2, 279
  Roli Roti Gourmet Rotisserie 127–8
  Saturday Ferry Plaza Farmers Market 125
  Tartine Bakery 121, 279
  The Tasting Room 132
  Zuni Café 130
  see also Berkeley
Santo Stefano Belbo 8, 10, 11
  Relais San Maurizio 11, 14–16, 275

Saturday Ferry Plaza Farmers Market, San Francisco 125
Sayer, Geoff 69
Schlesinger, Peter 45
Scuola Dalmata of St George and St Tryphone, Venice 153–4
Sea Crest School, Half Moon Bay 137
Shaffer, David 43, 44, 45, 46, 47, 48, 49, 78
Shaffer, Serena 43, 44, 45, 46, 47, 48, 49
Shearer, Charissa 53, 68, 110, 244, 268, 269
Shearer, Harry 53, 114–15, 119, 129, 130, 137, 139, 237, 252, 253, 255, 256, 257, 260
Shearer, Miranda 53, 68, 213, 264–5, 267, 268
Sheridan, Kevin 221
Sheridan, Seamus 221
Sketch, Berkeley 136
Slow Food Cheese Festival, Bra 10, 22
Socca Oven, Epicurious Garden 135–6
Somerset, Christmas 262–71
Soop, Epicurious Garden 134
Sorba, Diego 27, 28–9
Spender, Natasha 165, 166
Spender, Stephen 165–6
Sullivan, Steve 125
Susan (American) 193

Tamasin, culinary influences 43–66
Tartine Bakery, San Francisco 121, 279
Taste, Epicurious Garden 135
The Tasting Room, San Francisco 132

Temperley, Julian 104
Têtedoie, Christian 216, 220, 220-2, 223
Three Days of Rain (play) 252, 253, 260
Torino 22
  Salone del Gusto 24
Trillin, Calvin ('Bud') 258-9
Troisgros, Jean-Baptiste and Marie 224
Troisgros, Michel 225, 226
Troisgros, Pierre 225
trulli, Merge 197
Twelve Pins Club 232-46

Unterman, Patti 190, 193
Upper Parrock, East Sussex 51-2

Valdespino, Migueol 84
Valdivilla, La Cristina 10, 12-13, 14, 18, 275
Vaughan, Richard 68, 85
Vaughan-Williams, Ursula 66
Venice 145-79
  Al Marka 161
  Casa del Parmigiano 161
  Da Fiore 158
  Gelateria San Giorgio 156, 279
  Harry's Bar 279
  Hotel Metropole 149-51, 157, 157-8, 162, 279
  Mure S. Elena 160
  Osteria Alle Testiere 162-5, 177, 279
  Osteria Gatto Nero da Ruggero 172, 174-8, 280
  Osteria Oliva Nera 154-6, 280
  Ristorante Corte Sconta 170-1, 280

Verduno, Castello di Verduno 30-4, 36, 275
Vivaldi, Antonio 149

Waters, Alice 117, 120, 132, 134
Welsh, Nick 235, 239, 242, 243, 245
Welsh, Sal 235, 239, 243, 244, 245
White, E.B., *Stuart Little* 271
Wise, Jason 266
Woodforde, Parson 86
Wreathall, Clive 265, 266, 267

Zapata, London 45
Zarin, Cynthia 115
Zito, Pietro 208, 209, 210
Zuni Café, San Francisco 130